Carly Findlay is an award-winning w[...] activist. She writes on disability and appearance diversity issues for news outlets including the ABC, *The Age* and *Sydney Morning Herald*, and SBS. She was named as one of Australia's most influential women in the 2014 *Australian Financial Review* and Westpac 100 Women of Influence Awards. She has appeared on ABC TV's *You Can't Ask That* and *Cyberhate with Tara Moss*, and has been a regular on various ABC radio programs. She has spoken at the Melbourne Writers Festival, the University of Western England and Melbourne University – to name a few. She organised the history-making Access to Fashion – a Melbourne Fashion Week event featuring disabled models. She has a Masters of Communication and Bachelor of eCommerce. Carly identifies as a proud disabled woman – she lives with a rare, severe skin condition, ichthyosis. She also co-hosts a funny podcast called *Refreshments Provided* that could do with a few more listeners.

CarlyFindlay.com.au
facebook.com/tune.into.radio.carly
twitter.com/CarlyFindlay
instagram.com/CarlyFindlay
RefreshmentsProvided.com

Say Hello

Carly Findlay

Dear Lindy,

Shrill was a reason I
wrote this book.
thank you.
love, Carly x

HarperCollinsPublishers

Lines from 'You Get Proud by Practicing' (laurahershey.com) © reproduced with kind permission from Robin Stephens.

A version of the chapter 'Woman of colour?' first appeared on *Ravishly*. It will be included in *Growing Up African in Australia* (ed. Maxine Beneba Clarke), Black Inc., 2019.

All reasonable attempts have been made to contact the rights holders of quoted material. If you have not been correctly attributed, please contact the publisher so that appropriate changes can be made to any reprint.

HarperCollins*Publishers*
First published in Australia in 2019
by HarperCollins*Publishers* Australia Pty Limited
ABN 36 009 913 517
harpercollins.com.au

HarperCollins*Publishers*
Level 13, 201 Elizabeth Street, Sydney NSW 2000, Australia
Unit D1, 63 Apollo Drive, Rosedale, Auckland 0632, New Zealand
A 53, Sector 57, Noida, UP, India
1 London Bridge Street, London, SE1 9GF, United Kingdom
Bay Adelaide Centre, East Tower, 22 Adelaide Street West, 41st floor, Toronto,
Ontario M5H 4E3, Canada
195 Broadway, New York NY 10007, USA

A catalogue record for this book is available from the National Library of Australia

ISBN 978 1 4607 5503 7 (paperback)
ISBN 978 1 4607 0939 9 (ebook)

Cover design by Hazel Lam, HarperCollins Design Studio
Cover photography by Kristoffer Paulsen
Typeset in Bembo Std by Kirby Jones
Printed and bound in Australia by McPherson's Printing Group
The papers used by HarperCollins in the manufacture of this book are a natural, recyclable product made from wood grown in sustainable plantation forests. The fibre source and manufacturing processes meet recognised international environmental standards, and carry certification.

Say Hello was, for the most part, written on the land of the Kulin Nation. Thank you to Aboriginal Elders past, present and emerging for letting me work, learn and create as a guest on your beautiful land.

Thank you also to the leaders of the disability rights movement who have paved, and are still paving, the way for equity today.

This book is for everyone who has felt alone because of their ichthyosis, facial difference, chronic illness and disability. It's for Little Carly too. It is time to be the person Little Carly needed. This book is my truth, and researched to the best of my ability. I acknowledge that other perspectives may differ.

IMPORTANT INFORMATION

Contents

Preface: Say hello

Often the first thing people say to me is a comment or question about my appearance. Even before they say hello.

They blurt out what they're thinking – sometimes out of concern, and other times because they don't think. Things like:

'What happened?'

'What happened to your face?'

'Are you sunburnt?'

'I'm so sorry [for how you look].'

'Oh, God.'

'Look at her.'

'Whoa.'

'Holy shit.'

'Mum, did you see that lady?'

Occasionally, they stare – sometimes glancing quickly, but other times their heads turn, mouths flapping. They stop what they were saying to have another look, nudging their friends. *Did you see her?*

It never fails to surprise me that some people just don't know how to behave. I wonder whether they'd appreciate being asked personal questions as a greeting.

Conversely, some people are uncomfortable about my appearance. They avoid conversation and look away. They can barely mutter a 'Hello'.

So I invite all these people to say hello. To drop their preconceptions. To say hello to someone they might be afraid of, and see that I am approachable, friendly and ready for conversation *beyond my appearance*.

To be clear, I'm not trying to encourage the condescending contact and smiles that are all about making the other person feel good about interacting with a disabled person. I don't mean for non-disabled people to grin widely and say hello (and offer a pat on the head) to disabled people as they pass us in the street. It's about meaningful conversations in relevant situations. I think, when someone needs to engage with a disabled person, the first thing they should say is 'Hello' – not something inappropriate that they wouldn't want said to themselves.

I notice it, you see. I notice people treating me differently from the way they treated the person in front of me in a queue – I often receive a completely different reaction or level of service. People's expressions change when they see me – they place money on the counter rather than in my hand, and they seat me facing the wall in restaurants, so I won't scare away other diners.

Sometimes people ask me how they should behave around me, or others who have a facial difference or disability.

A quick answer: how would you behave around anyone else? And another question: would you need instructions about how to speak to a person from a different marginalised group?

Probably not.

How would you like to be treated if you had a facial difference or disability? Would you like to be stared at, or not looked at altogether? Would you want intrusive questions asked on a regular basis?

Or would you rather someone see you, smile at you politely and say, 'Hello'?

I think you know the answer.

I hope this book will help readers find the courage to look the world in the eye when the world sometimes looks away, or looks too much.

Go on. Say hello.

A note on language

This book uses a few terms that you might not be familiar with.

I use **disabled people** – rather than people with disability. This is because I see disability as being a key part of someone's identity, just like gender, race, sexuality and religion. It's not to be hidden. And while I love a good accessory, I don't carry disability around like a handbag. It's not an add-on to who I am.

It's my belief that saying the words 'disability' and 'disabled' rather than euphemisms and made-up words like 'special needs', 'differently abled' and 'diffability' reduces the stigma around disability.

Non-disabled people are people who don't have a disability.

I talk about **appearance diversity** and **facial difference** – these are self-explanatory – when referring to people whose faces look different from those belonging to most of society.

I refer to the **social model of disability** – whereby society is the disabling factor, rather than my body. Factors like the built environment, low expectations of disabled people, and discrimination are disabling. My appearance and body is not faulty or something to be ashamed about.

I talk about **impairment** – that's a diagnosis that causes an abnormality in the function or appearance of a person's body.

Ichthyosis is the rare, severe skin condition that I was born with. It causes red, scaly skin; it's prone to pain, itchiness and infections. My daily treatment is paraffin ointment applied to my whole body after a shower twice daily, and extra ointment on my face when needed, an antihistamine, and a mild painkiller if needed.

Sometimes I refer to **chronic illness** because my skin condition is ongoing, incurable, and it can make me very unwell.

Othering and **the other** is when a marginalised person or a group of people is treated differently because it's believed they don't fit the social norm. Othering might involve ridicule, exclusion, curiosity and the expectation to educate. 'The other' is regarded as different from 'us'.

Ableism is discrimination towards disabled people – it can be unconscious or overt.

And **microaggressions** are the everyday behaviours – like staring or avoidance, careless remarks or unconscious bias – that compound.

Disability pride means that disabled people can feel proud about our identity. Pride takes a lot of practice – especially because of the ableism, microaggressions and othering we face. Disability pride is also linked to **disability culture** – for me that's a strong sense of identity and community, resilience and shared stories and experiences.

I have written about my own experiences and reactions, and acknowledge that other people experience ichthyosis, facial difference, chronic illness and disability in different ways.

1

This face is not up for ridicule

When the bad guys on TV look like you, and the monsters in bedtime stories seem lonely like you, and you hear the phrase 'a face only a mother could love' and know the only person who tells you that you're beautiful is your mother, you learn that too.

Erin Kyan, *Monsters*

Every two months or so I receive an email from a TV production company or tabloid magazine – the type that run stories on people with rare medical conditions, ridiculing them for the way they look.

The TV shows set the tone with their titles – *Embarrassing Bodies*, *Body Bizarre*, *Born Different*, *The Undateables*, and so on.

You don't need to watch these shows to understand the type of public gaze they attract. Asking a person with a visible difference or disability to appear on a show with such titles, for other people's entertainment, is insulting and predatory.

While I haven't watched full episodes of all of these shows, I have observed that the subject of the show never tells their own story. It's narrated – I expect by a non-disabled person – with a camera zooming in on the most unusual part of the subject's appearance, and it's highly medicalised. For awareness raising. And entertainment.

And yes, that's right – I don't watch the programs but I have an opinion about them. I've taken some flak for that. But when people with disabilities, facial differences and rare diseases (sometimes the same type as mine) are featured on these shows, I *can* have an opinion. Because I live with the stares, the sniggers and ridicule from strangers, and the expectation to educate people, every day. I also live with the intimate parts of my illness – the shedding skin, the infections, the screams of pain. I don't need to televise this, or invite an audience to get their *Embarrassing Bodies* fix.

Regular viewers can't understand my disdain from these programs, chiding me for being outspoken about them. When my skin condition is featured on these shows, I always get messages from well-meaning friends telling me the show is on. They're excited to see someone like me on TV! Strangers I meet tell me they've seen ichthyosis on these shows too. They often claim to know more about the condition than I do, detailing how long it takes the people featured to bathe and scrub their skin. I guess I can thank these shows that I don't have to discuss my (much quicker) shower routine with a stranger, though!

A producer who invited me on to a show told me, 'I must stress that the name does not reflect the sensitive nature of the program.

The title is more of an "attention grabber" and not indicative of the human nature of the stories we cover.' But the titles are abhorrent. They're not sensitive or empathetic. Just like I don't want to be labelled embarrassing, I don't want my condition to be labelled as bizarre either.

And yet I am asked to take part in this tabloid media to 'raise awareness'. The pay offered is very low, $150 to $250. But the reach is wide – with regularly repeated worldwide broadcasts, and online shares.

In my early days of writing online, just as I was starting to get media interest, I sold my story to a UK-based tabloid – I was a bit dazzled by a media offer. They assured me it would be tasteful, and that I would have control of my story. They interviewed me over the phone, and said they could run the story by me over the phone, but not via email. They paid me a pittance. When the magazine was published, I was horrified. The headline screamed, 'I always look sunburnt!' It was full of woe and pity. They got my dad's name wrong too. I'm not proud of that decision.

I've been in tabloid magazines since, but I've written my own story, in third person, to have some control over how my story is told.

In 2016, an American casting director contacted me about a show he thought I'd be suitable for. While I usually say no to these, it sounded interesting and I'd just experienced a microaggression – so I thought that maybe, just maybe, my appearance might help change the thinking of people who are scared of my (and others') appearance. We talked on the phone a few hours later.

We had an interview via Skype to discuss my potential involvement in the show. It was on a cold Saturday morning in April. My husband, Adam, was not home. The director asked me a few questions, and it was clear he knew very little about disability politics or pride. The questions were quite pitying. I talked to him about Stella Young and inspiration porn (see Chapter 2) and said I didn't want my potential appearance on the show to be about that. I told him I often worried about the intrusiveness of journalists, explaining that was why I rarely engage in these interviews. He told me I could make a lot of money if I was cast, but not if I was difficult. (I guess he sensed from our chat that I can be outspoken.)

About 40 minutes in, maybe less – I don't have a recording – he told me we were wrapping up and asked if there was anything I wanted to tell him.

'I got married a month ago,' I said.

'Yeah, I was wondering …' he said, scratching his stubbly chin. I saw him on the computer screen, leaning back casually, his entitlement to my story just beginning to show.

I thought he might be about to ask me about my dress, or even an awkward question about Adam looking past my ichthyosis. Nope.

'What does intercourse feel like?' he asked.

He asked what sex feels like. He sat through the interview, thinking that the whole time.

Of course, I was shocked. I told him he had no right to ask that. He told me he was doing his job. My mind was racing, furious. I had told him, during the Skype call, that I've spent a lot of time writing about intrusive questions – and now he'd just asked me one. I recall him mentioning a woman with a severe facial disfigurement or disability who had never had sex, and that she wondered how it felt. I ended the conversation politely. Had the conversation been in person, I think I would have still been polite, though perhaps I'd have slammed the door on my way out.

I'm proud of my difference, and I'm not an object to be ogled at or ridiculed on social media.

I was shaking. I recall texting my best friend about it, telling her about the potential money and also that question. I don't even think I told Adam. I felt so used. So intruded upon.

I was scared to speak out about this at the time. I didn't want to be seen as difficult, and there was no proof on my end. This is how these types of men get away with it – it's a form of sexual harassment. I tweeted about it more than nine months later, naming him and the company he was attached to. And when I did, he threatened legal action, denying it all. I deleted my tweets. (Now, with the #MeToo movement, I'd be much braver about speaking out about this slimebag and the people who stood by him.)

Would he have asked a woman without a disability about sex? Probably not. His actions proved what I've believed about this exploitative media – that the subjects are modern-day freak show exhibits, shown very little respect.

I've had enough of exploitative media outlets implying my appearance is hideous, and that my private life is available for questioning by inviting me onto these shows. That's why I make my own media – to show I'm proud of my difference, and I'm not an object to be ogled at or ridiculed on social media. And to set a positive example for others living with my skin condition.

I know some readers will think my stance on this exploitative media is an absolute contradiction. People have told me so. Pfft. I blog, regularly write for the media, and quite enjoy having an audience. I am comfortable sharing my image across social media. I put myself out there. So I get it. Why wouldn't I want extra media attention? Why would I criticise this method of 'awareness raising' when I do it via the media too? Aren't I hypocritical?

I like to be able to tell my own story in my own words. I like to portray the condition realistically and positively (even the difficult things) with positive language. I don't want to be in the public gaze for voyeuristic entertainment. I don't want to be someone else's money-maker (for a small inconvenience fee). I don't want to be the subject of pity or inspiration, and I certainly don't want to endure the ridicule from viewers. I want to tell my story on my terms, changing the disability media landscape. And I encourage others to do the same.

Whenever someone with my skin condition, a parent of a child with the condition, or another disability or visible difference, says yes to being on these TV shows or in a magazine article, they're feeding the exploitation machine. They're showing the world our conditions are ugly and embarrassing and implying that the best way to raise awareness is through doing this.

How are the kids whose parents put them on the show in the spirit of awareness raising going to feel? What happens when they read the comments?

How are people with rare conditions going to see themselves when this exploitative media is one of the only ways that people like themselves are represented?

How do you love yourself when people invite you to be laughed at on television and social media?

The commentary around shows like *Embarrassing Bodies* is like sniggering in the schoolyard. News columnists are calling it 'the horror'. People are talking about it on social media. It's TV that you binge on – excited at the prospect and then throwing up at the gory details. I came across an audience analysis of what people were saying about *Embarrassing Bodies* online. Some described it as their guilty pleasure, and another said they 'can't wait to laugh at people then vomit'.

Evan, a child who I met in the USA, is the most delightful little boy. He loves Mickey Mouse and kangaroos. He has Harlequin ichthyosis – the most severe form of ichthyosis – and looks a lot like me. Evan was featured on a TV program in 2016, and the online comments were revolting. While the media company prided themselves on their sensitive storytelling, they contradicted themselves when they let commenters spurt hate speech, debating Evan's right to be alive, and making grotesque remarks about his appearance. I hope he never has to read them.

This isn't how I want my condition discussed. I don't want ichthyosis to be gratuitous fodder for someone to laugh at in their living room. And this isn't how I want my friends' disabilities discussed either.

I want to take back the power. I want disabled people telling our own stories, through blogging and performances and YouTube channels and standup (sitdown?) comedy and podcasts and even mainstream medias – inviting the public gaze in a much less gawkish way.

When we invite the public gaze in on our own terms, it can be very empowering. We are choosing how we want to be portrayed – taking on the tabloid and social media paparazzi predators.

I am a public person, a voice in the media, but I'm not here for your entertainment (or infotainment) unless I invite it.

Of course, sometimes the attention comes whether I invite it or not. Take my experience with the US social news aggregation website Reddit.

It was an ordinary morning in mid-December 2013. I woke up at 6.30 am – my then boyfriend (now husband) was off to work. I checked Facebook, Twitter, my email and my blog stats. There had been a big spike in traffic overnight, which surprised me because I hadn't blogged recently. The traffic came from Reddit. Shit. While I had shared a few of my blog posts there previously, I had also heard Reddit described as the bottom of the internet. I clicked on the link – and it took me to the 'What the Fuck?' forum. There was a photo of me, dressed up, smiling and holding a glass of champagne in a dark function room, with the caption, 'Made me say it' – the inference being that my face made them say, 'What the fuck?'

I scrolled through the comments.

What does your vagina look like?

WTF is that? Looks like something that was partially digested by my dog.

Lobster.

She looks like a glazed donut.

I dated a girl with a mild form of ichthyosis, once. Thankfully, she was Filipino so her skin was naturally brown, otherwise she'd be as bright red as her. I thought her skin was cool … it certainly wasn't unpleasant, but had a nice texture. Plus her boobs felt like underinflated basketballs … Very fun to squeeze :)

Seeing people like this smile makes me uncomfortable. It looks like a lie; they are only smiling in an attempt to fool themselves that their lives aren't horrible. You can see it in her eyes. The same rehearsed dead-eye mouth-smile in all her pictures. Gives me the willies.

And there were countless diagnoses (so many people educated by Dr Google) and assumptions of sunburn. They annoyed me a lot. Not to mention that that photo was actually taken on one of the happiest nights of my life, when I met the *Rush* TV show cast.

What the fuck indeed. My worst fear had come true. I was the subject of ridicule on the internet. This is why I had held off from sharing my photo online for so many years. (I think it took until 2005, when I set up a MySpace account, for me to share – almost 10 years after I started using the internet.)

There were some supportive comments, though.

> There, but for the Grace of God, go I. Parents, teach your children not to laugh at people that aren't what society deems as 'perfect'. That's my sermon for the day, keep your comments to yourself if you don't agree with me. I don't need any help, thanks tho. Except for her condition she has a smile that makes her look like Geena Davis.

One guy said he wished he hadn't missed his chance to ask me out on a date.

And this guy, he was a standout:

> You, madam, are the strongest motherfucker I have ever HEARD of, let alone met. If you are ever in Boston, I would be honored to buy you a beer.

A little shocked, I wrote a Facebook status about the Reddit post. And then I modified it, and posted a response on Reddit:

I knew the day would come that someone would create a Reddit thread about me, using my photo, having a laugh at my appearance. For years, that fear was why I didn't share photos of me online. But now, after gaining confidence and support through years of blogging, I couldn't care whether they call me a lobster or silly putty.

The love I have around me and success I have had through telling my own story to break down stigma like these Reddit threads is stronger than any of those words.

Yes, I have ichthyosis. Yes, that picture is me. Don't fear it and don't criticise it. I am proud of the way I look, what I have achieved and for telling my story.

FYI: I have two forms of ichthyosis – a mix of Netherton syndrome and erythroderma. My skin is shiny because I use paraffin. My body is less red than my face as it's not exposed to the elements, but it is generally more painful. Ichthyosis is survivable – I have lived a very full life.

My response quickly changed the tone of the comments.

The original poster gave me an apology.

I'm reading all this and I apologise! I was looking for 'champagne fridge' on Google images. When I saw your picture, I thought 'WTF!' and further: 'allergic reaction', also your hair looks a bit on fire so I put it here. Hopefully you see it as a good promotion for your blog and chapeau to you for being awesome!

A bit backhanded, but I thanked him all the same.

When this picture was posted overnight, I was content lying in the arms of my love, having just seen a band and eaten a great meal – a night filled with laughs. Meanwhile, these Reddit posters were making fun of a stranger on the internet. I think the location of this post, and the title, is a clear indication of the original poster's intent. However, I say the others who joined in with the ridicule and armchair diagnoses are just as voyeuristic.

I am resilient. I've got thick skin. These are just words on a screen. I am safe and loved, strong and intelligent, and can fight back with awesome. But I worry for those who can't. What about those people who are mocked online and do not have the strength or words to defend themselves? Or even continue living?

My blog about Reddit made national and international news. I took calls from CNN (I said yes to a story) and *The Daily Mail* (I said no but they published one anyway, and the comments were the loveliest). I was the top story on *News.com.au*, and other local outlets ran my story. I spoke on Studio 10. TV presenter Charlie Pickering mentioned me on *The Project* – saying that the Reddit post meant my writing would be discovered. He was right – it did boost my profile and career. And I was all over US, European and UK news. I couldn't keep up. But while I received lots of support from both friends and strangers, some of the comments on the news sites were worse than those on Reddit.

The Reddit abuse erupted twice more over the following couple of weeks, although it didn't make the news.

The second time was in a sub-forum titled 'I am going to hell for this', and the post was called 'A sophisticated lobster'. Commenters suggested I should be killed with fire. When I reported it to the administrator, he said, 'Sorry that happened to you,' but did not remove the post immediately.

The third time was in this same sub-forum, titled 'Guys, you've angered the lobster again'. I reported it to the administrators but they didn't respond directly. During these times, publicly they condoned it, and privately they were apologetic.

I called out the behaviour directly because I had the confidence to do so after blogging about my appearance for so many years. I thought I was brave enough to take it on (again), but I'm not. I can't stop this cruelty.

When you are threatened in the street, you know to call the police. But who do you call when you're threatened online? The founders and administrators of sites like Reddit have a duty of care to people's emotional and physical safety. I did not feel safe when people said I should be killed with fire.

Reddit was the first time I'd gone viral. Going viral felt out of control. While it was exciting to see the blog stats climb (80,000 hits in two days) – and I was constantly checking and screen-shotting them – it wasn't exciting to wake up to awful comments.

I couldn't control who saw my blog or commented on it or reproduced my story and photos. I couldn't unsee the hate speech and death threats – but I did pass on the job of comment moderator to Adam, and it wasn't so easy for him to read them either.

I still get a huge amount of traffic from that post on Reddit, and from some of the stories written about it. Stories about my Reddit experience pop up occasionally – in mid-2015 there was a spurt of international coverage, 18 months after the event. Today, my initial post about Reddit is still the most viewed of my blog.

It's the story that keeps on giving. Bullying is a pack mentality, but so is kindness. The amount of support shown soon overtook the number of negative comments.

People killed those trolls' comments with kindness. Minds were opened, the Redditors told me so. And I have been stronger and bolder than ever, writing much more focused content, because I now know my positive influence.

I want my work to reach as many people as possible – I want to influence the way people think about appearance diversity and disability.

Being a writer – online and through this book – and having a social media profile can help me achieve these goals. But I want my work and writing to reach the right people. Going viral is not the right way to make this happen. Longevity is not 15 minutes of internet fame.

Internet fame doesn't last long. For about a week I was that red woman who took on Reddit trolls. And for the rest of the year I was that woman that they'd maybe seen somewhere before ...

2

Why this book refuses to be 'inspiration porn'

Even though I want to influence the way people think about appearance diversity and disability, I don't want to inspire you, or anyone, just by existing. If I must inspire you, I want you to use that inspiration to create positive change.

Even before I started writing this book, I worried that it could turn into 'inspiration porn'. I wanted to do the right thing by the disability community – because we deserve to be represented better. But I don't want someone to read this book and think, 'If Carly can go out of the house with a red face, then what the hell am I complaining about?'

'Inspiration porn' is a term coined by the late Australian disability activist and writer Stella Young. It means the objectification of disabled people for the benefit of non-disabled people. Stella talked about inspiration porn in a TEDx Talk that's been viewed over two million times:

> I use the term 'porn' deliberately, because they objectify one group of people for the benefit of another group of people. So in this case, we're objectifying disabled people for the benefit of non-disabled people. The purpose of these images is to inspire you, to motivate you, so that we can look at them and think, 'Well, however bad my life is, it could be worse. I could be that person.'
>
> But what if you are that person? I've lost count of the number of times that I've been approached by strangers wanting to tell me that they think I'm brave or inspirational, and this was long before my work had any kind of public profile. They were just kind of congratulating me for managing to get up in the morning and remember my own name. [Laughter] And it is objectifying. These images, those images objectify disabled people for the benefit of non-disabled people. They are there so that you can look at them and think that things aren't so bad for you, to put your worries into perspective.

Stella Young was a comedian, journalist and disability rights activist. She described herself, in a piece she wrote about dancing, as both a political statement and an act of enjoyment, as 'less than a metre tall, and … a wheelchair user'. Stella challenged and changed the way I saw disability, and changed how I saw myself too. In a widely published letter to her 80-year-old self, Stella wrote, 'I devoured the memoirs of other disabled people. And I completely changed the way I thought about myself.' I feel this way when I read her work and that of other disability activists.

She gave me an opportunity to write for the ABC. Most weeks I re-read her writing and find something new to ponder over. I'm so grateful for how she changed the way disability is understood, in Australia and beyond.

Her words, in the *Ramp Up* piece 'Dance Like Everyone's Watching', reinforced the way I feel about the able-bodied gaze — stares and comments from strangers.

> Just as I am aware of my body in those moments, the way my muscles feel as I move, I'm equally aware of the able-bodied gaze. Heck, I'm aware of it when I'm in the supermarket, on a tram or wheeling through the streets. But there's something extra at play on the dance floor, and people not only look, they comment.

I know that people who call me an inspiration are well intended. They think it's a compliment. But for me, and for other disabled people, the word 'inspiration' can be tricky. Non-disabled people often call us an inspiration for doing not very much. That's because expectations of disabled people are so low.

When I was working towards my Masters of Communication, I was sometimes asked if I was at TAFE. Not that there's anything wrong with TAFE — but some people couldn't fathom that I could accomplish study at Masters level. Because of my skin and the way I look, their expectations were so low they couldn't fathom I could do postgraduate studies.

Some non-disabled people see our lives and think, 'What am I complaining about?' They marvel at us doing everyday things —

sometimes with the help of a prosthetic limb or mobility aid – and think we're superhuman. They cry at news stories about disabled people finding love – because they think no one could love us. And they congratulate us for being out in public – I've lost count of the number of times I've been told, 'It's great to see you getting out there!'

Sometimes, when one of my articles is shared via a news outlet's Facebook page, and my photo is attached, people will comment:

I see this woman on my train. She's such an inspiration.

I don't recall these people ever speaking to me on the train. And when I'm on the train, I am not doing anything particularly inspiring. I'm usually just scrolling through Facebook. Sometimes I'm writing on my phone. Sometimes I'm crammed in like a sardine, trying to avoid being poked by other people's shopping bags. I'm just going into the city like everyone else.

Of course, we can't control how others see us or what they're inspired by. There will still be people who are inspired by us, without considering their entrenched unconscious bias and discriminatory beliefs about disabled people. But I hope that by changing the narrative through writing and speaking, and just being visible and present, I can help a few people shift from seeing me and other disabled people as objects of inspiration and pity.

I'd like to be an inspiration because of my writing and work ethic, not only because I identify as disabled and am getting out and about. I don't want to be called an inspiration just for getting out of bed.

I do acknowledge that for some disabled people, it is a big feat to get out of bed, though. For some, the sheer act of getting out of bed and getting dressed expends so much energy that it can inspire themselves and others. I also acknowledge the ways disabled people can inspire each other – which is different from being objectified. We inspire each other by sharing stories, riffing off each other's experiences, seeing someone do something we were too afraid of doing, and connecting deeply.

One of the reasons I wrote this book is because Caroline, a friend with ichthyosis, told me that my writing had changed her life. The small act of my outfit photos on social media made her comfortable and confident enough to finally wear a sundress in public during summer – after almost 40 years of covering up.

> The more of Carly's articles I read, the stronger I became. It is a slow process but because of Carly, I wore a summer dress on public transport. A huge step for me in my life. I no longer feel ashamed for having ichthyosis and I have even posted publicly on social media that I have ichthyosis.
>
> Because of Carly's writing, my relationship with my skin has changed completely and I have accepted that I am not defined by my ichthyosis.

Caroline held her breath for so long, afraid to take up space, and my words helped her exhale. You can read a little more from Caroline later in this book.

I am happy to inspire other disabled people to get on the path of self-confidence, or think differently about themselves or disability. I am happy to inspire non-disabled people to think a different way – broadening their perceptions of what it means to be disabled.

But I don't want to inspire non-disabled people because they think my life is worse than theirs.

Many other disability activists have been key to my growth and knowledge. Blogging and social media and has been a big part of

I don't want to inspire you, or anyone, just by existing. If I must inspire you, I want you to use that inspiration to create positive change.

that. In the almost-decade that I've been blogging about ichthyosis, disability, chronic illness and facial difference, I've met some amazingly smart and dedicated disability rights activists online. They've given me a sense of community and taught me so much. I thrive on reading their articles and tweets.

I've also come to know myself. This book is a result of that knowledge. *Say Hello*, and my other writing, represents my own views and not the views of all disabled people. I don't speak for everybody in the disability community, because we all have different views and values. I am not the only disabled writer out there. Please go seek out other disabled writers online and in bookstores and libraries. Go see the art we make, hear us talk at events, invite us to work with you, and buy our work.

While I might not have as much privilege in the wider community, I am certainly privileged in the disability community – especially compared to many disabled women. I acknowledge my privilege. I work a few different jobs and live above the poverty line. I am in a heterosexual relationship. I have been educated to postgraduate level. I am able to travel. I can afford most of my medications. I have access to free healthcare. I can advocate for myself. I work in the media – and because of my profile, I am often offered further work. Many disabled people do not have these opportunities.

I try to use my privilege – and the power that comes with that – to fight for human rights and equity for all disabled people. I always endeavour to amplify the voices of other disabled people on my social media, pledge to their crowdfunding campaigns, invite them to work with me, tell them about media and speaking opportunities, put forward their names for work, and pass work on if I am able to. I want to use my work to raise the profile of others.

It's crucial that everyone recognises their privilege – even those in marginalised communities – and makes space for and hands over power to others. Stella Young did this – she made space for other disabled people to be visible and respectfully represented.

I sought Stella Young's family's permission to mention and quote her, and I really hope I've done her justice. I wish she was still here – to keep writing fierce and funny articles and for her friendship.

3

I was born this way

I came into this world at the Mercy Hospital in Albury, after a gruelling 32-hour labour. I was born with the rare, severe, genetic skin condition ichthyosis – diagnosed with erythroderma at birth, and rediagnosed with Netherton syndrome after genetic tests when I was 10 years old. I came out red and shiny, but I don't think I was in pain immediately.

Ichthyosis (ick-thee-o-ses) is a rare genetic skin disorder, which affects approximately one in 200,000 newborn babies. Since it's a genetic mutation, it isn't contagious – you can't 'catch' it. Ichthyosis causes the skin to build up and scale, and makes it extremely dry, among other problems.

Most types of ichthyosis are present at birth, and are life-long. Currently, there is no cure, only treatments.

I am red and scaly. My skin gets itchy and sore. My face is the reddest part of my body because it is exposed to the elements. I get infections easily – generally on my legs, but sometimes on my face. Sometimes my infections result in hospital stays where I am bandaged up like a mummy. Infections can make me very sore.

My skin condition affects lots of other things in my body. My eyes, ears, digestive system, temperature and metabolism are all affected to a degree. I see lots of doctors!

My parents met at a party in Cape Town, South Africa, in 1978. Dad grew up in Nottingham, England, and went to South Africa to work as an engineer in 1976. Mum grew up in what would now be called commission houses in Cape Town. They kept their courtship secret, trusting only close family and friends, because my mum was classified as a coloured South African, and my dad is white. Apartheid kept them from being together in the open. They were almost caught on two occasions – when Dad's car broke down on the beach and they had to seek help from strangers, and when the police visited Dad's flat to tell him his car had been run into. Mum hid on Dad's balcony, which overlooked the rocks and sea. Both times, Mum could have been jailed.

In late 1980, Dad proposed to Mum by saying they were going to Australia to get married. Dad had found a job in Sydney. Not so romantic – but the most practical option for them to continue their relationship legally and publicly. They had a pre-wedding honeymoon in Sri Lanka, Singapore and Thailand, and arrived in Sydney in January 1981. It was a condition that they got married within a month and Mum had to find work soon after, or she would have needed to return to South Africa. They did both. They married in Centennial Park in February – Dad, ever thrifty, proudly reminds me their wedding cost $87. Mum found work in a bank, thanks to a referral from their wedding celebrant. Dad found a job at a car parts manufacturer in Albury, country New South Wales, in October of that year, and so they moved to Albury. I was born in 1981 in Albury – population 37,350 at the time. Albury was then a small rural city surrounded by tiny farming towns.

Before I began writing this book, I asked Mum what she thought when I didn't look like her or Dad. 'To be honest, I saw you were red, I asked what was wrong, but I was too tired to even wait for an answer,' she said. 'You were on my chest straightaway, which was good. We got to bond. You weren't agitated.'

Mum said it was a while before she learnt anything about my diagnosis, because she was so tired. 'I went to sleep for eight hours. You were in the nursery in the humidicrib, with Dad by your side.'

The doctors and nurses hadn't seen a baby like me before. The obstetrician sent for the paediatrician that night, and he came with a dermatologist. The dermatologist diagnosed me straightaway, though he told my parents my skin should be perfect by the time I left the hospital.

I stayed in hospital for eight days after birth, but I contracted golden staph, which we now know is likely because my skin is susceptible to infections. This isolated Mum, because she wasn't able to have any visitors apart from Dad. She asked to go home before the 10-day period, knowing I'd receive the same care in the home.

At this stage, when my skin hadn't got 'better' – I was still red and scaly – the dermatologist accused my parents of not looking after me properly. Mum and Dad were very angry, and we didn't see this dermatologist again.

When I was born I was prescribed Sorbolene (a water-based cream) to my whole body, and Sigmacort (a mild cortisone cream) to infected areas. I used Sorbolene until late primary school, but it left me with a patchy, red and white face. Mum used to feel sorry for me, using a visible cream on top of my bright red skin. How embarrassing! Then I switched to paraffin-based ointment, which I've applied to my whole body twice a day ever since. I much prefer paraffin as it absorbs into my skin and leaves me feeling moisturised for a good portion of the day.

My parents are very resourceful. They just got on with it. 'We had to,' Dad says. They didn't blame themselves or anyone about my ichthyosis, nor did they sit around moping. They were new to the country, new to a small rural city, newlyweds, without family help, and just had a baby with a skin condition so rare and severe it was unfamiliar to most doctors.

But Mum's always optimistic. 'I wouldn't call it difficult. I didn't know what to expect. So I just took it one day at a time,' she says with shrug. 'The doctors did their best. I didn't think of a cure at the time.' Mum always maintained 'There's nothing wrong with Carly,' and the questions and comments about my skin didn't get her down.

Mum and Dad didn't get any counselling, although Mum was referred to a social worker – and at the time, Mum thought the social worker wasn't experienced or old enough to know what it was like to care for a baby with a serious illness. In hindsight, she realises that the social worker's advice – to be around positive people and to take one day at a time – wasn't negative, but encouraging.

The nuns from the hospital visited regularly to provide assistance around the house, and gifts at Christmas time. The care the nuns gave my family is the most positive experience I've had with religion. They didn't push religion – they were hands on. We visited them regularly as I grew up – my parents had a lot of respect for them. But a priest from another denomination told Mum and Dad they needed to go to church and needed to be saved. It was only then I could get better, he said. 'I threw him out of the house without dinner. I told him where to go. I still believed [in God] then, but he put me off,' Mum says. Later, I was sent to Sunday school and youth group, but was still told that if I was alive in Jesus' time, I'd be treated like a leper, and that my parents are black and white, so I'd paid for their sins.

Mum says I was a happy baby, laughing and giggling. It wasn't all sadness. But when I was sick, I was sick. More often than not.

I spent a lot of time in the Royal Children's Hospital in Melbourne – from when I was a few weeks old – because the skin specialists were there. But there were other problems too – I was born with a heart murmur, arm paralysis and dislocated hips. At one stage, I suffered a seizure on the day I was due to be brought home from Melbourne – and my parents had to leave me there. The doctors weren't sure how long I would live. (Even today, babies with some types of ichthyosis have a high chance of infant mortality.) The hospital was a long way from Albury.

Mum never grieved for a 'normal' life. She did hope I wouldn't suffer. It was hardest when I was very small – I couldn't tell my parents how my skin was feeling or ask for pain relief or temperature control, so they couldn't help me. At times, Mum asked Dad why I had to be in so much pain. But I never saw it – I only experienced positivity and encouragement from them.

In 1983, we moved to a new home in Walla Walla, a tiny country town 30 minutes from Albury. The summers were scorching hot and dry, and the winters were frosty. It was a farming community – sheep and cattle were raised for slaughter, and wheat would be harvested yearly. Most people were white and Christian and worked on the land or within Walla Walla. Mum and Dad moved into a tiny weatherboard house on half an acre, with a garden abundant with vegetables and sunflowers. I had a very happy time at home with Mum and Dad – sourcing photos for this book reminded me of that. I had love and encouragement and never went without.

Mum and Dad never invited the media into our lives – even though we'd see stories about disabled kids on *60 Minutes*. 'You were Carly, you were not an object, you were not a spectacle,' Mum says. (I see a lot of parents taking their kids' stories to the media now – and I cringe because so often the kid hasn't consented, and doesn't know the reach and implications of the media.) But they did expose me to other kids with more serious impairments like burns and cancer so I could gain some perspective. The head dermatologist at the Royal Children's Hospital (a doctor I still see today) recommended this.

My parents received a lot of advice. Everyone had a cure to suggest, everyone thought they knew more than my parents. Like Percy's Powder (bought from the side of the road in Porepunkah). We didn't know the ingredients then but Google tells us that Percy's Powder is now available in an online health store, and the ingredients are magnesium, potassium and iron (all as sulfate). It tasted like mud and did not make one scrap of difference to my skin. Mum said advice from others was well meaning, but it did get tedious, especially as I became a teenager. 'If it wasn't getting better by then, it would never get better,' she says. Most of the advice-givers had limited knowledge of ichthyosis. They only saw me outside of the house (at my relative best), and for all they knew, it was merely cosmetic. A lot of people pushed their pyramid scheme products – and they still do, years later, especially on Instagram. (People selling face creams and scented oils find me, I guess via hashtags like #ichthyosis and #skinconditions, and offer me products that will supposedly help me. Only, they're not doctors, and their products are very much cosmetic.)

My parents chose not to have any more children because I was a 24/7 baby. They felt they wouldn't able to divide their time equally – Mum had seen it happen to other families in hospital. Mum personally wouldn't have minded having another child to give me a companion, though. I did adult things and had adult conversations because I didn't have a sibling. Other children and some adults told me that if I had a sibling, it would be better if they had ichthyosis, so they could empathise with me – but they don't know what it's really like to live with the condition.

My earliest memory of knowing I was different was when Mum took me to daycare one day when she had an appointment. I had just turned three. I had been with other children when I went to playgroup occasionally, but I don't recall being teased or avoided, because the kids were used to me. These kids at daycare rode around me on tricycles, pinching and punching me.

I wanted to change how I looked. I didn't want to be red anymore because I thought then kids would treat me better. And looking back, I didn't want to be in photos because it would confirm I was different. There are a few photos of me at various ages scattered around my parents' home – mostly milestones like school and university graduations. In my early years, I was hesitant about smiling for the camera – sometimes I'd just screw my face up or shut my eyes. I didn't think I was worthy of having my photo taken when my face was different from most people's anyway. It was internalised ableism. I didn't like how I looked. But looking at the photos decades later, I wish I could have seen myself through Big Carly's eyes. So cute. So worthy of smiling for a photo.

I felt alone for most of my school years. Most kids don't want to hang out with someone who looks different. I tried to tell them about my skin and cream, but it just grossed them out. I was called names and laughed at. They wouldn't touch me, sit near me, sit where I'd been or hold my hand. They wouldn't touch me when we played heads down thumbs up. And I wasn't fashionable wearing a bee net over my hat – to prevent the flies from getting into my ears. Mum discovered flies buried in my ear when she was doing my hair when I was four. The flies were attracted to the smell of infected skin in my ears, and became trapped. I was operated on to remove the flies – and for a few years I wore a net. This contributed hugely to my low self-esteem. I felt repulsed that only flies wanted to get close to me, and that I had to wear such a daggy contraption to stop them. I looked like a junior beekeeper who hated the outdoors.

Aside from being spat on, which was cruel enough, there was never physical bullying. I suppose it was fortunate that kids didn't want to touch me – it saved me from being physically hurt. It was all name-calling, laughing and exclusion. I was called 'skinner', 'redskin', 'red light match', 'traffic light' – these are the ones I can remember. I wasn't invited to many parties after the age of six – I suspect this was the age when kids had a say about who to invite and who to leave off the list. Parties were a status symbol of being fully included in school and out. And so I felt pretty special when I was invited to the occasional one.

I went to a really sporty primary school – if you didn't enjoy sport, you automatically didn't fit in. Although I was often unable to do sport or swim because of the heat or the stress of exercise on my skin, teachers would make me sit and watch. I was exposed to the heat and flies anyway – and all I wanted to do was go into the library to read. Mum tried to keep me home on sports days, and thankfully she had good friends to look after me while she was at work.

Teachers didn't believe me when I told them how sad I felt about the bullying, putting the blame back onto me. How could I change so they didn't pick on me? Hear this, teachers: I could not change my appearance so the kids would accept me, but they could have changed their level of acceptance and got to know me. I hate it when people use 'kids are just kids' as justification. Those kids know what they're doing. They know how hurtful they're being. The bullying stuck with me for a long time – and occasionally, even now, I get nervous when I see groups of school kids out and about.

When I was bullied, my parents would confront the kids and their parents. This of course did nothing to help me make friends – no one likes the weird kid who gets her parents to defend them.

And it is hard to know how to be a good friend if you haven't got many friends. I didn't know how to treat my peers well because they didn't treat me well. I wasn't able to build trust, and probably came across as needy.

When I was nine or 10 I wanted to kill myself. I can't even say those words without a lump in my throat. I had had enough of being different, and the kids were saying I got special treatment from the teachers — being able to sit out of sport or spending lots of time away from school — both of which were not special at all. I never attempted suicide, I just told Mum. I feel so sick at the thought that I can't recall the moment I told her. Mum panicked, and called the paediatrician straightaway. They referred me to a child psychiatrist — I went to two sessions with my parents, and three alone. While the psychiatrist helped (I actually have no memory of these appointments), it was Mum who rebuilt my self-worth. Mum tells me that although the bullying continued, I had a better outlook. She taught me it was important to have self-respect, and not to worry what others thought, but she never justified or made excuses for other people's behaviour.

My social landscape wasn't completely barren. Due to my parents' work hours, I stayed with the Milnes — a large family — before and after school, and made friends with them. They ran the local pub, and it was quite an adventure. It was a really bright spot — I felt welcome and safe. They were a jolly, inclusive, and loud family — they liked horseracing and sport — very different from me. In the mornings, Mrs Milne would make us all a chocolate milkshake in the pub kitchen, and in the afternoons, Mr Milne would let us go behind the bar and help ourselves to chips and Coke from the machine. Their daughter Brigette was in my year at school, and I've recently reconnected with her. She told me she would always try to include me, but would get frustrated that I couldn't join in the outdoor sports and swimming, and wished I could. This gave me a new perspective — maybe some kids wanted to include me after all. And maybe I was so fed up with the bad experiences that I couldn't see the good.

As a result of being bullied and excluded, I spent a lot of time indoors, reading and being creative.

Dad was my mate. We spent hours making cheeses from playdough – he taught me the names of exotic cheeses as he shaped the playdough into rounds and wedges. Cheshire, Stilton, Swiss, Brie. And on Saturday nights we'd feast on real cheeses.

He was an engineer and so a lot of the projects were hands-on and messy. I'd spend time with him in the shed – making puppets, painting rocks, making rafts out of Paddle Pop sticks, and hammering nails into wood. I didn't seem to mind having to clean the paint off my hands with turps, even though it stung a little.

He built me a guinea-pig house – a double-decker palace – for five guinea pigs. We bought two from the pet shop when I was about eight. We were assured they were two males. But Cuddles and Dinky were a male and a female. It should have been obvious they were mating when they spent a lot of time sitting on each other. A few months later, three babies were born – Tiger, Rabbit and Mouse. It was my job to feed the guinea pigs, brush them and clean their cage. It was fun for a while, but they gave me worms. I'm sure this happens to most kids who keep rodents!

Dad is creative – good at storytelling. Every Sunday morning I'd get into bed with my parents, and Dad would tell me stories about Tippy the Elf, who lived in the park next to our house, as well as Marmaduke and Joe, who drove their red lorry around town, delivering things to shops. When I got to primary school age, I'd help tell the stories with Dad, taking them on tangents.

Mum and I would also make up stories, elaborating on fairytales, while she combed the scale out of my scalp. That was a nice time to bond – we talked about our day, and had a chance to be creative. As painful as it was, I cherished this time, although

Mum cooked dinner before she did my hair, and the chilli residue on her fingers stung my scalp. Mum couldn't understand why it was stinging. She'd also get annoyed with me because I'd complain when my scalp was so cold on a Saturday morning when we went shopping – she didn't realise how much ichthyosis affects my temperature regulation. (Having my scalp combed at night didn't affect me temperature-wise as we wouldn't go out afterwards. But going out in the morning just after my scalp was combed really hurt!)

I would stay up late reading on Friday and Saturday nights, devouring whole books at a time. I loved to read. I read books from a very early age – my first memory of reading is of the *Sesame Street Dictionary*. Once a week the Mobile Library (a truck filled with books – how fun!) would come to my little town. I'd go there after school, reading books on the floor, and borrowing a big pile for the next week. It transported me to other worlds.

I grew up reading Enid Blyton and Roald Dahl – *The Magic Faraway Tree* and Noddy, and *Matilda*, *The Twits* and *Charlie and the Chocolate Factory* were my favourites. My Aunty Diane sent me a tape of Roald Dahl reading *George's Marvellous Medicine*. I loved hearing his voice – despite the sinister message of the story, it was a lot of fun to listen to.

My parents bought me a personalised Cabbage Patch Kid book to accompany my Cabbage Patch Kid – Lisa Jacqueline. How exciting to have a book that was about me! The illustration that represented me didn't look like me, though – now I would love it if it did, but back then I rejected my red appearance.

The *Baby-Sitters Club* books were a staple in my final years of primary school, and every month I'd buy one from the Scholastic book club. Mum thought they were too old for me when I talked about boys snapping Stacey McGill's bra strap, but I read them anyway. It was the same with *Sweet Valley High*.

Craft was another pasttime. I'd spend a lot of time hand-sewing Barbie and peg doll clothes, creating animals from gumnuts and leaves, and knitting with a bobbin. I developed some skills in keeping house too – my parents were far from giving me special treatment – so I had to learn how to cook and clean. I enjoyed cooking much more than cleaning as a kid – and that hasn't changed as an adult!

I was lucky my sore skin afforded me so much time to read, write, create and imagine. Yes, lucky.

I asked Mum and Dad what advice they have for new parents. Mum encourages parents to take one day at a time. She also said that they need to show their child respect, and teach their child self-respect – even before self-love. She is matter of fact when answering strangers' questions, but gives parents permission to be rude if the questioner is rude.

Dad is ever practical. Stoic even. Carry on as normal, he said. 'Accept that skin debris and cream-tainted walls, books, phones and TV controllers will prevail. Buy a decent vacuum cleaner and commercial-grade washing machine. Tiled and timber floors are preferable over carpet.'

Both my parents believe in good doctors over naturopaths and herbalists, and discourage looking for a miracle cure and comparing whose child has it worse within support groups.

4

Woman of colour

When I was little, I wanted to have 'normal' skin. I would often pull up my sleeves and look at my forearms, showing them off to the kids at school — the kids who weren't really my friends. My arms were the part of my body that could pass as 'normal'.

If I were to wear a mask and long pants and just bare my forearms, I could pretend I didn't have ichthyosis. The skin on my forearms is, for most of the time, smooth and pale, although it does get red when I'm sore. Strangers often tell me, ignorantly, that ichthyosis doesn't seem to affect my arms.

I used to ask the kids at school whether I would be white or black or brown if I didn't have red skin. 'White!' they would say, nodding their heads furiously. White, the desired, socially acceptable shade. Were they trying to tell me that if I had a chance at being normal, I wouldn't want to stick out again in my small, white bread Lutheran town in country Australia with — gasp — dark skin?

My mum has dark skin. She's South African — classed as a coloured in apartheid terms. Her skin is like brown sugar, chocolate milk, iced coffee. Mum was one of the few black people in Walla Walla — there were a few exchange students at the private high school, but as far as I knew, she was the only black person to settle in Walla Walla in the 14 or so years that we lived there. My father has white skin. But my skin tone isn't midway: it's red. It's so far from the 'exotic' complexion I could have had.

I don't feel black. I don't feel white. How does being those skin colours feel, anyway?

It took me a long time to identify as 'Carly with the red skin'. It was so often associated with rude nicknames, and, of course, I just wanted to be 'normal'.

But how else would you describe my face? Red is a fair and factual descriptor. Not an insult. Not derogatory. Just a fact.

I've been thinking about my culture. I didn't grow up learning Afrikaans or listening to rap as my South African friends did, although South African curries were a staple meal, and I learnt about Steve Biko and Nelson Mandela, just as I called my parents' close friends Uncle and Aunty, even though they weren't relatives. My dad's English accent rubbed off on me, and I knew a lot about the Liverpool Football Club. But I just felt Australian. Aussie pop culture and barbecues and running through the sprinkler in the summer. Just before I started school, my parents insisted I get one of my Australian aunties to teach me the national anthem so I could sing it at school.

I fear I am a fraud to claim blackness when I haven't lived my mother's black culture and I haven't experienced the racism she did under apartheid. But in recent years, I've been called a woman of colour by other people – because of my redness, and by people who know my black heritage. If they see me that way, I give myself permission to see myself that way too. I've been saying I've got black heritage more and more. I'm talking to and reading more from black women, and the more I read and hear, the more I want to learn. I also relate to some of their experiences because of my experiences with disability and discrimination, but I know that it might be false equivalence. I don't want to presume to understand what it's really like. Whiteness and blackness are more than skin colour – they're about levels of privilege.

I worry that the furore over Rachel Dolezal – and others who 'pass' as belonging to a minority for some kind of personal gain – has made it hard for people like me to talk about race. Rachel Dolezal is an ethnically white American woman who claimed to be black for years before she was exposed in 2015, and who still identifies as 'culturally black'. She wears her hair in dreadlocks and has darkened her face, but her background is not black. Of course, I'm not making any false claims, but is racism my issue to take on, when I don't identify as either black or white? Online discussions around race make me quite uncertain of when to speak up or butt out. But if there's a place at the table for me, I'll listen.

Mum's experience was different from mine. She hasn't considered her colour as part of her identity. Her colour has never bothered her. For her, it just is. But like me, she does believe it's up to others to accept our differences – rather than us changing to fit in.

Mum's skin is ageless. A bit like my skin – though for different genetic reasons. The smell of Oil of Olay is long gone from Mum's dresser. She doesn't rely on beauty products to keep herself looking youthful.

A few years ago, while sitting in the Emergency Department – I had cut my thumb severely – I told Mum that I thought her neck needed a bit of moisturiser. She was nearing 60. She pulled at her neck and said, 'No. I've always had great skin. It's never been a problem.'

'Thanks for passing it on to me,' I chided. We both burst out laughing, which encouraged those patients who overheard us to laugh too.

I've asked others with ichthyosis how they see themselves, especially if they are red (there are many types of ichthyosis, and it presents in different ways – sometimes noticeable and sometimes not). Some who are red like me see themselves as white, because that's their ethnicity. A couple recognised their colour – red – said it was a fact, as I do. Some didn't want to see their colour, and that's often to do with other people's reactions – they were called derogatory names, or told they ruin school photos, or accused of being sunburnt or dirty. Some were very defensive and wouldn't answer.

I don't generally talk about race as a factor in the ableism and discrimination I face. Culturally, I feel like a middle-class white woman. I live in inner Melbourne. I listen to Aussie rock music. I earn a decent wage. I'm married and have travelled internationally. But I have felt discriminated against because of my skin colour – perhaps in ways both similar to and different from my black family and friends. And I also see my skin as my identity, finally.

I look at my family now: a blend of South African and English, and my husband is Malaysian-Australian. And those ichthyosis genes have created a uniqueness and bond that only a few others in the world understand.

It doesn't matter how we got like this

It doesn't matter how we got like this. Really. If you're just sitting next to one of us on the train, or taking our order at a cafe, you don't actually need to know.

Stella Young, frankie magazine

One time when I was a baby, Mum had to run into the chemist before catching the bus. She left me with a stranger – Albury was pretty safe in 1982 – and when she returned, a group of strangers was crowded around my pram, peering in. My follower count started early! That moment in the pram was the start of what life had in store for me.

It can be relentless. I can't think of a day outside of the house when I haven't been stared at, intruded upon or abused because of my appearance. Sometimes people look away – which can hurt as much as the stares. These reactions can change my mood. Most days I start off feeling happy, excited, anticipating a great time ahead, and feeling good about my skin and appearance. Even though the stares, comments and discrimination happen frequently, they're always unexpected. I'd like to think the next person I encounter will simply greet me with a smile, or I'll just be able to get through the day, comment-free. I'm optimistic, yet prepared.

I don't notice the subtle stares if I'm immersed in whatever I'm doing, or even just doing something simple like walking through a shopping centre. I'll see my husband's head moving, following the stares, and that's how I know. But if people are blatant – head turns, questions and comments – I notice. It can compound. The more people who stare and ask, the more it wears me down. And when I'm sore, the physical and emotional discomfort exhausts me.

Sometimes I feel all eyes are on me, particularly if children are staring and pointing. There is always a scene – everyone wants to see what the kid is pointing at and shouting about. Other times I feel isolated and invisible – like when I am ignored in a shop, or treated worse than a customer before me.

I have become intuitive to the microaggressions – people who are unfamiliar to them might think I am oversensitive when I write about my experiences.

When I am with friends, they never know how to respond. Do they intervene or not? I have become so used to speaking up or ignoring people that I do it on autopilot, but sometimes it is good to have an ally who speaks up. Though sometimes they are more aggressive than the stranger, which I don't want. Friends often tell me that through spending time with me, they become more aware of people's ableism.

I can't let the bastards win, though. I will not put my life on hold because of other people's rudeness. Leading an active, fulfilled and successful life when people stare, comment and ridicule is an act of defiance. I have the courage to look the world in the eye when the world sometimes looks away, or looks too much.

And then the discrimination. That's a thicker dossier than my hospital file.

I was leaving a conference dinner on a Wednesday night in July 2013. 'See you tomorrow,' I said cheerily to Debra – a friend who had hired me to speak. I was due to speak at the conference the next day. Debra insisted I take a Cabcharge voucher. 'I'll take the train,' I said, assuring her I catch it regularly. She handed me the voucher. 'I want you to be safe,' she said. I waved her goodbye and the hotel concierge booked me a taxi.

I got in the taxi, the driver fiddled with the meter for a minute, and then turned around to ask me where I needed to go. He saw my face, and then asked, 'What's that smell?'

'What smell?' I asked him. He turned on the light and had a better look at me. (Because that's what happens when you have a visible difference. People look twice, to see if they saw it right the first time.)

'What's on your face?' he asked. 'You smell.'

I asked him if he wanted me out of his taxi. He said no, but that he was worried my face and smell would damage his car. We had not driven anywhere.

I got out straightaway. I did not feel safe. Before shutting the car door I looked him the eye and said, 'Fuck you.'

I have the courage
to look the world
in the eye when
the world sometimes
looks away, or looks
too much.

I returned to the hotel lobby, asked for another taxi, told them briefly what happened, and burst into tears.

I didn't get the taxi driver's number. But the hotel did, and I made a report – three in fact.

While I have met some lovely taxi drivers, this was not the first time that I was questioned about my skin in a taxi.

I was once told not to touch the seats of a taxi as I was taken home from the airport – the driver was scared my skin would ruin his seats – he told me he was very concerned for future passengers. And once, after a concert, a friend and I shared a taxi home. Before I got in, he asked my friend how much I'd had to drink. She let me answer. I'd had three drinks very early that night. I was not drunk. I was not disruptive. I just wanted to get home – it was 1.30 am. He thought I was drunk because my face looked flushed, like someone who had been drinking. And he told me that previous passengers, as red as me, had been very drunk.

It is not my role as a paying passenger to justify how much I've had to drink when I am clearly not behaving drunkenly, nor why I look the way I do.

I blogged about the taxi driver's discriminatory behaviour, which then made it into the media, and also formed the basis of my complaints to the taxi company (who couldn't reprimand or train the driver because he left the job soon after the incident), the then Victorian Taxi Commission (now Commercial Passenger Vehicles Australia) and the Human Rights Commission. Efficiency is writing a blog post that can be repurposed into a complaint!

I met with the Taxi Commission and Human Rights Commission to give them a verbal statement. In the three complaints, I said that I believe the taxi industry needs mandatory training about diversity, visible difference disability, tolerance, respect and social etiquette. I have been with disabled friends who have been refused a ride because of their disability. I've heard of Indigenous Australians being refused a taxi because of the colour of their skin.

One of the outcomes reached in mediation and meetings with all three organisations was to develop better training for taxi drivers — to teach them that disabilities may not be so obvious, and to ask them to treat each customer with respect and patience, regardless of disability. The taxi company worked with me and a number of other disabled people to create a video about the diversity of disability, and how we deserve to be treated with dignity and respect. As I said on the video, disability is wider than wheelchairs and guide dogs. And I asked the taxi drivers to think of the way they treat people — what if this was your sister, wife, daughter or child?

I still catch taxis. Sometimes the drivers ask what I do. 'I am a writer,' I tell them.

'You should write about taxis,' they say.

'I have …' I reply, my voice trailing off.

Here are some examples of what it feels like to look different.

The following was a conversation I had with woman on the tram, one cold Saturday (after I had moved over for her and made polite conversation about the cold day):

'What's happened to your face?'

'Nothing.'

'Are you sunburnt?'

'No, I was born this way.'

'Oh, that's a shame.'

'No, it's not. I'm quite happy with my appearance.'

'Well, it is. You look like you're permanently sunburnt or something.' (Laughs.)

'No need to comment further.'

'No.' (Laughs awkwardly.)

She was about my mum's age, maybe a bit younger. She looked and spoke like she was middle class. She was carrying a walking stick. Soon after our conversation, she got up and moved.

Another time, I picked up a parcel that had been delivered to a newsagent by DHL. Both staff asked me what had happened to my face. One stared at me like a deer in the headlights before asking what happened, the other sorted the transaction and then asked me whether I was burnt.

I just wanted my fucking parcel, no questions!

Another time, I went to see Jimmy Barnes at the Regent Theatre in Melbourne. Twenty minutes before the show, I queued up for a bottle of water.

A woman, probably in her fifties, turned around and saw me. She laughed at me.

I asked if she was OK. She said, 'Your face!'

I said, 'No need to laugh; I was born this way.'

She continued to laugh. One of her friends – she was in a group of four or five – asked her what was wrong.

The woman answered, 'Look at her face,' and continued laughing.

I told her how rude she was, and again, that I was born this way.

The woman said, 'What?' and looked a bit confused.

'Who did that to your face?' one of her friends asked.

'No one. I was born like this.' Exasperated. Nothing was getting through.

The friend said, 'She has a skin condition,' and apologised to me. The woman who laughed did not apologise.

Her friend then said to me, 'It's OK, no one understands unless they know you.'

After I got my drink, she and her friends were discussing what happened, as though I was the rude one.

I entered the theatre. I was shaking. So angry. When I took my seat, a lovely social media follower spotted me and we had a chat. I debriefed to her. She couldn't believe it.

The show was amazing. I loved it. But I still could not believe that any adult (or child over five) thought it was OK to laugh at a stranger's face.

Almost four hours later, I walked out of the theatre behind the woman and her friends. The departing audience was a big crowd so I was surprised to see them again.

I tapped her on the shoulder and said, 'Excuse me, I'm the woman whose face you laughed at. It's not OK to laugh at a stranger's face.' She did not speak to me.

'She wasn't laughing at you,' her friend told me. 'She just smiled. You've got it wrong.'

I said, 'I deal with this every day, I know people's reactions.'

Her partner said, 'You're stalking us now.'

I was not stalking, I was walking through the crowd, with the other audience members.

Nothing would make them see the problem with laughing at a stranger's face. But I felt brave for speaking up.

I was shaking from this encounter. Having to explain myself, being laughed at, people's poor excuses for ignorance. Ultimately, I'm sick of going from minding my business to enduring rudeness from strangers.

The people who act this way aren't monsters, they're human. They're not the other. They're concert-goers, music lovers, tram catchers – just like me.

People can also be really curious – which is often assumed to be well intentioned, but can be tiring and sometimes offensive. Curiosity is often mistaken for kindness. They also often blurt out what they're thinking. I've had strangers and acquaintances ask me what my life expectancy is, whether I can have sex, and if Adam has my skin condition too – usually accompanied by hands flailing around their face, which is the international language of 'I'm not sure what to say about your face'.

Curiosity does not have to be satisfied. Someone told me that they thought it was their responsibility to answer everyone's questions about their child's appearance. No. There's no obligation to do so. And doing so sets up an expectation that intrusive questions are acceptable. If I do not know you, I don't have to share my medical details with you.

I also think that curiosity drives interactions in which people feel they are familiar with me, or clumsily try to help. After I spoke at a Women's Day event about how my body is often medicalised by strangers, an audience member approached me to congratulate me on my speech, and then started scratching my arm. I suppose she saw me scratching on stage, and thought she was being helpful. But I did not need her scratch. I didn't tell her how inappropriate she was, as I didn't want to make a scene. It was such an odd situation, and when I recall it, I do laugh a lot.

Unwanted prayers from strangers are not helpful. They imply I'm less than others, that Jesus loves me *even if* no one else does, and are self-serving – making the pray-er feel good about themselves. They sometimes suggest I've committed a sin and need forgiveness. A woman once followed me off a tram and into a bookstore to tell me that I'm beautiful and Jesus loves me. Another time, a man in a shopping centre asked me to put my head on his shoulder so he could pray to heal me.

Good intentions can be rude and presumptuous. I hate that people think my life must be so bad that I need prayer and pity from strangers. I hate that the prayers they offer may be attached to a sense of personal guilt about feeling uncomfortable around me. Especially when I'm clearly not suffering, I am just going about my day doing the things that they're doing too.

Pray-ers put me on the spot because there's an expectation that I'll be nice in response to their 'kindness' – that, especially because religion is associated with kindness and charity, I will be polite. And so I am polite – I just smile and walk on. But these misplaced good intentions are rude, intrusive and condescending. I want to tell pray-ers to fuck off.

I wonder, do people pray for disabled and chronically ill people because it makes them feel better about themselves? Because they see us as objects to be pitied? Because they can't interact with us as human beings? I've been told it's because they want to spread the word of God. I guess I can see that – I occasionally recommend a product I like to a stranger in the supermarket. But it's not the same. I get the sense that strangers believe we need to be granted forgiveness for past sins, to be healed of a grotesque affliction.

I acknowledge this is an angry chapter. I'm owning my anger because it's accumulated after all of these years. And there's a constant expectation from the world that I'll be polite and respectful when on the receiving end of impoliteness and disrespect. No!

So, what can people who want to offer prayers to disabled strangers do?

Say hello. Always say hello before launching into what could be an awkward conversation.

Don't assume that the person with a disability or visible difference is suffering.

Get to know the person before asking about a condition or offering prayers.

Help in tangible ways. Ask politely about our disability (after saying hello). Ask how you can help us – make a donation to an organisation that supports us, take the time to learn about our condition, tell others not to make a judgement about the quality of our lives.

Never assume someone wants to be fixed or healed, or can be cured.

Don't pray for us and our disability as a way to feel better about yourselves.

Never assume people have the same beliefs as you. Don't force religion upon us.

Don't take offence if prayers are rejected.

Don't tell us we've sinned and that's the reason we are disabled.

If you must pray for us, do it in private, and don't mention it.

These things just happen. I don't bring them on. Someone laughs at my face, or tells me how ugly I am or asks a stupid question. And of course I recognise these incidents straightaway, because I've become pretty attuned to body language and tone.

For you, it might be the first time you've seen someone with a facial difference. You're surprised, shocked, disgusted, pitying, curious, scared or even amused. I see the range of emotions on your face in the first few seconds of our interactions. Your face moves in slow motion. You nudge your friends, thinking I don't see. You stop what you're saying mid-sentence when I walk past you. Your kids point and persistently ask what is wrong with me. It's all new to you. But for me, living with a facial difference is my everyday. Your reactions are my everyday. And responding to rude, curious, and even sympathetic and concerned, questions is tiring.

Even though I share these experiences in writing and speaking, people still don't seem to understand the impact. People 'ablesplain' – invalidating my experiences by telling me how to feel. They say curiosity is natural, or justify it by saying they too ask questions of people, or excuse the behaviour due to mental illness. They want us to educate constantly, even when we're tired. I feel these kinds of justifications are as tiring as the incidents themselves.

When I share my experiences online, I often receive comments that autism or another impairment justifies bad behaviour. But I'm of the opinion that disability isn't an excuse to forget manners. A facial difference doesn't give you the right to know. If you wouldn't like being asked, don't ask. Disability isn't a free pass.

If you're non-disabled, and a disabled person tells you their experience, take the time to listen. Don't play devil's advocate and try to get us to see it another way. Don't tell us how to identify because you might be uncomfortable with the word 'disability' or disability itself. Just show some genuine support, and change your behaviour if you're naturally curious and feel it's OK to ask strangers about their appearance.

Having a facial difference means I work really hard at first impressions. I don't want to shock people – or to see their shock. I want to make them laugh, make them think, and make them remember me in a good way. I aim to be well dressed, approachable and a good conversationalist. While ichthyosis has made for some difficult encounters, I have met some wonderful people – from celebrities to people on the train or in cafes. I'm spottable and memorable in a positive way, like the time the security guards at a Kings of Leon concert gave me a heap of free merchandise in Melbourne, and then remembered me when I was in New Orleans. 'What are you doing here? Don't you live in Australia?'

Having ichthyosis can be a positive thing. I've had so many great opportunities that I might not have had if it weren't for ichthyosis.

Bright stars shine through dark skies. I often meet lovely people during difficult situations, like those who stand up for me when I'm abused. I feel so lucky sometimes.

6

Grief. And hope

If you google ichthyosis it can be really scary. This has a lot to do with the tabloid media that sensationalises the condition. There are photos of newborn babies encased in a shell of skin, red and raw. Some say they look like aliens. And this is one reason I created my blog – to develop a resource for new parents; to reassure them it's really not that scary.

When a baby is born with ichthyosis or another chronic illness or impairment, the parents often grieve. Unless they had a prenatal test, they've been expecting a healthy baby, and all the milestones that come with a healthy baby.

They've likely been told useless platitudes, like 'God only gives you what you can handle' and 'Everything happens for a reason'. But life is turned upside down. Many parents become resigned to the fact that they will not have the life they anticipated.

The grief is often linked to the immediate diagnosis – a baby they weren't expecting. And then the grief extends to the future – with the worry that their child won't achieve the life goals that so many of us disabled adults are, in fact, achieving. They lament not being able to run and tumble with their little boys, or dress their girls up in pigtails and lace. They believe their child won't have loving relationships, and won't get married or become a parent. Marriage and children are seen as the pinnacle of normality for disabled people. Anything for the world not to see them as disabled. But these children are only little. These are adult-sized plans. What about getting an education? Finding independence? Travelling? Forming friendships? More importantly, what about loving themselves?

And sometimes they're angry about how their child's skin condition inconveniences them – from ointment on their clothes to skin flakes scattered on the floor and on furniture. They detail meltdowns and toilet habits of children with other impairments. The internet projects these (preferably) private thoughts and conversations into the public. Mummy bloggers write articles titled 'I don't want to be a [my child's diagnosis] parent anymore' – mourning the fun life they were hoping for, free from therapy and non-normative bodies. They love their child, but … They write about grieving a living child as though that child has died.

How would it feel for their child to read this? As a disabled adult, not even related to the grieving parent, *I* find it very difficult to read. The impact of other people's grief on disabled people is very real. Friends have told me their parents blame themselves (or each other) for passing on a disability or chronic illness – this blame stays with them for years, if not a lifetime. Or their parents have become over-protective if they've acquired a disability or chronic illness as an adult. And sometimes, siblings of disabled people blame them for a bad life. Friends have told me heartbreaking stories about their family's grief and blame – it extends well into their adult years.

Caroline, who I wrote about early in this book, has told me about the shame she felt growing up due to the way her family dealt with her skin condition. She has continued to feel self-conscious in her adulthood, so much so, it's hindered her intimate relationships. Caroline says:

> When I was young I lived in the country, and if my nana was visiting, my mum would do my after-bath routine in front of her. I was very close with my nana, but that was embarrassing for me. Having family and medical professionals involved or included in private routines and states of undress was always humiliating as a child. I knew I was different and I felt like a freak.
>
> Medical staff picked up parts of my body and discussed them as if I wasn't there. My mother would explain my routines to my nana as my arms and legs were swabbed with lotion and wrapped in clingwrap, because that was the latest medical suggestion. Being naked just added to the feeling of being totally exposed. There was no covering up.
>
> I have no doubt that my parents loved me unconditionally and equally to their two 'normal' daughters. They wanted to protect me from the universal belief that being different is a bad thing. I was told to be grateful that I didn't have [ichthyosis] on my face and I could cover the rest of my body and no one would know. Neither side of the family had any skin conditions and each made it known that it must have come from the other side. I believed this thing I have is so bad and disgusting that no one wanted to be related to it and I should keep it hidden. There was no

value to me and I was lucky that anyone wanted to be around me. I would never risk a friendship or relationship by revealing myself to their friends or family, so I would always cover up at social events. I don't want to embarrass anyone through association. As an adult, I thought about getting therapy for the way my skin condition affects my self-worth, but that would mean telling a psychologist that I have it. And I am too ashamed.

Your response to your child's illness can stick for life.

I am fortunate that my parents never grieved over me or blamed themselves or me (nor did I blame them for passing on a genetic illness). My dad proudly declared this during a speech I gave at a school. 'I want to confirm Carly never blamed us,' he said, during question time. Oh, and how I beamed. This was so different to stories I've heard from other people. But I've been told by extended family that I'll be a burden on my husband. This hurt so much – even though it's not true – we work as a team, and I've been in stable employment for almost two decades.

I think grief is linked to ableism, and the belief that disabled lives aren't as valuable as non-disabled lives. Disability is believed to be a bad thing. Ally Grace, an autistic woman, feels the same way as me. In her blog *Suburban Autistics*, she writes that grief isn't natural, but a product of ableism. Ally writes:

Because we assume disability to be inherently tragic and terrible, people likening having a disabled child to having a dead child is seen as natural and healthy. But when we look closer at the systems that nurture and cheer on ableism, I think it becomes apparent that grief is not innate or a given, but just another product of seeing disabled children as less than, as less desirable than, the non-disabled ones, and as People Gone Wrong.

It's hard to hear about parental grief. I acknowledge it exists, realise how scary it must be to have a very sick baby, and hope that parents get the support they need. I hear you. I hear your disappointment and despair. I also know how it feels to be your child, and for their sake I want to offer you hope.

But I feel that when they are grieving over their child with ichthyosis, they're grieving over me. They're grieving over my friends. They're overlooking our identity, and forgetting that many of us have forged ordinary – and extraordinary – lives.

Some parents think of grief differently – they grieve over the social barriers their children encounter.

Deborah, the mother of Sam, a child with ichthyosis, told me:

The grief I feel as the parent is the grief of worry over the discrimination and discomfort my child will feel. All parents know that their child will face difficulties at some point in their lives. For those of us with affected children, we know what many of those difficulties will be: bullying, prejudice, self-esteem problems. And knowing these things HURTS OUR HEARTS! It is almost unbearable to see my child struggle for something that is completely out of his control. To struggle in ways that others don't have to. In ways that I myself didn't have to. It's terrible. So I don't grieve the 'normal' child I assumed I would have ... it's not like that. It's grieving for the pain my son will have to go through.

While it is a privilege to be one of the first people with ichthyosis that a parent talks to, a conversation with a grieving parent whose child has ichthyosis can be hard.

Once, I talked to a parent of a young person with ichthyosis. They were worried, hopeless and in denial.

'They won't be normal.'

'I have no hope for them.'

'It never gets better, does it?'

The questions were hard to hear, but I answered truthfully. I told the parent how I was like their child, without friends for a long time, lonely and wanting to be without red skin, and then I found my tribes through uni, part-time work and the disability community. I suggested connecting with others; I offered to talk to their child. No, the parent was adamant their child didn't want that. I told them that I lead an ordinary life, something I once didn't think would happen.

They just kept saying, 'I have no hope; this is an awful life.'

I had to call my mum and debrief. I was so upset and worn out. And I was so thankful to have a mum like mine – who never gave up hope. If a parent is not behind their child, who will be?

I think they wanted me to tell them a lie – that my ichthyosis was cured when I reached a certain age, that I am less red. But that hasn't been my reality. It got better when I found my tribe, found role models and got to know myself through writing.

I didn't want to hug them and say, 'I understand.' I wanted to shake them and tell them there is hope, that I wish their child could meet me and others to see what they could become.

Hearing a parent say there is no hope for their child diminishes the experiences of others thriving with ichthyosis. It stops important connections from forming, because of denial and dismissal of our

It's hard to feel proud when someone is grieving for a life that could have been, when you're still here.

collected experiences. It also creates fear for other parents – they too will worry there is no hope. I'm sure their child picks up on their hopelessness and helplessness too.

There are many adults with ichthyosis leading wonderful lives – highly educated, well travelled, with covetable jobs at Disney, the UN or writing for popular publications, in relationships and becoming parents. There are children who are thriving academically and socially. Of course, it's hard – with sore skin and social challenges. But it does get better – even if ichthyosis doesn't go away, the very fact that I am here, leading an ordinary and successful life, even with the pain and social difficulties of ichthyosis, means it does get better.

But it's hard to feel proud when someone is grieving for a life that could have been, when you're still here.

Some people believe disabled people are better off dead – and they don't mind saying so. Perhaps this is well intentioned, said to console the bereaved after a disabled person has died. But the truth is, anyone who says this cannot imagine a disabled person's life to be fulfilling, happy or purposeful.

In a *Medium* essay, disability activist Rebecca Cokley wrote about the way society reacts to disabled people taking their lives, compared to non-disabled. Non-disabled people are encouraged to seek mental health support, yet disabled people are regarded as having little to live for. Rebecca writes that in eulogising them, their disability is erased:

> Mainstream society reacts differently to disabled person killing themselves than a non-disabled person. When a disabled person commits suicide you typically respond with 'Well, now they're in a better place.' Or 'God has made

little Jimmy walk now.' (If Jimmy used a wheelchair.) Even when eulogising a disabled person, non-disabled people find it appropriate to erase their disability or minimise their difference: 'He was small, but the biggest person I ever knew' or 'In Heaven everyone is beautiful.'

I've seen deeply religious people have hope for better skin with the promise of heaven. They've openly wished for the day their child reaches heaven – where skin will be perfect for eternity. How can a child can feel proud and confident when they're told their best life will be when they're dead?

I want these children to know they have perfect skin *now*. It might not be perfect according to other people's standards but their skin *is* perfect. It allows them to smile beautifully, holds kind hearts in place, and stretches over curious, smart minds. It's also pretty special because it renews quickly, meaning fast healing of sores. And because of their skin, many other people with ichthyosis have come to know each other.

They will grow up and have amazing opportunities. I can't wait to see all of the places they'll go!

I hope they come to love themselves while they're here on earth, and know they're perfect right now.

When parents talk about hope for their child, they're often talking about their child's disability disappearing. They hope for a life without disability. They long for cures, fixes and normality.

Hope is tied to fixing the body, wishing away the reality of disability. But the reality is, most impairments are here to stay.

Hope is linked to the body – but what if hope was accepting disability and focusing on interests and achievements and wider life? What if hope was connecting with others who have similar impairments? What if hope was finding role models – other people with the same impairment, or disability activists, creatives and leaders like the late Stella Young, Vilissa Thompson, Keah Brown, Jessica Walton, Emily Ladau, Sarah Blahovec, Melissa Blake, Fi Murphy, Gaelynn Lea, Imani Barbarin, Kurt Fearnley, the late Stephanie Moore-Turner, Jane Rosengrave, Dylan Alcott, Jeanette Purkis, Cara Liebowitz, Alaina Leary, Elizabeth Jackson, Autistic Hoya, Leigh Creighton, Simon J Green, Sinéad Burke, Robert Hoge, Kelly Vincent, George Taleporos, Karolyn Gehrig, Jenni Grover, Christina Ryan, Emma J Hawkins, Elisha Friday Wright, Leah van Poppel, Ariel Henley, Rachel Edmonds, Michelle Roger, Ellen Fraser-Barbour, Belinda Downes, Kate Hood, Erin Kyan, Andrew Pulrang, Caroline Jones, Daniel Monks, Jordon Steele-John, Pauline Vetuna, Fiona Tuomy, Sarah Houbolt, Lawrence Carter-Long, Amy Marks, Liz Carr, Julie McNamara, Kiruna Stamell, Nicole Lee, Emily Ladau, Stacey Christie and Alice Wong? All of these people – and many, many more – have lived or are living great lives, and are changing lives.

That's hope.

7

Letter to parents

Dear parents,

I know your world has been turned upside down with this diagnosis – the great unknown. It's a whole new world with ointments, infection risks, weight gain difficulties, pain and skin. So much skin.

Maybe you're grieving a life lost – and that's expected, that's OK. But a life hasn't been lost. That little life you have in your arms is a new challenge, but also a life full of happiness, fun and achievements to be celebrated. As an adult patient with ichthyosis, I want to tell you that at times, life will be hard. But it will be OK. Good or great, in fact. And who knows what life will bring – for any of us – but I recommend taking life one day at a time.

Please never blame yourselves for your child's genetic condition. You don't need that added stress. They don't either. You probably didn't even know you carried the gene. I have never blamed or resented my parents for passing on the gene. It's not something they could control. People ask me if I am angry at my parents – and I am always saddened by the question. No. They did the best they could when an unexpectedly unwell baby came into their lives.

Maybe your child's diagnosis was made years after birth? I guess life doesn't have to change or get harder with this diagnosis – because you and your child have not known any different, and this diagnosis is just a word. It's not defining or a curse. What it does mean is that you can get some treatments specific to the condition, which might be a big help.

People will stare and make comments. Sometimes their comments will be rude. Don't take these as a reflection on your child's appearance or on your parenting. They're a reflection on the person staring and making the comments. You can give them an explanation, but you don't owe them that. It will be tiring, and you will get frustrated. But sometimes the curious (polite) encounters will spark up an interesting conversation, and may even be the start of a wonderful friendship

If you are struggling with guilt or feeling overwhelmed with the daily treatment regime, see a counsellor – it's good to talk to someone.

And on the topic of talking to someone – emotional support is just as important as medical support for a condition like ichthyosis. The feelings from isolation and bullying can be as painful as a skin infection. Ensure that you have a team of physical and mental health specialists – for your child and you.

It's important to connect with others who understand and are living with this condition each day. Support groups are good for this – they're filled with adults with ichthyosis and parents of children with the condition. But sometimes support groups can be overwhelming – full of comparisons as to who has it worse, resentment for those who have it 'better', guilting others for their choice to have more children with ichthyosis (or not), and all sorts of recommendations, including from snake oil peddlers. Don't fall into that trap – comparison is the thief of joy. Remember that a treatment that's working for one patient may not work for another, and so don't take treatment recommendations as gospel. Talk to your doctor before trying something new. And listen to other patients with the condition as much as you listen to other parents – after all, we've lived with the condition and know it firsthand. And never guilt others for their choices or happiness – we're all in this together.

Listen to disabled adults. The way (some) parents of disabled kids talk to disabled adults astounds me. They assume we don't know what treatments work for us, that we can't provide peer support, that we aren't experts on our condition, and that we should reject disability as part of our identity. The thing is, your kids will need us, *will be us*, one day. It's important not to reject our experiences.

Know that there's more to your child than their condition. They are, or will be, smart and funny and beautiful. I bet your little one is the best thing that happened to you. Encourage them to read widely and talk to lots of different people and to take every opportunity presented to them – even if it means they're (and you're) a little out of their comfort zone. Don't think it will be too hard or impossible because of their skin or the way people may react to it.

I believe it's important to tell your child about their condition. Be honest and use simple terms. My parents never hid that I was different from other kids. They explained my skin factually and medically, as much as I could understand. That meant I was able to articulate my condition from an early age, and assert my needs. They were also open in talking about my medical situation to the doctors with me present – nothing was ever hidden.

Teach your child that they don't owe anyone an explanation about their appearance; that if they don't want to disclose, to give standard responses like 'I was born this way' or 'It's rude of you to ask'; to be polite as possible; and also that it's OK to be rude if you're totally over it. The questions never end, but you get better dealing with them.

Encourage your child to connect with others with disability – with their impairment and with other impairments. Set up a penpal system or have Skype chats. Why not find pictures of role models with their condition or other impairments and show them to your child – so they can see what's possible for them? It can help to form connection and a sense of identity, and show them they're not alone.

Consider the impact of your comments or complaints about your child's skin, creams or lengthy care regime. While you might think it's insignificant parental complaining, your child may grow to become very self-conscious of the 'mess' they make because of their skin or creams left on surfaces, or the time you're taking to care for them. Be especially mindful of this if you're complaining online – that's part of their digital footprint too. What you write about your child online will follow them forever. The language you use to describe your child's skin, or other disability, might mean a lifetime of internalised shame for them. Don't be too quick to share your child's story with the media, either. Let them make that choice when they understand the reach and ramifications.

Be proud of your child, show them that you're proud, and show others that you're proud of them. That's the best gift you can give them. When you show your child you're proud, you give them pride. Teaching them self-acceptance is as valuable as teaching them how to read, write and add up.

I can't tell you what creams will cure your child, how to take away pain or even how to handle bullies — because I am still learning, and what's worked for me might not fit with your values.

But I can tell you how the condition makes me feel — how my eyes get stringy from discharge, and that sometimes a good sleep in a warm bed is just what I need to calm my skin when it's sore, and that I love waking up each day knowing something good is going to happen. I can tell you that instilling a sense of self-worth and self-belief, resilience and the courage to dream in your child is as important as all the medical treatments you all go through. And I can tell you that life with ichthyosis can be a blessing.

I wish you and your child all the best. And I thank my mum and dad for instilling these values, confidence and pride in me. You are ALL doing a great job.

Much love,

Carly

8

I don't want a cure

'Is there a cure for that?'

'I couldn't handle looking like you.'

'I'd kill myself if I looked like that.'

'There will be a cure one day.'

'Try this cream/juice/recreational drug. It worked for my friend with eczema.'

'I know a really good naturopath.'

'I distribute stem cell treatment that I'd like to give you.'

'I saw an article on your condition once, how do you pronounce it?'

'I'm sorry, that must be awful to live with.'

All of these things have been said to me, almost always by people who don't know me, often at the beginning of a conversation. The conversation ends pretty abruptly after I say I'm not interested. Sometimes strangers interrupt me at dinner or run after me as I leave a building to give me a card, because they're so sure they've got a miracle cure. It's often well meaning – people wish I didn't have to endure the pain, so they offer me a cure. But it's also presumptuous and under-informed, and often very rude.

First, there is no cure for ichthyosis. You can't cure a genetic condition, although there's opportunity to eliminate it through genetic selection. If there was a cure, I'd probably know of it, because my dermatology team are like family – they were invited to my wedding, so we're pretty close. I'm sure they'd be the first to tell me the news. I'm sure I won't find out about a cure by someone tagging me in a tabloid news video about cannabis oil on Facebook.

There are treatments that lessen the redness and scale. But they don't make the condition disappear. The treatments that are available – some of which I've been on – carry huge side effects. I made a decision when I was about 10, after exhaustion and peeling from retinoids that kept me from school, and peeling large pieces of skin, that I would no longer take these treatments.

I'd rather be fire-engine red than unable to live a full life because of meds that make me sicker than ichthyosis does. I have heard pregnant women can't put cream on their children who have ichthyosis because the chemicals in the cream might harm the foetus inside of them. What's this cream doing to the child that's already in this world? I wonder. What would it do to me? (Some of the treatments I've been on or been offered could affect my future children, so it's advisable not to be on them if I want to get pregnant.)

Some treatments – like infusions – might help reduce infection risk, boost my immune system and increase energy levels, but I'm a busy woman and I don't have time to sit at the hospital for three hours once every three weeks. It can be exhausting having yet another hospital clinic to attend (on top of regular dermatology, pain, ear, eye and immunology clinics), it takes time, and it means a lot of time away from work. I guess I could read or work while I'm plugged in, but let's face it, I'd probably just scroll through my socials. Plus, I often get an infection from a cannula, so that might be counter-productive. I was also offered a treatment that is given to cancer patients. I was told I couldn't drink alcohol while on it. Immediately I said no, because while I don't drink a great deal, I do like to have a wine on the weekend. I don't want any interruptions to my life! For me to consider any new treatment, it not only needs to make a beneficial difference to my skin, it has to suit my lifestyle too.

(Please note that these are my experiences and if you want to seek similar treatments, I don't discourage it. I do advise you to see your doctor to talk about the benefits and risks.)

Second, I've tried a heap of woo-woo that people who aren't doctors claim will cure me. From goat's milk to Percy's Powder to noni juice (Mum was talked into the benefits of noni juice by a well-meaning bank customer once, and she passed it on to me. When a bottle fell from my cupboard one day, I was convinced it was just really expensive Ribena) – I've tried it all. Still not cured. And none of it tastes good. Why can't these consumable 'cures' be made over on *MasterChef*? Then I'd consider it. Joking! I'd rather spend my money on fancy brunches featuring sides of smashed avocado and salmon to give me all the good fats than Percy's Powder-infused panna cotta seasoned with truffles, wild berries and gold leaf.

Third, and it's something that might be hard to fathom, I don't want a cure. I use ointments and take medication to manage the dryness, pain, infection and itch, but I see that as maintaining a good life. I'm not saying no to treatment, but I'm choosing what works for me. I've found a relatively basic mixture of products that allows me to live my life. When the pain gets unbearable, I do wish there was a magic pill to eradicate that, but I wouldn't want it to change how I look.

A man I once had dinner with asked whether I'd want a cure, even just a treatment – to look more normal, I guess. The conversation was uncomfortable – telling of his perceptions of a life lived looking different. He went on to say that if I changed my appearance, it would be so much easier for me – fewer questions, comments and stares. I'd be being kinder on myself, he said. His rationale, while not considering the pain aspect of ichthyosis, was partly compassionate, and partly because he admitted not being able to cope if he looked like me. 'I'd do myself in' were his exact words.

This conversation was full of beliefs and personal insecurities being pushed onto me. My dining partner may as well have asked, 'Wouldn't it easier to be straight?' or said, 'Use a little face-whitening cream, it'd be kinder on yourself in this white society.'

Once I picked my jaw up off the floor, I answered no. I wouldn't take a pill to cure or drastically treat my ichthyosis.

The projection of a cure onto me is inherently ableist, especially when phrased in the ways I mentioned at the start of the chapter. I don't understand why people think it's OK to tell someone that they couldn't live with disability or a facial difference. Imagine thinking someone's life is so bad they'd rather kill themselves than exist. Imagine projecting suicidal ideations on a stranger.

Those people think disability is a tragedy, that it must be so hard to live like this. (Their ableist attitudes are harder to deal with than the medical stuff.) They are uncomfortable about disability and facial difference – perhaps not having any friends who are disabled, and certainly too scared to look us in the eye because they're scared of catching it or being associated with us or something. This happens to so many disabled people.

Disability and illness is often seen by doctors, the media and wider society as something that is to be erased and eradicated. Prenatal testing is offered to all expectant parents, which reduces the number of disabled babies born.

Once, I delivered a university lecture, talking about ichthyosis and how life has been hard yet amazing, the importance of self-acceptance, and that disability pride and culture is an actual thing. And a student came up to me after the lecture, too scared to ask a question publicly. She asked if I fell pregnant would I have an abortion if the foetus was diagnosed with ichthyosis. Even after I had talked firsthand about life with ichthyosis and the struggle and relief to feel pride, she saw my life as a tragedy.

Disability and diversity is a rich part of the human condition – our lives are worthy, and it is not for anyone to tell us we should change, or shouldn't exist at all.

This might be a radical concept for you, uncomfortable reading even. It's uncomfortable for me to be told my identity should be erased. It took years before I could look at myself in the mirror and be happy with my appearance, and put photos of myself in front of thousands of strangers. Disability culture and pride is a big part of my life and community. Ichthyosis is a part of who I am – it's why I have so many stories, and the reason for meeting wonderful people. A cure would strip me of part of my identity – and I don't want that.

The people who suggest I might want a cure haven't seen the years it's taken to build up this confidence and to be proud of how I look and embrace disability and appearance diversity as part of my identity. Disability is not all bad, and I am sure if I told the cure-pushers that I've never had to have a bikini or leg wax because I have no body hair, they'd be pretty envious and might shut up for a minute.

The medical model of disability positions our bodies as the problem, in need of fixing. The social model of disability says that environmental and attitudinal barriers are more disabling than our bodies are.

Of course, my body lets me down, but the discrimination and ableism I face is an even bigger barrier to my happiness and progression.

My body was medicalised from an early age. I was poked and prodded, stared at and used for research.

When I was about six, I started to attend dermatology conferences, where skin doctors from all over the world would look at patients with rare skin conditions. The doctors pitched these to me as a way to find a cure for my skin condition. Almost 32 years later, there's no cure. And these conferences (and genetic research) still continue.

These weren't two-way participatory conferences. The doctors would look at me, discuss me, and I wasn't able to say anything because they had to diagnose me based on appearance alone. I'd lie in a cubicle – sometimes with thin wooden walls, other times just with a makeshift curtain on a rail – and wait for doctors to come in and observe me. I'd lie under a white hospital-issue cotton waffle blanket, wearing nothing but underwear and one sock. I was cold, a specimen, no more than a diagnosis. They didn't even say my name. I was alive, but I may as well have been a cadaver.

Doctors' voices floated above me, their voices booming – talking about me and never to me.

'I've never seen a case this rare before.'

'Netherton syndrome. Diagnosed with ichthyosis form erythroderma at birth.'

'Was she a collodion baby?'

'Her eyelids are ectropion.'

'You'll see her skin's abnormality – showing ichthyosis linearis circumflexa.'

'This is a rare case.'

'It is estimated to affect one in 200,000 newborns.'

'A rare case indeed.'

'A difficult patient.'

'She wasn't expected to live past a few months old.'

It was cacophonous, repetitive. They saw me as a tragedy. They saw me as a statistic. I was rarely humanised in those conferences – my 'rare patient' status meant they had won a prize. It erased me as a person.

Sometimes I would charge money for a look – like a medical peepshow. I could never do this as an adult, but childhood cuteness and bravado made me a few dollars.

Outside of the conferences, at regular checkups in the hospital, I would participate in medical photography. We went down to the hospital's basement and followed a long red line down sharp corridors to a cold photography room. I stood, near naked, shivering, in front of the cameras.

There was no need to smile for the camera. I found copies of these photos years later – I pushed them under the pile, unable to look at them. My skin was terrible, and I felt more like a specimen than a person, as the photos were just close-ups of body parts – not many of my face. I don't know where these photos ended up.

It wasn't until my breasts budded that I knew I didn't want my body stared at in this way.

Sometimes my body is medicalised by a stranger, or someone I'm on a date with, or I'm told that I should change my appearance for someone else's comfort. That hurts. That's when it can be hard to practise pride. When other people's default is pity, how can I feel good about myself?

A cure was pitched to me from an early age – from everyone including doctors, naturopaths and strangers on the street. Alternative therapy pushers have said to me:

'There will be a cure in 20 years.'

'Jesus loves you.'

'Here, drink this powder.'

'I couldn't handle looking like you. I'd want a fix for my face.'

'You're not cured because you don't believe in God.'

'Jesus loves you.'

'We'll pray for you.'

'Is there a cure for that?'

'I couldn't handle looking like you.'

'Have you tried eliminating dairy?'

'Jesus loves you.'

Throughout my life, the way people spoke about my body made me think I should change it. But now I realise this is who I am. Why should I change myself to make other people more comfortable?

I still see others who face the loneliness, isolation and unemployment that comes with having a rare and severe skin

I don't want a cure for my ichthyosis. Instead, I'd like a cure for other people's ableism.

condition, and the tiredness and grief that comes with searching for a cure. I'd love for them to see that while life can be hard, it can be wonderful if you let it, and that so much time can be wasted on wishing for a cure rather than living life. Instead of ichthyosis charities pushing for a cure, I'd love to see them raise funds for holistic therapy that includes medical treatment and also counselling, connections with other patients, confidence and esteem development, career skilling and relationship building.

I don't want a cure for my ichthyosis. Instead, I'd like a cure for other people's ableism. Offers of cures are exhausting, and in some cases, they're putting someone else's comfort before mine.

Sidenote: Can someone come up with this invention, already? One symptom of ichthyosis is that my body doesn't regulate its temperature.

In the summer, it can be very hard to cool down because I don't sweat. I used to have an old car without air-conditioning, and in the summer, my body would heat up so much that when I got to my destination, I would have to rush to the toilet and sit on the cool tiles. (Since then, my cars have had air-conditioning, and I also recently got a disability parking permit so in the summer, I can park close to my destination and not have to walk far in the sun.)

The lack of temperature regulation means I also get very cold. I wear many layers, and I regularly sit with a blanket over my knees at work.

So any inventors – any magicians out there – how about a tablet to cool me down and warm me up? That would be great!

9

The really shit stuff

Even though I fully accept life with ichthyosis, it can be full of really shit stuff. Luckily not all the time, and luckily not outweighing the great stuff. The really shit stuff falls into two categories: pain, and other people's behaviour towards me. Life can be going fine, and then bang! I get sick. Or I face ableism and discrimination. And my threshold for ableism and discrimination is much lower when I am sick, of course! I just want to curl up in bed with my favourite music on repeat, and a hunk of soft cheese and wine on hand. That's my comfort food.

When the really shit stuff happens to me, I get tired. I get angry, because I never know when I will encounter pain and ableism – because my body and other people are unpredictable, and when it comes to discrimination, I wonder how much people have progressed since the last time I encountered discrimination. And as my public profile increases, I worry I didn't handle my response to the discrimination right – was I too angry in the moment, was

I a pushover, should I have said more? But I rarely cry. I write about it, dust myself off and brace myself for the really shit stuff to happen again when I least expect it. Discrimination is just another thing that happens and I've become so hardened to it. Yet others are surprised and outraged when they hear of the really shit stuff happening to me, because they don't believe it happens.

I also try to inject a bit of humour into the situation. It can be better to laugh than cry when discrimination happens – like the time a taxi driver worried that my face would wet his car seats when I was on my way to talk on *The Project*. I told the panel what he had said and asked, 'Is this a sexual thing?' on TV. It got a lot of laughs.

The pain makes up half of the really shit stuff. Oh, the pain. While I don't want a cure for my appearance, I'd often jump at a cure for the pain.

I cannot explain pain. That makes it hard to describe it to dermatologists. How can they empathise when their skin looks so perfect they could be on the cover of *Vogue*? Have they ever been so sore that moving their bedsheets over their body is unbearable? Can their partner sense when they're in pain just from the heat coming off their body?

Dr Leah Kaminsky writes about the language of pain on her blog – the inability of patients to describe their pain, and of doctors to understand it:

> This inexpressibility of pain weighs heavily on my patients, made worse by the difficulties I face as their physician in trying to elicit expressions of pain from them. Where the hell are words when trying to describe Hell? A 93-year-old patient described their pain so beautifully.

Every time I ask her, 'How are you?' she replies in Yiddish, using first-person plural, 'Mir lebt.' We are living. 'How can we be?' she says, going on to list all her complaints: 'Our head feels like last week's leftover kugel, our feet are so swollen we may as well be wearing puffer-fish slippers, rats and cockroaches are running up and down our spine, gnawing away at our nerves, our hair is falling out so we are beginning to look like a mangy old boiler hen ready to volunteer to dive head first into the chicken soup pot. But what's the use of complaining, Dr Leah? How could you ever understand the pain we are in?'

This description is beautiful, even though pain is compared to food scraps and vermin. I feel that I've failed as a writer if I can't describe pain. I only have words like 'throbbing' and 'burning'. Skin screams as it tears from my legs, leaving them bloody. I can merely whimper.

Perhaps I'm too distracted by the pain to think deeply, or maybe finding the perfect metaphor will mean the pain is real, when I prefer to shrug off the severity. When you write something down, you confirm that it exists. I prefer to be stoic and resilient. There is no beauty in skin pain; it flakes, oozes and smells. And I am so guarded about who sees me at my most vulnerable that I don't want to describe it in detailed writing.

During a hospital stay in 2012, I was asked what number I'd rate my pain at, at that moment, on a scale of one to 10. I said seven. The doctor said that was really high, close to unlivable. That I didn't have much room to go on the scale. I don't feel as though the pain is unlivable, but when I am aware of every movement of my legs, every scrape of pyjama pant against my ankle, and every thump of pain, it isn't something I want to live with.

I became so aware of my skin during that stay. I think it was because of the painkillers. In the past, it's been difficult to take more than Panadol, as I'm allergic to codeine, and strong painkillers can make me feel nauseous. And so that time I was in hospital, the doctors prescribed me a four-step pain management plan. It's a cocktail that I wasn't entirely comfortable with, but my body benefits, and it's physically comfortable. So I tried to forget my perceptions of painkillers and appreciate that they were needed, and they were helping me. There's this strange perception I've got about painkillers – I should be strong, I don't want to get addicted, and I've read so many media reports about celebrities who died of a mix of alcohol and strong painkillers. I have to remind myself that my doctors are the best, and they know what they're doing, and my body needs the painkillers occasionally.

As the painkillers set in, I could feel my legs lighten, like I had kicked off my heavy shoes for the day. And as they wore off, the thumping, stinging pain washed over my legs. If I stood up, I had to dance on my tiptoes like a frail ballerina, shifting the weight from leg to leg. I went to the cafe in a wheelchair, just to escape the four walls of my room, and even the small bumps as the chair was wheeled into the lift entrances hurt me.

Sometimes warmth helps, being under my quilt, with the electric blanket on, but the heavy cotton blankets in hospital don't warm me in the way that I want.

I felt sore, but not sick; tired but alert. I didn't feel I was healing quickly. *I will be OK soon*, I lied to myself. It's weird how skin can determine your entire existence.

I am never well when I get out of hospital. Well, by my standards, anyway. Hospital is a place for treatment and discussions with doctors, and educating nurses about a condition they've never heard of. But it's not a place for rest. Sleep is interrupted by my legs peeling off a plastic mattress after the sheet gets crumpled (I'm never taking a fitted sheet for granted again!) and the nurses wake me up in the middle of the night to take my blood pressure. My 2012 hospital stay showed me just how needle-phobic I am – thrashing and shaking and cry-perventilating over a tiny butterfly needle inserted in my wrist to access the cannula. Ironically, the site that was treating my infection hurt more than my infected legs because of the cannula. I couldn't even look at the cannula site in the shower; I needed to keep it bandaged. I don't know how this phobia got so bad.

My body often goes through a big peel after hospital, and also after big events like my wedding or travel. Sometimes it just happens, for no reason at all – only every two years or so, fortunately. Big pieces of skin fall off – first my legs, then my torso, and my hands and feet peel last. They're the worst parts – my palms and soles are left without a protective layer of skin, which makes it hard to touch things and walk. My shoes hurt my feet and I wish it was OK to wear sheepskin boots in public. And I spend five minutes gently taking my stockings off before a shower – they stick to my legs, pulling at the weepy bits, taking skin with them. So much of me is left behind.

During the big peel, I am acutely aware of my skin. The old skin stretches and shrinks. It's like milk skin. Strudel pastry. Thinly rolled pizza dough, before it's been topped and baked. (Though not delicious, because it's on my feet.)

The old skin, which has been growing for a long time, is thick. It sheds, revealing new skin. The new skin is initially soft and supple, but it's a long wait until it fully covers my body. The old skin sheds in parts; it's a slow process. By the time I lose the thick layer, the new layer is almost as hard as the old layer was.

When the big peel happens, it feels like my skin is too small for my body. There are little bloody cracks on my feet where they're trying to burst through the scaly layer of skin. My legs are the worst – throbbing and thin-skinned, bleeding when I scratch them. I get bumped by people's grocery bags when I travel on the train and I am too embarrassed to ask people to be careful. What kind of person bleeds because they've been bumped by someone's dinner ingredients in a plastic bag? I feel cold but my skin is too hot for my husband to snuggle me. Peeling every day makes me look youthful. Who needs microdermabrasion when you've got ichthyosis? But the big peel is tiring and raw. I've read about how angry snakes get when they shed their skin. One animal carer said he observed a skin-shedding snake to lose most of its vision and wouldn't let anyone near him. The shedding process is called ecdysis. Ecdysis is a necessary process for growth and movement, and happens to snakes, lizards, turtles and iguanas. These animals go off food, and they're very sensitive to touch during and after the shed. And I expect dinosaurs experienced ecdysis too. Imagine how angry they'd get during a shed!

I know that after the big peel I will feel like my usual self. But it's hard to remember what no pain is like when there's so much pain. I try to see the positives in everything. Maybe my skin is shedding for new life. Is this what being a butterfly is like?

I have seen a pain specialist in recent years and it's helped a lot. Not only to get adequate painkillers, which work miracles – and make me sleep-talk – but also to be listened to and have my pain acknowledged. Having pain acknowledged as being real and severe changed my life. I have something stronger than Panadol if needed, and I have mindfulness iPhone apps that I can use if I need. I am no longer scared of painkillers as I'm on the right ones for my body. And I don't take them every day – only when I'm extremely sore.

And now to the other shit thing – discrimination. My face often worries people – because they haven't seen someone like me before – and their fear results in shocked, ableist and discriminatory behaviour.

In early 2016, my face scared a post office worker – he was so shocked when I peered in the afterhours porthole, he jumped. Ironically this happened as I picked up a delivery of my wedding photos – wherein memories of my face looking quite beautiful were captured.

At the end of 2016, my face scared the cleaner. So much so, she ran away without completing the job. The agency said they'd talk to the cleaner, rather than engaging me in providing training. This is what I envisage happened. The cleaner got a talking to. She giggled to her friends about seeing me. She won't be rostered on to work with someone 'different' again. And her small-mindedness and reluctance to see anyone who looks different as human will continue. The cleaning agency dropped me as a client – they were annoyed with me labelling this incident as discrimination.

It's exhausting having a face that can scare people. And even more exhausting worrying that I sound like a victim as I recall events like these. But my editor said I should tell the truth about the shit stuff, and this is it.

People who don't get it say, 'It's understandable that people are scared' or 'Of course they'll be startled if they haven't seen someone like you before ...' But they never say, 'This must be tiring.' I am expected to be polite, to educate, to take it – because my face is unexpected. But I'm angry. And upset.

These are the microaggressions I face – about my face – on a regular basis. It is not up to me to make someone else comfortable about the way I look.

It is tiring. There's so much emotional labour that comes with reactions to my appearance.

I acknowledge that of course discrimination doesn't happen all the time, and the majority of interactions are positive.

But when something like the cleaner being afraid of my face and leaving the job happens, or when I'm abused by a taxi driver, or even when I'm surrounded by high-pitched children demanding to know what's wrong with me, I can be on guard in case of the inevitable next time. I notice sniggers and glances from my peripheral vision. I see the gaping mouths and hear the sudden silence as I enter their space. I jot down the cab numbers before I've put my seatbelt on, and I put a smile on so as to not scare the children.

These are the things I've become accustomed to doing because I look different.

I try to be polite, but I cannot guarantee that I will respond to each microaggression (or outright discrimination) in a chirpy, educative way. But that's often expected of me, including by people who experience ichthyosis – as a carer, or sometimes a patient.

'You should have welcomed this opportunity to educate,' I am sometimes told in the comments on my blog. It's bitterness, they tell me. They also assume that I'm not comfortable with my appearance if I see stares and comments and fear as negative experiences. (Wrong.)

Then there's the peanut gallery of people who look on the bright side. Usually people who have never been judged by their appearance alone.

'They probably didn't mean it.'

'It's natural to be curious.'

Even, 'Maybe you're taking things too personally?'

And then there's always my own high-achieving self, telling me that the way I respond will shape a stranger's experience of dealing with a disabled person or someone with a facial difference. It's a huge responsibility to get it right. And I don't want to be seen to be scary and difficult. That angry red woman. Because I'm not.

I write about the discrimination I face because it helps non-disabled people to understand what disabled people endure. When I share my experiences, many people are shocked – they find it hard to believe that this is the way some people treat and speak about disabled people. I want to use an awful experience that happened to me to help create change for others.

I write blog and social media posts about discrimination with a view to use them in official complaints. But taking it to the media can be more effective than making a complaint. It is wide reaching, cathartic for me and educates the public. A complaint takes a long time and there is often no direct impact on the offender. The taxi driver who said my face would ruin his cab had long quit by the time I made a complaint. I wasn't able to mediate with him – I had to mediate with the head of driver education instead. So the taxi driver did not learn, nor have any chance to sit down with me to talk and see how he can do better next time.

When the really shit stuff happens — both the pain and discrimination — it's often assumed that I've caused it myself. I'm asked what I've done differently to make my skin so sore — and while I know stress and excitement are factors, sometimes I wake up with my face on fire for no reason at all. The pillow cases and sheets are fresh, I had eight hours sleep, I don't have a cat, and nothing was different from the previous night's sleep. Face infections just happen. And of course, I've been asked whether I've brought bullies and discriminatory behaviour on myself. The thing with ableism and discrimination is that so many people don't believe it happens, so they think we must have done something to cause it.

Most of the time I'm hardened to the really shit stuff. But occasionally it happens and I find myself frustrated to the point of crying. 'Not again,' I think, never prepared but always on edge for how far the really shit stuff might fly.

These are the times I feel unsafe (like the time a drunk woman on the tram told me I should be dead), or humiliated (like the time a woman threw me out of her store because she said my face would ruin the clothes hanging on the racks), when I feel powerless and I know the person doing the really shit stuff sees me as a threat — as someone to fear or a literal security threat. This often comes about due to cultural and language barriers.

Take the times I've had to self-advocate in an airport. Overseas. In one instance with a language and cultural barrier. Travelling alone. It can be a nightmare. It's never as straightforward for me (or other disabled people) as it seems for my non-disabled friends.

Domestic travel is pretty easy. I pack my stuff and go. No doctor's letter, only the clothes I need for the trip, one container of ointment and a small amount of painkillers/antihistamine/antibiotics. I am never questioned when I ask if I can take the aerobridge instead of the stairs if I am sore. I travel for work monthly, and only once have I been questioned about my skin.

But travelling overseas is quite an ordeal. I pack enough for a month or more — that includes upwards of 10 jars of ointment (five kilos, because I don't know if I can get the same ointment in the same consistency or at a reasonable price overseas), and lots of tablets plus a doctor's letter (laminated so it doesn't get greasy!). I call the airlines in advance, label my medication, and have my doctor's letter out when checking in. I request extra legroom and water while on long-haul flights. Most airlines I've travelled with have been excellent, but I have sometimes been made to feel like I am the problem. When I booked for my honeymoon, one airline customer service person's first question was 'Are you contagious?', rather than 'How can I help you?' On a different trip, when I flew back to Australia from London, I found that my Access needs had not been met, even after emailing and talking to the airline six weeks prior to flying. I enquired about the lack of communication at the gate, and when I arrived in Australia, I discovered that someone from the airline had created a fake Facebook account to tell me I was a 'stroppy bitch' at Heathrow. The airline said it was a social media glitch.

There have been two standout occasions when I've been frightened I wouldn't be able to fly, or would have my medication confiscated.

When I was at the airport in New Orleans, airport security pulled me aside and told me I could not take my ointments on board or in checked luggage. I still had four weeks of my trip ahead of me. I showed them the doctor's letter and the chemist stickers on the ointment jars. But they told me they couldn't trust that the documentation was not counterfeit. They were worried my ointment was an explosive. I spoke to many staff, all of whom were abrupt. I cried. When I was finally let on the plane – and my ointment came too – I asked if I could contact the airport I was next due to fly out of, to notify them of my medication. They told me I could phone ahead, but when I did, I was told nothing would be noted on my file. I worried I'd have to endure all that again. But fortunately, when I flew out of New York, everything went smoothly.

On that same trip, I flew home from London via Abu Dhabi. I was eager for a shower during my three-hour stop at the Abu Dhabi airport. I had the security process down pat – placing my ointment and doctor's letter in the baggage tub for staff to see. Suddenly, I was pulled aside, while my items were going through the X-ray belt. I no longer had my doctor's letter to refer to. Security staff did not speak English.

I was asked to sit down and wait. I worried that I might miss my connecting flight. That I might be strip-searched and accused of drug trafficking. It was a long 15 minutes. Other passengers were taken to makeshift rooms – matched with a staff member of the same gender. I expected to be taken to one of these rooms too. Twice the security stood around me, speaking about me in their language. When I stood up, asking for my bags and my doctor's letter, I was told to sit down. Eventually, a doctor came.

'I don't need a doctor,' I told them.

'But your face,' he said.

'I always look like this,' I said. I wanted them to see my doctor's letter. But they didn't look. They conferred a minute longer. And then I was allowed to go. I was extremely relieved.

Travel within different countries can be overwhelming too. I live in Australia and exist within Australian prejudices, but travel reminds me prejudice is everywhere – at various levels. And I have every reason to worry.

There are still instances of children with ichthyosis killed or hidden away in developing counties, because villagers believe they're cursed. People with ichthyosis are asked to leave public transport like my friend in Hong Kong, or refused service at a nail salon or sacked from work like my friends in the USA.

Language barriers mean I can't simply answer questions when people are curious. I really should find out the translation for 'I was born this way' in every country I visit! Though I've had difficulty in English-speaking countries too – in New Orleans, the middle of the day drunks were disconcerting, in my face, laughing, pointing and asking questions. I didn't want to tell my then fiancé how scared I felt. 'I'm having a great time,' I reassured him. But I wasn't.

I wrote on my blog at the time:

> Drunks stare blatantly. They snigger or burst out laughing. They are more brazen with their questions, they have a right to know. They react more in a group – loudly and intrusively. They point and turn their heads and get in my face.
>
> Yesterday, while on the food tour, three men, shirtless and intoxicated, circled me as I crossed the street, hollering, 'Where did you get your tan? Can I have a tan like that?' It was unnerving. I didn't want to engage so I ignored them and kept walking. Some of the tour group asked if I was OK – and truly, I was OK, but this interruption meant that I wasn't having the great time I had hoped to have.
>
> But these sorts of reactions do stick with me because I sometimes feel like my personal space and even safety is

compromised. I never know how much someone has had to drink, or whether they're also affected by drugs, and how they might react if I respond rudely. And so I prefer not to respond at all.

The drunks' reaction to my ichthyosis can be likened to the way women are objectified on the street or in a bar – wolf whistles, loud comments and crass remarks. It's intrusive, rude and scary. And can really hinder a good time.

When the really shit stuff happens to me and to others, I lament about whether things are improving for disabled people. And the wasted time of admin – preparing airlines or lodging complaints or satisfying strangers' curiosity – mounts up. Mostly, though, I just want to get on with my day.

10

I wanted to be normal ... but I was saved by fandom

I went to high school in Albury. The school was known for its technology focus, and also for being quite rough. I had hoped the social side of things would improve when I got to high school but it didn't. There were a few people I called friends, but only one that I hung out with after school. This was Fiona, a girl who I first met when she came to my primary school for a while in Year 4, and who came back into my life in Year 9. She was also a bit of a loner, coming from a large droving family that never settled in one place for long. She was loud, dyed her thick mop of hair all sorts of colours, and couldn't care less about what people thought of her. I thought she had the self-confidence I could only hope for, but in reality, she was probably a lot like me – trying to find her way. And she had a heart of gold.

I still hardly went to any parties — apart from Fiona's. There was no one like me at school. No one else looked different, no one that I knew of had a disability. I just wanted to be like others — even though the others were not at all how I wanted to be. I wished I could dye my hair like the cool girls, and that my legs didn't get sore from wearing a short school dress. I didn't want to be mean or a bully, which is how I saw so many of the other kids — people make fun of and exclude the different, especially when they are egged on by their mates. But I admit to taking part in the high school hierarchy — not wanting to hang out with the other friendless kids by default. Most of all, I wished it was OK to be myself.

Most of my lunchtimes were spent in the library, alone. When the library wasn't open, I'd hang around the school office. I was called names but the isolation was the worst.

I couldn't have imagined getting up on stage to make a speech when I went to school — I'd have been afraid no one would clap or they'd snigger and whisper among themselves. So when I gave a speech at my high school as an adult, I was so grateful I was now more confident — though I wished those kids from my day were there to hear it.

I think it would have made all the difference if I was in touch with someone with ichthyosis, of a similar age to me, when I was in high school. We could have exchanged war stories and told each other that things would get better.

I was quite an immature teenager, which I think stemmed from not being exposed to my peers' teenage hijinks. I also still relied on Mum to help with my skin; she was washing my face until Year 8. My skin improved a little when I learnt to have the right touch, and manoeuvre it as I needed to.

I didn't meet anyone with ichthyosis until I was a teenager. A woman, much older than me, came to lunch with my mum and me after a dermatology conference. She too had ichthyosis. She told us she was on strong drugs – they took the redness away from her skin, but her internal organs were ruined. Liver failure, I think. She couldn't have children while on the drugs. She was moonfaced from steroids.

Was this happiness? I wondered. Was this what it was like to be 'normal'?

I asked Mum how this woman could be happy spending all her life looking for a cure. When the treatment was worse than the condition itself, how could you choose this path?

It was then I realised I didn't want that for me. I had longed to meet someone just like me as a kid, so I could feel less alone. But how could she be my role model when she wanted to change the way she looked?

In the mid-1990s, when the internet came to Australia, the school librarian suggested I try to connect with other people with ichthyosis. I hadn't even considered this possibility – for me, the internet was all about finding other Savage Garden fans. (More about Savage Garden later!) But I took her advice – it was safer to look up ichthyosis than Savage Garden in the open-plan school library – and found the ichthyosis message boards. I got chatting to adults – and instantly felt less alone. From my little town in country New South Wales, I was now in touch with others like me. I don't think I saw their photos at the time – nor did I understand the difference between types of ichthyosis. In my mind, they all looked like me.

Some of the people I chatted with were married or in relationships, and had careers. They led ordinary lives. This is what I hoped would happen when I finished school – a tertiary education, someone who loved me as much as I loved them, a career and a life in the city. (I now have it all!)

Others I spoke to had depression, were unemployed, and had been sent to disability institutions as children. They resented their skin condition, and wanted to be fixed. I couldn't fathom how they were placed in institutions, not given the chance to thrive and interact in the wider community. And because I didn't see ichthyosis as a disability then, I wondered why they were classed as disabled. My internalised ableism meant that I thought they should be getting on with life, like I was – not receiving government handouts or using mobility scooters. This was a very unfair judgement from me. I now realise that the rejection and isolation they faced through their lives meant that depression and the welfare cycle were hard to escape.

I just wanted to be 'normal'. I wanted to have smooth skin – in any 'normal' skin tone other than red. I wanted to have my hair plaited by the girls in my class and be invited to more parties. I hoped that others would stop being too afraid to touch me, and I tried to win my not-really-friends over with Christmas gifts from the discount store.

It was so hard being different. I wasn't disabled enough to get the assistance I needed at school, which was a private space to apply my creams and to be able to sit indoors and read or do craft while the other students swam or played sport. But I was just disabled enough for my peers to call me names, leave me out of activities and avoid sitting on the seat I'd just sat on.

Dancing lessons in PE were the worst. A few years ago, a man I went to high school with told me he was one of the only boys who would hold my hands during dance class. The other boys covered their sweaty hands and sniggered to their friends when they had to dance with me. But not him. He braved my rough, oily red hands. He felt good about having been one of the few to actually hold my hand, although the other boys gave him shit for it. My heart sank for two reasons – remembering the time when people were too immature and repulsed to hold my hand, and because my now-friend was telling me he took a hit for the boys' club. Such a great guy for telling me this.

As Clementine Ford writes in *Fight Like a Girl*:

> We have to resist the urge to respond to basic decency by treating it as if it's some kind of enormously magnanimous gesture. It isn't. There shouldn't be anything astonishing about a man who doesn't degrade women, hurt them or treat them as somehow less than him.

I was actually revolted at this former classmate's admission of decency, and my revulsion was confirmed when I read Clem's words. I wish I'd had the guts to say these words to the people I went to school with at the time. Thanks, Clem, for making me realise that just because someone says they took one for the team, they're not a good guy. They are still contributing to the bullying.

My parents sent me to a church youth group, to give me the chance to form friendships outside of school. But members of this group told me I was a sinner because I was not baptised, and because one of my parents was black and one was white – and that was why I had red skin. So I left.

I didn't understand how my parents could love me so much when I didn't feel loved by others. I only felt accepted and understood when I was in hospital. I remember telling my parents I'd rather be in hospital than at school because people liked me there.

When I turned 17, things changed. That was the final year of high school – the end of feeling alone was near. It was the year I got a job, working at a department store for six hours a week after school. It was the year I learnt there was a wider world out there – with people who were nicer than I'd experienced at school. Perhaps it was because Kmart had a workplace code of conduct, or maybe they were just genuinely good people. In the first few months, I was just dusting shelves and folding car seat covers back into their packaging, but it was so much more than a mundane job. At Kmart, I made friends that I have to this day. I developed valuable life skills there: customer service, prioritisation, leadership and managing work and study. Most importantly, I learnt how to handle questions and comments about my appearance in an assertive yet professional way. I worked at Kmart for four years, until I moved to Melbourne – a big city three hours away – and I only wish I'd started working at the department store earlier.

One day before my shift, I was queuing to buy a CD. Music was my life then. I think I'd just turned 18, and was still fairly timid. A customer asked me something – I was in uniform so he recognised me as an employee. And another customer referred to me as 'the lobster over there'. I was upset, but I also didn't know how – or even if – I could speak up about him calling me a lobster. And so I met with the store manager – a big deal for a junior employee. We talked about ways I could handle customers' questions and rude comments. The store manager said I was able to be politely assertive and I had the choice in passing the customer on to a colleague if they were really rude. I didn't have to work on the main checkouts where questions about my appearance came as quickly as customers' items on the conveyor belt. This was one of the most empowering things ever to happen to me. I was given permission to take control of how others reacted to my appearance.

Andrew, the man who hired and managed me at Kmart almost 20 years ago, died while I was writing this book. In my sadness, I reflected on how he changed my life. I wasn't locked away working out of customers' sight, as some people expected me to be. I was visible, representing ichthyosis in a very public job, even though I didn't realise it. I was paid award wages, which gave me freedom and control. And I was truly included in mainstream employment, which led to full-time work in the government. I regret not telling him this when he was alive. It was more than just a casual job on my days off uni. Thanks, Andrew.

Another thing that gave me strength in those years was being a fan. Yep, I'm a fangirl. And I'm going to call it: Savage Garden and Darren Hayes helped to shape my identity. Their music gave me something to believe in. It was there through my headphones when I had needles, and posters on my wall when I was sick in bed. The music was a friend.

There's something special about being a fan. It's the anticipation of your idol's arrival. It's the passion of seeing your team or band or actor do what they do best. It's the camaraderie, the chanting, the cheering. It's the safety of being in a concert, never having to explain your difference, because everyone's the same. It's that look you get from other fans – the feeling of sharing the same excitement. It's that intimate moment when your idol looks you in the eye or sings you that song. It's knowing that your passion has a place in your heart for life. It's the most alive you'll ever feel. And I'm never embarrassed to admit my fandom.

The most memorable Monday night of my life was when I saw Darren Hayes launch *The Tension and the Spark* at the now defunct jazz club Manchester Lane, back in 2004. Darren's family had organised a ticket for me. (I met his parents after waiting outside Savage Garden's hotel when I was 16. We stayed in touch for a few years.) I was beside myself with excitement.

During 'I Like the Way', Darren looked at me. After all these years, he was staring at me. And then during another song, he reached down and kissed and hugged me from the stage. He then took my camera and took a selfie – selfies weren't really a thing then. My beaming face was in the background.

I went to the launch on my own. When we posed for group photos, Darren asked me, 'Do you want a photo just with me?' Of course! Oh my god! I wasn't able to concentrate at work for a week.

I've been a fangirl for as long as I can remember. I think it's because of my dad. He is a staunch Liverpool fan. 'You'll Never Walk Alone' was as familiar to me as nursery rhymes when I was a tiny girl. In the days before we had SBS, we would listen to Liverpool matches on shortwave radio in the middle of the night. Additionally, every night at quarter to eight, he'd tune in to get the sports scores. Sometimes he'd travel to Melbourne to watch games on SBS in hotels – this worked well when I had a hospital trip. Football is his life. When I got married, he had to leave the wedding by 11 pm so he could watch the Liverpool match.

My parents raised me on the music they listened to – The Beatles, Fleetwood Mac, Simon and Garfunkel and The Hollies. They'd play records on Saturday night and sometimes we'd dance.

Instead of chocolate eggs at Easter, my parents would buy me records. When I turned six, I picked out Kylie Minogue's *Enjoy Yourself* because I adored her, and loved the sequinned hat on the record cover. I knew every word on that album – listening to it on repeat in my Walkman on car trips. While writing this book, I played this album on Dad's record player – and I still knew every word.

The first band I really obsessed over was Southern Sons, in the summer of 1990–91. I got into them because of my cool babysitter, Simone. Jack Jones, the young singer, was cute – I liked his cheekbones and long dark hair. 'Heart in Danger' – the song of Simone's summer – quickly became my song. I was as captivated as she was.

My pocket money went on *TV HITS* and *Smash Hits* magazines – for a short time, they were filled with posters and articles about Jack Jones. I quickly filled my scrapbooks with his photo, drawing hearts on each page. I was nine, which in hindsight was far too young to be this into hairy man bands. Jack Jones was only nine years older than me – which would be fine when I reached 18.

My mum's young colleague Jason was also a big influence in the bands I was exposed to. He recorded Southern Sons' album onto cassette for me – Boom Crash Opera was on side B. Jason helped Mum buy me a Southern Sons T-shirt for my 10th birthday. He got extra-large. It came down to my ankles then, and my knees now. It's still in my drawer at my parents' house. I sometimes wear it to bed when Adam isn't there.

My next fandom was over Shane Warne. I hate cricket but I loved him in the Just Jeans ads. So I'd take time off school to watch test matches — boring! — and get excited when Ian Healy said, 'Bowled, Shane,' out of the corner of his mouth. Once again, I filled scrapbooks with clippings. I bought his biographies and cricket cards. When Shane married Simone Callaghan, I sent them a wedding present. It was a photo frame — nothing unusual. But I put a photo of me in the frame. So embarrassing. I was 12 at the time, OK? Shane wrote back on a Nike promotion card, thanking me for my love and support in silver pen. That card was quickly laminated and was stuck next to my bed for a year. I soon fell out of love when I saw news of his partying ways — his values were very different from mine. Bye, Shane.

I wrote some of this chapter, aptly, listening to the other love of my life — Darren Hayes from Savage Garden.

It was August 1996 when I first saw Savage Garden on TV. I noticed a video clip featuring a long-haired young man (Darren Hayes), and a short-haired man (Daniel Jones) on the back of a truck — and back then, long-haired boys were my thing. I decided that this would be the band I would love forever. And I remained committed.

Later that year, *To the Moon and Back* was released. 'Do yourself a favour,' Molly Meldrum said. And I did. I was a ravenous fan, collecting CDs from Australia and around the world, covering my walls and school books in posters, and dubbing recordings from music shows onto one VHS tape.

My friend Fiona and I went to their 1997 underage concert together, at the now bulldozed Palace Theatre in St Kilda. I was too small to even see the stage, and it was very dark and very loud, and far too crowded, but Oh. My. God. *We were there in the same room as Savage Garden!* I planned my outfit — just like I thought

Darren would dress. Levis, denim jacket, marble-red Doc Martens and a maroon velvet shirt. I still have the Doc Martens (they fit me) and the velvet shirt (it doesn't fit me, but I can't bring myself to throw it out). I was so excited. I finally felt part of something. The crowd had Savage Garden in common and we were united by our love. Feeling electric, part of a community at a concert was a stark contrast to school, where I sat alone in the library at lunchtime.

In the late nineties, I had many penpals – mainly due to Savage Garden. I found them in the classifieds pages of *TV HITS* magazine, as well as through the *Savage Garden Fanzine.*

In my final year at school, my music tastes expanded. There was in fact a world outside Savage Garden, and my love for poetry meant I explored singers who wrote beautiful lyrics. I spent hours in my bedroom doing art projects (badly) while listening to U2's *Achtung Baby*, and in the school library studying for my HSC, listening to Silverchair's *Neon Ballroom*. I'd write my own poetry, inspired by Silverchair and Douglas Stewart, the twentieth-century Australian bush poet whose poetry I studied in Years 11 and 12. My poetry was a conglomeration of dark teenage thoughts set in the Australian bush. Weird, hey?

Savage Garden announced their break-up in 2001. I was devastated, immediately calling other fans. I wasn't sure if life would be the same – this band had been in my life for five years. But I had to move on. There was plenty of other music to discover and enjoy. And some of that music had a profound impact on my life, just like Savage Garden did.

It was because of Silverchair that I chose which government agency to work at. I had been offered a job at the ACT Public Service in Canberra, and the Australian Tax Office in Melbourne. I had Silverchair tickets in Melbourne, and if I chose the job in

Canberra, I wouldn't have been able to go see Silverchair. When the then Tax Office Commissioner asked me why I chose to work there, I told him the truth. He wasn't expecting that. I guess he was expecting me to say it was my dream to work there. That is the absolute truth – I chose a job because of one Silverchair concert in April 2003. And I stayed for over a decade.

During my early years in Melbourne, I saw bands most weekends. I made a few friends there, but I didn't experience fandom like I had with Savage Garden.

In 2006, I wanted to reinvent myself – even though I'd just been to see Darren Hayes at the Sydney Opera House, 10 years after I had first discovered him. I tuned in to Triple J, and found Gotye, Angus and Julia Stone, Kings of Leon, and Regina Spektor. The singer that stuck with me the most, though, was Bob Evans. 'Nowhere Without You' was on high rotation. I bought *Suburban Songbook* – his second album. I loved the lyrics and sounds, and knew he, like Darren Hayes, would be a long-term influence. My first concert was at Chapel off Chapel in late 2006, and I've seen almost every Melbourne show on every tour, plus a couple of shows in Sydney and the Gold Coast.

In my early stages of fandom, I could never have imagined sitting down and chatting with my idols – they only existed in magazines, through my speakers and on my TV screen. But guess what? Darren Hayes was the first person that I messaged about my engagement after I told my parents and best friend. And after 10 years of being a Bob Evans fan, I asked him to sing at our wedding. He said yes! He sang three songs after dinner. It was such a beautiful gift. For a moment, I wasn't sure what to be more excited about – getting married or having my own private mini Bob Evans concert. Adam and I had our first (and only) dance to 'Wonderful You'.

Every time
someone stops me to
say they love my
work, I get a little
giddy. It means
so much.

My fandom has rarely been influenced by others. I'm used to being laughed at because my idols haven't been the coolest. But I have listened to music outside of my immediate tastes to impress boys. I spent some years trying to enjoy Pearl Jam and the Red Hot Chili Peppers to get closer to a boy I loved, unreciprocated. And I can thank another man, who I loved but who never loved me back, for introducing me to Sia's music, which I adore.

My fandom brightened my life. It lifted me from the depths of loneliness at times, and the lyrics helped me find myself. Contact with my idols has been very special – from a hug to a tweet – it has often soothed the emotional and physical isolation I've felt, even as an adult.

During the many times I've felt lonely or rejected or love-lost, or even so overwhelmed with love, I have immersed myself in their music. I can still be reduced to a puddle of tears (rather than screaming with awe) when faced with Darren Hayes in person.

Thanks to social media, my idols have come to know me a little more too. I can't quite believe it. The look Bob Evans gave me when I told him I had a book deal was similar to my face when I see him play live.

My writing and speaking profile has meant that I now have fans. Every time someone stops me to say they love my work, I get a little giddy. It means so much. I want to give them the same time and interest in their lives as the people I admire give me. They tell me they're fangirls, and I say, 'So am I.' Sometimes they ask me for a selfie, which makes me squeal inside, because it's a long way from people being too scared to look at me. I recognise the fandom I have for others in the people I meet. How wonderful that it's come full circle.

11

No apologies about my skin

For years – almost my whole life – I apologised about my skin interfering with others. And now I have stopped.

My need to apologise stemmed from other people, including my relatives, being outwardly inconvenienced by my skin – vacuuming where I'd walked, wiping surfaces down after I'd touched them and not feeling as though they could kiss or hug me because they didn't want to get me on them. These attitudes shaped how I interacted with people. I often apologised because I get cold when the air-conditioner is on, or when I couldn't sit outside because it was too hot, or people were smoking. Sometimes I'd get looks as though I was being a princess, so sometimes I just put up with the discomfort. I apologised for my needs, and for inconveniencing others.

I spend a lot of time wiping up after myself. It's a little about etiquette and leaving things nice for others, but a lot about apologies. I see how gingerly people touch things that I touch, I've heard them complain, and I want to avoid that. Years ago, when I was at primary school, Mum used to give a woman a lift to work. She complained because the seatbelt – which absorbed my cream – left a mark on her top. Mum was upset and probably even angry, and she no longer gave the lady a lift.

The need to stop apologising for my skin and cream came to me with a bang at Stella Young's memorial. That lady has taught us so much in her life and death – a big reminder for us that we get proud by practising. I met Stella's family for the first time that day. At the end of the memorial, I hugged Stella's sister. She was wearing a gorgeous pink blazer, and I left a face imprint on the side of it. My cream darkened the fabric. I apologised to her, and she said, 'Don't worry about it, I've probably got my own makeup on it anyway.' And then I felt so stupid. Because Stella – her sister – never apologised for getting in the way. She wrote:

> I stopped unconsciously apologising for taking up space. I'm sure you can scarcely imagine that now; a world where disabled people, women in particular, are made to feel like we're not really entitled to inhabit public spaces.

If Stella's sister is reading this, I want to retract that apology. I am not sorry for getting my cream on your blazer. I am not sorry, because Stella stopped apologising years ago, and now, so have I.

I retract all of the other apologies I've made – because my needs do not inconvenience you. It is your attitudes that constrain us. Those who really know me, who really love me – they don't care whether I leave cream on their clothing or make their floor oily from where I've walked. And those who feel inconvenienced, well, they don't matter.

It's not as though I make a mess purposely. I take good care. And my love, he keeps reminding me not to apologise.

When we stayed at my parents' house – which has tiled floors to help prevent allergies – Adam showed me his socks. The soles were thick with my skin.

I said, 'Sorry,' and he shook his head.

'No sorrys,' he told me, waving his hands to suggest the conversation was finished. 'Stop apologising for what you can't control.' And I loved him so hard.

When Adam and I fell in love, some people assumed I would be a burden for him. They asked, with prying condescension, whether I will pass on ichthyosis to our children. They marvelled that he looked past my red face, and congratulated him for taking me on. I felt that I should apologise to him for being a burden.

But he doesn't do any of this. He sees me. He tells me I have beautiful on my face. He carries my skin in his pockets so I'm with him at all times. And he loves my body even more than I imagined a man could.

I am no longer apologising for my skin and cream. And you shouldn't apologise for your skin or cream or whatever else makes you different either.

12

Looking for love

Finding love is often seen as the holy grail for disabled people. Gosh, I chased love, and for much of the time, it was because I wanted to feel like everyone else.

Society and the media desexualise disabled people. When's the last time you've seen a lingerie ad featuring a disabled model? Plus, it's assumed we can't find or don't want either long-term or casual relationships, or that we should only pair with other disabled people (think disability-specific dating TV shows, websites and dances to keep us 'safe'). And disabled men are often encouraged to hire sex workers for exploration and pleasure, but what about disabled women's pleasure?

The TV show *The Undateables* suggests disabled people are, as the name suggests, undateable. There's no room us on shows like *First Dates* or *The Bachelorette*. That's right. Like most things disability-related, we are segregated, in a show of our own, with an undignified name, because we couldn't possibly find love with someone non-disabled (sarcasm font of course).

The Undateables shows people with visible differences and disabilities trying to find love. The participants have many disabilities and visible differences – Tourette Syndrome, OCD, short stature, facial differences, Down Syndrome, autism and Asperger's, learning disabilities, brittle bones and paraplegia (in Season 2 alone). They sign up to a dating agency and are matched with potentially compatible dates. The program highlights the struggle people with visible differences and disabilities face with self-esteem, being accepted and also the discomfort that society sometimes has around being in the company of a person who looks different.

While the show is a fairly sensitive portrayal of disability, I completely disagree with the term 'undateable' being used to label someone's appearance. It is labels like 'undateable' or 'beast' (in the case of *Beauty and the Beast* – a TV show that pairs someone with a facial difference or skin condition with a very vain, cosmetically enhanced person) that create negative perceptions and exclusion of people with visible differences and disabilities. And I believe the titles create a sense of othering – a divide between people with disabilities or visible difference and those without. The TV shows become curious case studies of how the different live, making disability a spectacle. I also believe there is a 'feel good' moment for the audience (on the verge of inspiration porn).

In 2013, *The Guardian* reported that 21 complaints were made to the British Advertising Standards Board after the ad for Season 2 of *The Undateables* was aired. Complainants said the title was offensive and derogatory towards people with disabilities, suggesting they were 'inevitably dateless and incapable of having a personal relationship'.

Sadly, programs aimed at raising awareness, such as *The Undateables*, can perpetuate discriminatory attitudes towards appearance diversity, amplified by social media users, who have an immediate and sometimes vast audience. There is often hate speech on social media during *The Undateables* and similar TV shows.

My friend Steve, who has a facial difference, was on several seasons of *The Undateables*. He married Vicky, who he met on social media because of the show, in 2015. The couple loves to travel, hang out together at home, and want to start a family one day. Steve loves being recognised in the street as a star of *The Undateables*, but it hits him hard when he's the subject of ridicule by online commenters. After his wedding special aired on *The Undateables*, Steve discovered an article on a personal blog with the headline, 'The couple from *The Undateables* wanting to have children is the most selfish thing I've ever heard'. The article argued that because of Steve's disability, he and Vicky should not have children. The writer said Steve and Vicky should be killed, and any potential children might be subject to a tortured childhood. Steve was hurt, labelling this as hate speech, and considered reporting it to the police. The hate speech Steve (and his wife) endured on social media brought me to tears, with people suggesting the couple should not have children because of the risk of passing on Crouzon Syndrome. The public gallery weighed in on their right and ability to start a family. Of course they did. Soon after Steve found the article, he demanded that it be removed – and it was.

I wish I had been more assertive while I was dating. I needed Sophie Monk on *The Bachelorette* to tell me that it's OK to reject someone if they weren't keen on me. I cheered when she got rid of that guy who wanted her to change. I kept the losers around because it was nice to feel wanted.

Crushes started when I was at school. Always the popular boys, never reciprocated. And this went on for years. I was either gently let down or laughed at. A guy I liked for years kissed me and then told me I was too good for him, and our friendship was unsalvageable. If he thought that much of me, why wasn't I good enough to be his girlfriend?

In my late teens and early twenties, my self-worth hung on whether a man found me attractive or not. When I met a guy at a pub and pashed him, I felt just like my friends without ichthyosis and other impairments. Feeling wanted and loved by others was the epitome of acceptance – by others and of myself.

When I was a teenager, my goal was to find love. I wanted it more than getting into journalism at uni, and I wanted it more than finding a cure. I thought that if someone else loved me and wanted to hold my hand and kiss me, it would mean I'd conquered ichthyosis. That I'd be 'normal'. And so I really tried to find a boyfriend – with no luck. Anyone I showed interest in at school would be laughed at like I was, because it wasn't cool to have the red girl crush on them.

And then the internet came along, so there was hope.

Even before we signed up to the internet at home, I was chatting to boys online. I met a 17-year-old in a chat room while doing work experience at the local radio station, on my sixteenth birthday. We chatted online for a week, and then he sent me Lynx-scented letters until we started talking on the phone. On Valentine's Day, he sent a giant box filled with a teddy bear and a card – and I was so shy about telling my parents. We met about nine months after we began talking online – our date was at La Porchetta, the night before my hospital appointment in Melbourne. He brought me a giant bunch of flowers – and my first kiss was a shy peck on the lips. He lived in Melbourne and drove up to Albury to stay with me a few months after that. Things faded out, but we remain in touch, online, years later.

When we got the internet at home, I chatted to strangers online via ICQ. I also started a blog on *Diaryland*. I met boys and girls from all over the world, chatting about everything and nothing. I found some of the boys I met online attractive, but I mostly used ICQ and *Diaryland* for friendship. The internet opened me up to a world of judgement-free communication. As Brodie Lancaster wrote in *No Way! Okay, Fine*:

> When you're told your whole life that it's what's inside that counts and that your outside is not worth writing home about, online relationships seem like a godsend: they're a safe space where you can be sure that someone is getting to know you for who you are rather than just what you look like.

I'd waited 15 years to talk to people without having to explain the way I looked at the start of the conversation.

As seen on MTV's *Catfish: The TV Show*, so many people with visible differences (usually overweight or transgender – I've never seen a disabled person on *Catfish*) deceive their online suitors because they're embarrassed or ashamed. And rarely do the suitors want to continue the relationship when they see the person is different from the pictures they provided. Even though they fell in love with a personality and a conversation. These people were afraid to disclose. And so was I – though I never deceived anyone I met online.

I could tell them about my appearance and skin if and when I was ready to – usually after months of chatting to build trust. I'd scan my school photo on my clunky scanner, and apologise profusely about my face. I explained that I wasn't contagious, and told them I understood if they never wanted to talk to me again. I wish I never had to do this. I wish I had pride then. If they didn't like my beautiful teenage face, full of wonder and possibility, and so very smooth – stuff them.

It wasn't like that with my first true love. He liked me for me. We met on ICQ in 1999. Uh-oh, indeed.

He came into my life on Monday 30 August 1999. I'd taken the day off school to listen to the radio debut of the appropriately titled 'I Knew I Loved You' by Savage Garden.

We chatted online for four months before he told me he was beginning to love me. I convinced my parents that this guy wasn't some 70-year-old paedophile (but how did I really know?), and I was allowed to give our home number to him.

I knew I loved him during our first phone call on 10 November 1999, the night before my Year 12 history exam.

He called me every night for two months. We would speak for up to seven hours at a time, about our day's events, how we loved each other, and how we both had unusual traits, which made us perfect for each other. We spoke of our future. He sent me generous birthday and Christmas presents – an opal necklace, a Savage Garden clock and a CD of his favourite band, Coal Chamber. I bought him a lava lamp and wrote him really long letters.

We met in person on Friday 14 January 2000. Before we met, he told me he was going to be a father – he'd found out his ex-girlfriend was pregnant. We spoke for hours that night. We were going to make things work. He cried. I cried. Then I stupidly told my parents, who flipped out. My dad was so angry. 'He's not Jesus, you know,' Dad said about my love for him. Still, my parents let him stay after meeting him when he arrived at the airport.

He'd come from interstate to stay at my house for nine days. A big expense on an apprentice's wage. He was everything I hoped he'd be. Funny, cute, alternative, had a job as a chef, into cool music, smart. Different and eccentric. He had 11 piercings and dressed like a gothic punk rocker crossed with the Australian cricket team. My parents, as strict as they were, and although reluctant to have a stranger in their home, liked this guy as he was polite, respectful, and taught them how to sharpen their kitchen knives properly.

He was a myriad of firsts for me. I felt accepted. And loved. I still remember him and the time we spent together so vividly. He was willing to hold my hand and kiss me. Unafraid to touch me – he knew he wouldn't catch my condition. He accepted me and loved me. And I knew I loved him a million times more in the nine days we spent together.

When he left to go home I was devastated. Absolutely devastated. I've never seen him again.

We kept in touch by phone and internet, on and off – on his terms – for five years after meeting. We couldn't continue our romance because he was to become a father. He got back with his pregnant ex-girlfriend. He told me about how badly she treated him, and that if she wasn't pregnant, we'd be together.

In March 2000, his mum died. I sent a condolence card. He told me not to talk about my dog that'd just died because it upset him too much.

The baby arrived, a daughter. I sent a card and a dress. He told me stories of what progress she was making – milestones – first steps, preschool, school. He told me how his girlfriend left him with his daughter, to be a single father.

He told me he still loved me. He told me he wanted nothing to do with me. Then he came back.

Months apart. Time after time. Calls at all hours. For six years. I remember saying to Mum that I felt he and I would always have a connection.

I thought I had no reason to disbelieve him. But actually, I did have reasons – four reasons. One: before we met, he sent photos of himself that looked like him but were actually of a musician. Two: after we met he'd send me poems he wrote, and just by chance (reading a music magazine) I found out they were Marilyn Manson lyrics. Three: I never saw photos of his daughter. Four: his phone would often go dead when he called me.

'You'd better watch out for the quiet ones,' was a frequent saying of his. He said it to me; he said it to my mother. I wondered what he meant, but didn't overly focus on that detail because to me, he was the world. He was a quiet one, and perhaps that's the reason I found him on ICQ.

Six years after we first chatted online I found out that everything he ever told me was a lie. In July 2005, his then girlfriend called me. The first thing she asked was how I knew him. She was angry. She said my number was all over his phone bills. That he spoke about me a lot.

When she calmed down and found out I was not a threat and didn't know about her (I'd always ask if he had a girlfriend and he said, 'No, why do you think I'm calling you?'), we got to know each other.

She revealed some truths. There was no baby, his mother was not dead — she actually lived with his mother. The mother of his 'daughter' was a woman he'd met once, and when we contacted her, she was as freaked out as we were.

To be honest, this guy seriously fucked me over. I was 17 when we met online. Impressionable. Naive. Wanting to be loved. He was one of the first people to show me attention, emotionally and sexually. I was so wrapped up in him. I stopped looking for other relationships because things might have just worked out with him.

While he hurt his then girlfriend — she left him after he 'accidentally' sent a picture of his penis to my phone — he had shattered six years of my life too. Before I told him I found out his lies (by writing a letter to both him and his parents), he would call me while his then girlfriend was in the other room. Once, he called me on my mobile while she was on my home phone.

The only things I really know about him are his name, age, occupation and location. Oh, and that his warning about the 'quiet ones' rang true. This 'quiet one' was telling similar lies to other girls he met online, though none quite as large has those he told me. He had my love, so I trusted him, but he also had the distance between us in his favour, which meant that I'd probably never find out his real identity. And he had the benefit of a saved message history to keep track of his lies.

I took it surprisingly well. Of course, I was angry, hurt, numb and sad. I can't say I grieved for the man who wasn't — I had already spent years before that grieving that we weren't together. On the upside, I was excited to have a topic for my upcoming journalism assignment.

I asked him why he did it. Why he maintained his lies for six years. He said he wanted to be better than he was so I'd love him. I realised he was very unwell, aside from his drinking and drug use. A pathological liar. I was lucky my emotions were the only thing he harmed.

I often wonder if I hadn't found out the lies, would I have continued to put myself through the hard times he caused with his toying? Finding out was a good thing. About a year later, he called me at 3 am. I told him that I loved not having him in my life and never to call me again.

I've become friends with his ex-girlfriend. We met when I was interstate in 2007. She's lovely. We recently saw him on Facebook, looking well beyond his 30 years – so washed up. He has a real baby now. Neither of us have contacted him.

Even though this awful thing happened to me, I am still willing to form online (often to offline) relationships and trust people I meet on the internet. I am always cautious, though. You've got to watch the quiet ones.

In 2000, I wrote this poem. And it now reminds me that the revelation of his lies meant I was no longer alive just to please him – for so long, being on call when he wanted me made me feel that way.

draw a life, name it blue
because sometimes it's that way
and place me in the corner
I'll be the one you can play with
when you're sick of it all –
looking for something more
and I'll obligingly return
when you tire of me
I'll bathe in misery
to have the smallest part of you

do you want me for my plumage,
or for the idea that
I could make your mind
fly?
From here.

I did internet dating for years. I could choose how much to disclose or not, and I kidded myself that the guys I was chatting to were interested in my personality and were not put off by my skin. Most were put off – even though they reassured me through our witty email exchanges that they were really interested in me and were FINE with my skin.

Internet dating became a thing for me when I moved to Melbourne in my early twenties. It was much harder than chatting to high schoolers on ICQ. I was chatting with a fierce intention to find love. I felt the pressure to disclose my skin because there was a likelihood I would meet the men I chatted to online. I did so apologetically, even telling the men that I understood if they rejected me for a girl with smooth skin that wasn't red.

There was always a power imbalance between the men I met through online dating, though. I always liked these men more than they liked me. I'd build up relationships in my mind, based on chat conversations and phone calls. It was always unequal.

On most occasions, I'd be rejected either when I told them about my skin, or after we met. Of course, they wanted to let me down gently, so I was rarely told that my appearance was the reason.

Many online conversations were rude and lewd (on their side) – brash guys talking with their penises.

Back in 2010, when I volunteered as a presenter on community TV, a rather cute guy said he liked my profile. Good start, I thought.

I told him what I do. My day job. That I am a writer and a TV presenter. He said, probably ignoring what I told him, 'Are you interested in meeting up for some sex?' No.

Then he said, 'I may want a relationship in the future, but for starters, I just wanna fuck you.'

Wow. Flattering. Forward. Gross.

He asked me what I did again. I told him again. A writer and a TV presenter.

'Now I really wanna fuck u,' he said. 'I have never fucked a TV presenter before. That would be fucken mad as.'

And then he asked for my number, and said, 'I have seriously never fucked anyone famous.'

Block!

Another guy asked me, 'Does your disability stop you from sucking cock?'

Block!

Disabled men were not immune to rudeness, either. I started chatting on a dating site with a guy who had a disability. He pounced on me, spilling out his whole life story (which I'd already read in his profile), gave me his phone number and said, 'Where to from here?' in the first two minutes of chatting. I said I'd like to get to know him better, and he told me that's all there was to know about him. I said, 'Surely there's more,' and proceeded to ask him about the music he likes. 'Pink Floyd, U2, Cold Chisel, I have a big sex drive'.

Block!

The semi-anonymous and fully unaccountable nature of online dating means people can say what they want, with little consequence.

They can say things that leave others feeling uncomfortable, unsafe and repulsed. I wonder if these things said through dating apps would ever be said face to face, in public spaces? I gave it up a few years ago, but my friends who are still doing the Tinder and Bumble thing tell me the dating scene remains just as bad.

I dated guys who treated me awfully. If I were my friend, I'd have told me to run. But instead, I'd hang around them, because I thought their goodness shone so brightly through their bad behaviour. Everything was on their terms. I hung out with guys who didn't share my values or lifestyle (smokers, alcoholics and drug takers). In hindsight, I think I saw them as fixable – guys I could nurture and who would need me. Only they didn't need me. I helped a man get his life back on track, and he rewarded me with dick pics. He told me that he shouldn't send me any more photos after he met a woman on Adult Match Maker. I was devastated – because I believed our connection was so much more than dick pics. I really loved him. My life improved significantly when he dumped me – I didn't unfriend him on Facebook because I wanted him to see how great things were without him.

I eventually let him go.

Five years later he looked me up on Facebook to tell me he realised how badly he'd treated me. I'm happy, and I hope he is too.

When #MeToo began (in the wake of the Harvey Weinstein sexual abuse disclosure), I thought about times where sexual abuse happened to me: a blind man who I volunteered with guessing my bra size – it was laughed off as 'his shtick' by those who had worked with him; the man at a pub who grabbed my hands and told me how disgusting I looked; ongoing misogynistic rants and the expectation of my time and attention from another man who placed me on a pedestal only to abuse me when I didn't meet his expectations; online comments describing the way a man should rape a woman with my skin condition; and the guy in the Mickey Mouse costume on Hollywood Boulevard who groped my breast.

Me too, I guess.

Society positions the sexuality of disabled women in two ways – they are either regarded as asexual and de-sexualised, or used as sexual objects, existing only to be abused.

The de-sexualisation of disabled women means that I've never been wolf-whistled or cat-called. I'm stared at but not in a lustful way. I've never wanted to be cat-called, but I have definitely seen that I am treated differently from my conventionally attractive friends when we walk down the street together.

Once, when I was walking to dinner, there was a group of men drinking at a pub table on the footpath. They had a dog with them, and it barked and growled at me as I walked past. The men egged it on, encouraging the dog, I guess because I looked so ugly to them. That has stuck with me – I didn't deserve cat-calling, but an aggressive dog coming at me was fine.

When a disabled woman speaks about the abuse – sexual or not – she's endured, she's often doubted. We are seen as difficult, complainers, over-reactors. People play devil's advocate – questioning the other person's motive – writing them off as concerned and kind, having a bad day or mentally unwell. Intellectually disabled women are regarded as unreliable witnesses, so often their stories of abuse are not heard.

We are often expected to be quiet, to be grateful for attention received, and not to rock the boat. For many disabled women (and

It's imperative that when disabled women speak up about abuse, we are really listened to and assisted.

men) who are abused, the abuser is the person in charge of their 'care'. And so speaking up can be more dangerous than not speaking up, because it could lead to further abuse, or even homelessness and a lack of access to essential services.

Disabled People's Organisations Australia states:

- People with disability experience higher rates of violence than the rest of the community.
- 90 per cent of women with intellectual disability have been sexually assaulted, 60 per cent before they're 18.
- Children with disability are three times more likely to experience abuse than other children.

While all women should speak up and be heard, it's imperative that when disabled women speak up about abuse, we are really listened to and assisted.

Women also become disabled due to abuse – I have a friend whose life has changed irreparably because of domestic violence. She acquired physical impairments, her appearance has changed significantly, and the emotional impact has been enormous. Every time she is asked why she looks the way she does, she has to relive the horror of her past. This is a big reminder not to ask a stranger about their disability.

Reflecting on my stints with internet dating, and desire to find love in order to feel validated, I want to tell my younger self that it's perfectly fine to be alone – if only to be in a respectful and fulfilling relationship with myself. I endured so many awful encounters, and it stripped that self-respect my parents worked so hard to instil in me. When I stopped this desperate search for love, and stopped trying to make things work with men who didn't treat me with the love and respect I deserved, I focused on developing me.

13

So can you have sex?

To everyone who has felt it is their right to question me about my sex life ...

None of your fucking business.

14

Work ethic – and the ethics of work

I moved to Melbourne in 2003 to start full-time work. I got a graduate program position at the Australian Tax Office. I don't have the love or skills for working with numbers, so I found a lot of the tax-based graduate program really hard (what did I expect?).

I stayed in the public service for almost 15 years (including a year without pay), working at three different agencies. For the most part I enjoyed the work, especially in communications and events, but I found it very hard to progress. No matter how much experience I gained in writing for the media, I still wasn't good enough to get a permanent communications job. Of course, it felt like unconscious (or conscious) bias but I could never say that. Towards the end of my public service career, I had a public media profile, with my opinions being widely read – which did not sit easily with being a junior in the organisation, unable to say a lot to my superiors. I was discouraged from being too 'passionate', which I read as meaning that they saw me and my work in the media as a risk. There was a weird moment when I spent my lunchtime doing a speech, opening before the former prime minister Julia Gillard, and then returned to my day job, doing extremely menial work.

I am not sure if I truly made an impact in the public service, but I did make some good friends and am happy that my superannuation is healthy.

When I started my first job in Melbourne, I thought that I was suited to a desk job, not predicting the emotional impact work would have on my physical health. In hindsight, I wish I had known that my body wasn't suited to full-time work.

A couple of years after completing the graduate program, I started a new job within the Tax Office – and it turned out I wasn't so great at it. The job involved numbers and a fast-paced cycle, which I wasn't prepared for. I felt lonely and like a failure. The pressure of work impacted on my health, and my ichthyosis was exacerbated.

Six months into the job, in 2005, I found the courage to request part-time work, because I thought it would make it easier on my health. I was nervous – this was the first time in my career that I acknowledged the impact of ichthyosis on my work. As I said earlier, I was raised to believe I could do anything.

My request to go part-time was refused. I asked if I had a baby could I go part-time? Yes, I could, I was told.

Unbelievable.

Lots of women in the organisation worked part-time. As far as I knew, they were all mothers. I couldn't see anyone like me – young, childless and with a medical condition – going part-time.

Perhaps the issue was that I wasn't seeing many other disabled and chronically ill people in the workplace at all.

I was young, and I looked like I had just come out of high school. I was called 'kiddo' by someone I worked with until my late twenties. I wondered whether it was because I looked so young that my request wasn't taken seriously. I decided to give a speech to my colleagues, showing them my ointments and tablets to prove how serious ichthyosis is. Perhaps if I raised awareness, that would change how I was perceived? I took in red snake lollies to represent scaly red skin – and to win them over. I articulated that ichthyosis wasn't just cosmetic. I had 20 minutes in the tearoom for this talk, and I sensed my colleagues just wanted to get back to work.

I was terribly disappointed. I know Gen Ys get a bad rap for being entitled, but I did expect to be better supported. I wondered if this was discriminatory. The union couldn't tell me much, and all an OH&S assessor advised was changing my desk height and layout. But for me, OH&S reasonable adjustment was about feeling supported at work, and reducing my hours when needed.

I had chosen a 'flexible workplace', under the impression that it would accommodate people with medical conditions. I wasn't about to get pregnant so I could drop back to three days a week.

The right to request flexible work because of disability didn't exist in 2005. Flexible work was written into the *Fair Work Act 2009*, and amended to include disabled people in 2013. But employers can still refuse.

When I returned to the job I wasn't good at after a hospital stay, a colleague asked, 'Who did you expect to do your work when you were away?' I was devastated. I felt like such a burden in the workplace. And then my health spiralled into a cycle of pain.

I carried the expectation to do it all. To work a well-paying, secure, full-time job. And I felt I had to prove I was worthy of a place in mainstream employment – that despite my skin condition, I could do it. I pushed myself to work, even when I was sick. I didn't want to let anyone down.

With pain comes guilt – especially in the workplace. And guilt can be crippling (yes, that word was used intentionally).

When I worked in a traditional office-based workplace – even when my managers and colleagues were supportive and understanding – I grappled with the guilt of being absent when I was sore. Apart from walking slowly when I'm in pain, I look the same every day, so I worried that colleagues would think, 'She looked fine yesterday, so why is she sick today?' And some didn't get the pain: 'Oh, yeah, I had a hard session at the gym this morning,' was said to me in 'empathy'.

The guilt would often surface in jobs where I was relied upon as the sole worker – office manager and executive assistant or event planner. Who would do my job when I wasn't there?

So I'd often attend work when I was just too sore. This contributed to the soreness cycle – not getting enough rest, not staying off my feet, and thus having more time off than I would have needed if I'd just given myself a break when the pain started.

Once, I'd spent all day excitedly telling people I was off to see a band after work. I went home, had a shower, and went into the city. I felt my face getting hot, burning up more as the stage lights got brighter. Infection started to crawl over my face – hot, yellow and sticky. I remember sitting on the far side of the Toff in Town stage, watching the band play. My face pounded with the beat. It was on fire, and not in the exhilarating way I usually feel when I see bands.

The next morning my face was still sore. It was so infected that I didn't want to look anyone in the eye. I went to work after washing my face twice.

When my managers arrived, they asked me how I was. I immediately burst into tears. I told them how sore my face was. They both asked, 'Why did you come into work today?'

And I told them I was worried about how my absence would be perceived. I saw a band the previous night. They knew that. I didn't want them to think I was out drinking all night. I couldn't take a sickie. I had posted a photo on social media. What if colleagues saw that? I wanted to prove I was capable, even more committed than my non-disabled colleagues. I had come in, in immense pain and with great self-consciousness, because I thought I had to. I was overcompensating because I thought I had to.

I cried some more. And they sent me home. I was due to see the band again that night. I cancelled – the first and only time I've done so.

Years later I talked to one of these managers, when she managed me at another organisation. I told her that I still carried the guilt of being sick. Every time I was sick, I would call or text, outlining any work that needed staff attention (like the dishwasher being repaired, or the travel documents in the commissioner's in-tray). She'd reply, 'Take it easy.' I spent each sick day doing nothing, because I felt guilty. Yet my mind was active. And being alone, in pain, is isolating. I spend a lot of time in bed. Doing nothing when I'm naturally a hard worker and a big thinker feels lazy. I could have written, lined up freelance opportunities, watched some documentaries even. But I didn't. I told her this.

I also told her that I worry about the somewhat public life I lead, and the questions I might receive about working across two industries. The truth is, most of my writing is done in bed. I had a sick day when one of my articles was published in *The Age*. I celebrated in bed, elevating my legs and napping it off.

The guilt is enormous.

My manager understood. She told me she wondered whether her telling me to relax placed extra pressure on me — that I should just lie there and do nothing, because that's what being sick means. We talked about the Protestant work ethic — that my family expects me to work, that I just have to get on with it.

When you are disabled, there's so much stigma around work. On the one hand there's the stigma of being unemployed, the stigma of welfare — the notion that disabled people are a burden on society, that we're bludgers if we claim welfare. On the other hand, there's stigma within the workplace — the sickie culture, and the idea that disabled people can't contribute or pull their weight to the workplace.

In 2016, I was finally able to take the leap to part-time and freelance work. I took a year's leave without pay from the public service so I had a safety net, and when I saw how much I loved part-time and freelance work and that I didn't need to ask my parents for money, I resigned in 2017. I work part-time and supplement my income with a range of writing, speaking and training work.

I didn't go part-time for health reasons, but to develop my own writing career. But the health benefits have been remarkable. I worked a part-time job at a not-for-profit for six months, and built my freelance opportunities. And then I decided to go it alone until I resumed part-time work for an arts festival in February 2018.

I admit I'm a little tired, but I'm so happy and fulfilled. I'm doing meaningful, enjoyable work, meeting interesting people, earning a decent income, setting my own schedule for the most part, and sometimes working with my idols. My sick leave and soreness is at its lowest ever. And perhaps it's because of this new work–life balance, including being able to write in bed, that I lasted a year without taking a strong painkiller.

Part-time work has changed my life.

When I finally identified as being disabled (more about this later), and had excellent managers, I talked to them about my accessibility needs. These didn't involve an ergonomic desk assessment and adjustment, but time. Time to get ready slowly in the morning if I was sore. Time to go home early if I couldn't manage a full day. Time off for hospital appointments. The ability to purchase extra leave in case I ran out of sick leave. My health was much more stable knowing I had time to take care of it and get better.

My freelance work means I mostly work from home. In my pyjamas. Sometimes from bed. I write most of my pieces on my iPad in bed. (I once wrote a job application from my hospital bed – and got the job – and I felt like I'd set a ridiculously high standard for my future work at the organisation. If I could do such a great job from my sick bed, imagine how amazing I'd be when I was well! I wasn't amazing at that job and didn't last long.)

I have a busy schedule, and with this and regular travel for my speeches and freelance consulting, my skin is surprisingly resilient. I travel interstate at least once a month. While my skin is impacted by the changes in shower water and air-conditioning in hotels, my health is impressively stable.

I went to my quarterly dermatology clinic soon after I quit the job I wasn't good at. I was working solely for myself, with a somewhat regular income thanks to a training contract. They asked how I was. I didn't have any soreness or irritation to report. My skin was the best it had been in two years.

Perhaps it's because I am my own boss – setting my own schedule – that my skin improved. I work different hours as a freelancer; longer but often from the comfort of my home, and in comfortable clothes.

I think it's mostly to do with my work being so intertwined with my skin and appearance. Because of my openness about pain and social barriers, my clients are more understanding and accommodating. I write about the barriers I face because of my skin, and my editors are very understanding about me being so sore that I can't write to deadline. I speak about the pain, and so I am more comfortable in asking for a chair at an event.

I won a tender for a big training delivery job – designing and delivering disability training to 400 staff – and I still can't believe it. The night before I was due to submit the training workbook, I was in a lot of pain. I was zonked out on painkillers. I wasn't able to do any work – if I did, it might have been compromised by synthetic opiates. I was in tears with Adam, worried that being unable to complete the work on time would leave a bad impression. I sent an apologetic text to Mick, the guy who hired me, and told him I'd have to send the document a day late. 'Don't sweat it,' he told me. 'Monday is sweet, or let me know if it's difficult. You don't need pressure on top of being crook. Rest up.' I sighed with relief. That guilt was lifted. The tone was set for the rest of our working relationship – my health came first. Sometimes I was so sore that I delivered the training with a blanket over my knee. But I delivered it, and I delivered it well – always with a laugh.

I have been really lucky to have regular, well-paid work since I left university. Of course, it's been a struggle at times, but I acknowledge my privilege as a middle-class woman who hasn't experienced the unemployment and poverty that many other disabled people have.

Disabled people face discrimination when looking for work, and in the workplace.

Disabled people are looked down upon when they are welfare recipients, but the physical and attitudinal barriers preventing people getting a job can be enormous. And the statistics around disability and unemployment are alarming. In 2015, the Australian Bureau of Statistics reported 53.4 per cent of people with a disability aged 15-64 years participate in the workforce, compared with 83.2 per cent of people without a disability.

A lack of employment leads to decreased economic and social participation in the community. It leads to disabled people living in poverty. PriceWaterhouse Coopers reported in 2011 that 45 per cent of disabled Australians live on or below the poverty line.

Further to this, equal pay doesn't extend to many disabled people. Disabled employees who work at government-supported Australian Disability Enterprises (ADEs) are paid mere dollars. In 2016, the ABC News reported that some disabled workers were offered $2.79 an hour – which is $15.50 less than the 2017 minimum wage.

ADE employees – who often have an intellectual impairment – do menial piecework, which includes packing boxes, packaging seeds, laundry, preparing frozen meals and mowing lawns.

While some argue ADEs allow disabled people to connect with others and gain a small sense of independence, the work is not meaningful, doesn't give them equal employment opportunities, and the pay is degrading. When people protest about overseas workers who are exploited in sweatshops, I wonder if they realise this happens in Australia too?

Additionally, some mainstream organisations run programs for new recruits who are disabled, but these programs don't extend past entry level. So even if a disabled person is highly qualified and experienced, they might not be able to enter that organisation at a more senior level (or progress past that level once they're employed). I am frustrated with the entry-level programs for disabled people. They almost always pay entry-level wages, and so the work assignment is rudimentary. It assumes lack of experience and qualifications and doesn't always provide meaningful work. These programs, while good opportunities, perpetuate low expectations of disabled people.

I put a call out on my Facebook page to help someone find work. Tish Peiris, a regular Facebook follower, left a comment on my post, telling me about her qualifications and inability to be placed in a job suitable for her. She acquired a traumatic brain injury during an internship writing about war and refugees in Sri Lanka. A recruitment agency once suggested she sell newspapers since she used to write for them.

Tish told me:

> I have two Masters, in International Law and Journalism, and a Bachelors in Political Science. My last disability recruitment place sent me for a job collecting tickets at the railway station in North Shore Sydney. I kid you not. It is tragic, actually – think of all that wasted potential that could be building up Australia. My background was as a serious political journalist and my ambition is to work

in human and disability rights, not collecting railway tickets, mate!

Tish, like me, finds it better to make her own opportunities than be placed in work that doesn't match her qualifications, skills and experiences:

I totally make all my own opportunities. I am a struggling filmmaker and I have written most of a film script about a soldier in Afghanistan but I'm much more interested in international disability rights. I find that even though I have multiple university qualifications, people are very uncomfortable about giving me a fair go.

And that's the kicker. Disabled people are given work below our capability, offered work for little or no pay, and aren't given the same opportunities as non-disabled people because we make employers uncomfortable. Christina Ryan, Founding Director of the Disability Leadership Institute, says:

As long as we knock on the door and ask, we are disempowering ourselves. We need to create our own strong space that is desirable to others, so we need to support each other, skill up, skill each other up, and ensure we back our success stories. By becoming experts, ground breakers, change agents, and so on (for example, I have skills in shifting UN thinking that not many have and which should be considered highly valuable), the mainstream will increasingly want what we have and the approach that we take. We need to make them come to us.

While it's important that we create our own opportunities, it's also important that organisations improve in their employment, retention and promotion of disabled people.

Now that I am a freelancer, every month or so, I get an 'opportunity' to work for free. For exposure. No payment. No money to buy food or pay for the rent or buy my medications. No money for holidays or pretty dresses either.

I receive emails and messages with soul-crushing invites to work for free – if they came in a paper envelope, moths would fly out of them, like a depleted wallet.

Come speak to us! We'd love you to write for our website.

I scroll down. The closing line is: *We're sorry but we can't pay you.* I've become accustomed to this – especially if it's a disability organisation or publication. A disability organisation should ensure their writers are paid – for our time, skill and lived experience. I understand not-for-profits (and some media outlets) run on a shoestring – but it's only fair that a disability organisation leads by example and supports disabled people who provide content to them. I know that some people with disability (and parents) would be pleased with the opportunity for exposure – but it's not feasible to ask for free labour.

It happens with large mainstream organisations too. When an organisation commits to inviting disabled people to provide advice on accessibility or inclusive language, for example, it often fails to back up that commitment with a budget. And they don't consider that we must take time from our paid or voluntary jobs to give this free advice. It's as if we are given unpaid opportunities as a

Do they think our lives are so unfulfilled that we're sitting at home just waiting for a generous offer of working for nothing?

gesture of inclusiveness; or worse, that our qualifications, opinions and experience aren't worth money.

They seem to believe that we should be grateful for opportunities – that at least it's something for us to do. I feel there's an assumption that, because we educate incidentally in life, we don't mind educating large audiences for a low fee or for free. Do they think our lives are so unfulfilled that we're sitting at home just waiting for a generous offer of working for nothing? We are seen as charitable, rather than employable.

I often provide my time and expertise for free. I volunteer. But I will not write for free when an organisation's business model is to source free content for their websites. This perpetuates the devaluing of writers' work.

Also, to the writers who write for free – please reconsider. You're devaluing our craft and saying that it's OK for organisations not to pay. You set the expectation that disabled people don't want or need to be paid. A person at an organisation wanting us to work for free may think, *Carly said yes to working without pay, so we'll ask others too.* And word will get around. Know your worth and know the worth of others.

So when is it OK to work for free?

Of course, it's fine – more than fine – to volunteer for charity. But when an organisation (a charity, not-for-profit, government or corporate) invites a disabled person to work for free, while their other staff are being paid, alarm bells should ring.

I am able to do a few things for free because my paid work allows me to. I do some work on ABC radio. I've been Clare Bowditch's arts reporter on ABC Melbourne. It was unpaid but my book writing process was often mentioned, and they linked my social media accounts to theirs. And I got tickets to arts events for review purposes.

I also did a piece to camera for ABC RN's Facebook page – advising journalists and editors on how to write about disabled people and centre us in the media. This video was shared in some writing groups I'm in, and a couple of people asked me to write and speak for them after seeing it.

There are no hard rules about working for free, but I do encourage you to consider the costs and benefits – both for you and for your community.

15

Teacher not patient

I've been a hospital patient my whole life. It used to be that the doctors only provided me with advice on how to manage my skin condition. They prescribed me medications and creams for infections, and admitted me to hospital when I got very sick. Even though I've been very vocal about my treatment, and even though I know my condition very well, they've always led the conversations in the consultation room.

When I was a child, my hospital stays were frequent and long – often for a few weeks at a time.

Mum would take time from work to stay with me at the Royal Children's Hospital in Melbourne. Her workplace offered her work in the hospital branch – I hope the same would still happen now. She slept in the playroom, and mothered other patients whose parents did not sleep at the hospital.

There were times I wanted to stay in hospital rather than go to school. The doctors and nurses had time for me – and the other sick kids had far more empathy than my peers at school. I felt understood and valued. I met wonderful people there. The hospital school and playroom were where I socialised and flourished. Rosemary, the teacher, encouraged me to be creative – I made Garfield cartoons on the computer, made collages and read books. I had a trip to the zoo once, although I was very sick and it took a while to recover afterwards.

I've made life-long friends in hospital – the Kirleys and the Joneses have been family friends for years. I met their children – Erena Kirley and Nigel Jones – on the wards, and we've been in touch ever since. Erena is from a family of 10 children, and my mum and dad and I have gone to their family farm every Boxing Day since 1989. The table gets bigger, with partners and children always being added.

I talked to Nigel a lot when I was in the Albury Base Hospital. He was three years older than me – and his brothers are one year older and one year younger. His family is involved in car racing, and each time I saw Nigel, he'd have a new autograph or photo of a sportsperson to show me. Nigel had a degenerative disease – and died when he was 18. His family and I are still close – his brother Mitch wrapping me up in a bear hug each time I see him. I am sad my friendship with Nigel wasn't able to reach adulthood, but I am so grateful that we met and for his family's warmth and friendship.

I have regular hospital appointments rather than frequent stays now. I usually talk to the doctors about how my skin is feeling, and renew my scripts. But the conversation extends beyond that. We talk about managing the emotional aspects of the condition, as well as how to cope with the pressure of being somewhat of a patient authority in ichthyosis. My hospital file doesn't only contain notes – there are clippings of my articles in there too. Sometimes student doctors come in, but I am always able to choose whether I want to see them, based on how I am feeling. I often make time for them, but if I am unwell, I don't want to have to recite my whole medical history to a student. I am grateful for this choice.

In recent years, my role as a patient has changed. I've become a teacher to these doctors. My senior doctors have asked me to be a guest at their training classes. I've given speeches to young dermatologists, geneticists and medical students about what it's like to live with ichthyosis. I've talked to them about the social aspects, my challenges and achievements, and about resilience. My story is something they won't find in their textbooks. At the start of one of my speeches I joked that this was the first time I had attended a dermatology training conference wearing so many clothes, and I thanked them for that.

The doctors and students have responded very well to me. I have seen some of them when I have an appointment at the hospital. They've thanked me for my talk, and for making them laugh! I even bumped into one of them when I was out seeing a band – such are the joys of being easily recognised!

Not that I'm a stranger to teaching doctors about rare skin conditions. As a child, I attended dermatology conferences, as mentioned previously. I was frustrated, physically and emotionally, by both the cold environment and the doctors' cold bedside manner. Not being able to wear clothes, and the impersonal consultation, made for a difficult time.

My last conference was when I was in my early teens. As well as the doctors who examined me, I met a few people with various skin conditions. That was a real eye-opener – they were in search of a cure, but were also miserable with their lives. I did not want to be like that.

That last conference was an unpleasant experience. I felt the doctors only wanted to learn about my condition, not me as a person. I felt like an exhibit at the zoo, a little exploited. I told Mum that I wanted to leave early, and so we did.

Eventually, I grew to love my body – this definitely came about when the doctors stopped looking at me like a specimen.

When my geneticist invited me to a training day a few years ago, she gave me the option of being a patient or a speaker. I immediately said I wanted to be a speaker. 'Good,' she said, 'that will change the power balance!'

It was strange being in a different role. While my dermatology team is fantastic and mostly realise that I know as much about my condition as they do, and they respect my medical choices, there is always that superior/subordinate relationship between us.

That day, I spoke about my desire to see greater representation of diversity in the media, the intrusive comments people make to me, and my Master's thesis on blogging, chronic illness and identity. I also referenced British disability rights activist Jenny Morris's book *Pride Against Prejudice*, which was pivotal in changing how I saw disability identity and pride. I talked about more than just the medical aspects of life with ichthyosis – I talked about the social and emotional aspects, which aren't often discussed between patients and doctors in the clinic.

The head dermatologist, a doctor I have been seeing for most of my life, walked me to the lecture theatre, and he was so proud of me for doing this speech.

These hospital talks have led to guest lecturing to medical students at Melbourne University each year. I am so proud to join my geneticist in the lecture hall to talk about media and genetics, and how I have chosen to tell my own story through writing and speaking.

The medical students find it useful to have a real-life case study in the lecture theatre.

I am always going to be a patient. That is inevitable. But when I first gave my speech, the roles had shifted, and I was a teacher.

One day while I was at the hospital, in my mid-twenties, I talked to my dermatologist about ways I could get involved in delivering messages about body image. He put me in touch with the Chronic Illness Peer Support (CHiPS) program at the Royal Children's Hospital. The program is for young people aged 12 to 25 who have chronic illnesses. I mentored there for three years. I assisted at meetings and went to camps – the highlight of the year.

As a mentor, I felt that I got as much out of the program as the participants. I saw that the barriers we faced were similar, even though we had different impairments. The young people all spent lots of time in hospitals and doctors' waiting rooms. They had time off from school and work. They felt like people who weren't chronically ill didn't understand their experiences. The environmental and attitudinal barriers they faced were the same as those I faced.

One night at camp, I comforted a young woman with a physical impairment who was afraid to be seen before she showered in the morning. She needed help to shower too, and she was embarrassed by this. I told her we could use sheets as a makeshift curtain around her bed. She told me I wouldn't understand how she felt, because I didn't have her impairment. I told her that I don't want anyone to see me before I've showered either, because my face is dry and crusty, and from this anecdote she realised that our diagnoses don't separate us. We have more in common because of the barriers we face – just as I had realised some months earlier.

I received a 'warm fuzzy' after each camp – a book of words and pictures from campers about the difference that I made to them. Camps were often emotional. The young people (and me included) challenged themselves to do physical and emotional activities – high rope climbing, rafting or songwriting. Some of the young people were mobility impaired and modifications were made so they could participate in physical activities they couldn't do outside this supervised, accessible environment. It was so wonderful seeing them achieve what seemed like the impossible – swinging on a flying fox or building a hut from scratch. And these achievements made everyone emotional – the young people, the volunteers and the nurses and doctors who assisted at the camps. So the warm fuzzy messages were often of awe – describing what it was like to see someone achieve a goal or push themselves. These messages remind us we can, when we think we can't. I treasure my warm fuzzy books, reading them when I need a pick-me-up or to remember that I've made a difference to someone. I know the young people I mentored value their warm fuzzies as much as I do.

I built friendships and the peer support I needed when I was young. And I gave myself permission to identify as having a chronic illness. I fit in with these bright young minds. Finally.

It takes a good doctor or nurse to realise that the lived experience of patients can be an integral part of our own treatment. If you want to play a part in educating young doctors and nurses about your disability, I encourage you to ask your senior doctors about how you can get involved. It's a great feeling to be a part of a doctor's education. Not all of their learning comes from a textbook!

Mine have come to trust me for advice about my own treatment. I advise them against intravenous antibiotics because the wound site often becomes infected too. They also ask me to spend time with new parents of children with the condition, which is a huge privilege. It's lovely to see the kids grow up, healthy, happy and confident. And I've worked with my dermatologists in educating new dermatologists and medical students.

It's a relief to have my lived experience valued. In 2016, I was experiencing more pain than previously, for unknown reasons, and I was referred to the pain management unit at the hospital. It was good to make a plan to manage my pain. While it helps to have painkillers, and some advice about mindfulness, it was just as good to be listened to by a doctor who understands what pain feels like. They talked it through with me, and validated that yes, my pain exists and it is in fact chronic.

On the whole, I feel in control of my treatment. I'm also lucky that my appointments are free through the public hospital system, although the cost of prescriptions can add up quickly.

My pointers for health professionals:

Listen to us. You can learn as much (maybe more) from our lived experience as you can from a textbook.

Talk to us about our whole lives. It can be uplifting for a doctor to be excited about what's happening for us, away from our conditions.

Don't show too much excitement at treating a rare patient for the first time. When you show excitement in seeing my diagnosis for the first time as a doctor, it sometimes seems like you've won a prize.

Let us help others who may be struggling with similar conditions. Invite us to speak at medical events or put us in touch with families.

Mind your language, especially if you're a doctor who writes for publication or uses social media. Terms like 'healthcare burden' are really damaging. Also, I don't 'suffer from' ichthyosis, I 'live with' it.

Take a step back to reflect on how far your patients have come, because of the treatment and empathy you've shown. Many of us owe our lives to you. Thank you.

16

Skin hunger

This chapter is about skin hunger. Skin hunger is the craving to be touched. I've created the chapter from a series of blog posts that I wrote over four years — from when I yearned for touch to when — well, I don't want to spoil the ending. (And you'll have to wait until Chapter 22 to find out what happens. Sorry!)

UNTOUCHED – 2011

For most people, being touched is something they take for granted. It just happens. A hug from a friend, a hand being held, a pat on the shoulder for reassurance. These small moments of physical affection aren't milestones for most people. Touching often happens without thought — like drinking a glass of water, doing up buttons, putting one foot in front of the other. For me, these small moments of affection are shelved away in my memory like wines in a cellar. And for the big moments of physical affection,

I want to hold a press conference, telling the world that I've been touched.

I received lots of physical affection from my parents as a child. I would sit in between them on the couch and Dad would curl my hair around his fingers. 'Curly-lurly, curly-lurly, curly-lurly,' he would say, letting each ringlet spring like a piglet's tail. He'd give me animal rides on his knee, usually diplodocus rides. And each night, and sometimes Saturday mornings, Mum would sit with me on the floor, me lying on her lap, while she combed the scale out of my scalp. I cannot imagine letting anyone else do this – it's such a private experience. Lots of skin being removed, my scalp and emotions often equally raw. The feel of the comb on my scalp was both pleasurable and painful. My scalp would feel so tender, especially when I went out in the cold. Void of its protection. I'd tell Mum what happened in my day – often how kids at school were afraid to touch me.

There's a line in Darren Hayes' song 'Unlovable' that I related to so much. He asks if his skin is untouchable. I felt like we had something in common, that he *might* just know my feelings of skin hunger, and people's reluctance to touch me. In 2004 and 2007, at small concerts, Darren hugged me from the stage. In 2007, he kissed my face. I can still feel his bristles against my cheek if I think hard. A celebrity's touch is pretty special – especially when for so long no one ordinary wanted to touch me.

Being bullied at school was, fortunately, not often physical. Kids were too afraid of catching my skin condition. Stabbing me with a protractor, pushing me off my bike or spitting on me were options, though – leaving enough distance between the bully and me that they didn't catch anything. Despite the isolation, teasing and name calling, I still wanted to join in on their playtime – much of which involved some sort of physical contact. I wanted to have my hair plaited by the other girls, to have my thumb touched in heads down thumbs up, to have my hand held by a friend. This sometimes happened, and I was so excited when it did. It meant that I was normal, like everyone else.

My dad is not a big hugger – nor were my grandparents. I think it's an English trait. Our hugs are clumsy and brief, like two humans in bear suits, just patting each other's backs gently. I was never allowed to sit on my grandfather's lap because I'd make it dirty. This is my main memory of time spent with him as a child.

Hugs and kisses as greetings are so commonplace now, even between strangers. Sometimes in a group situation, other people are hugged and kissed hello or goodbye and I am left standing there awkward, and waiting. I do not initiate hugs or kisses. I never know if someone wants their cheek to be smeared in my ointment, or have their black clothes peppered with my skin. People close to me don't mind if this happens. I remember feeling my most valued in the workplace when a male manager reached over and pulled some skin from my hair. Awkward but valuing.

I wonder if people's reluctance to touch me is not of fear for themselves – and it probably isn't, we are no longer in the playground – but out of genuine worry that their touch will hurt my skin. It generally won't.

Casual touches can feel miraculous to me, despite their innocent intent. A pat on the arm that means it's good to see me can make me smile all day. Even a sales assistant's hand brushing against mine when they give me change can give me shivers. I wonder whether the sensitivity of my skin is why the feeling of being touched is physically and emotionally heightened. I don't think my nerve endings are more sensitive than the norm, but it's like my skin is more receptive to touch because it isn't an everyday occurrence.

Intimate touching is literally etched into my memory forever, but I have to concentrate really hard to make the memories surface. After so many years of people's repulsion at touching me, the times when I've been intimately touched have been amazing. Not necessarily sexual touch, but the hand-holding, the brush of the arm to indicate interest, a kiss on the face. They're all electrifying. The best feeling in the world. I can remember every single caress during the first time I was in bed with a boy – even though it was in January 2000. I remember everything about how it felt.

When I had boyfriends I'd often want to go to bed extremely early in the evening, just to revel in more than eight hours of physical contact. I never felt like I woke up with my skin dry like I do when I sleep alone. It's as though touch nurtures me.

A number of years ago, a strange thing occurred. As I slept in a man's arms, it felt so amazing being held that the feeling of touch was squared. I dreamt of him holding me as he was doing so. And then I wondered whether this was my body's way of responding to a form of deprivation, drinking up the sensory overload of being touched.

SKIN HUNGER – 2012

I used to think about touch a lot. I'd think about how long it had been been since. I don't get touched a lot, and when I do, it feels amazing, and sometimes heightened, even just a tap on the shoulder. It's not necessarily sexual touch that I crave, it's just the feel of skin on skin that I want. A hand held, a hug. I've got skin hunger.

Skin hunger is the yearning to be touched. It is a form of sensory deprivation. Shortly after the end of World War II, when babies in orphanages failed to thrive, psychologist Harry Harlow used baby monkeys to study the effects of skin hunger. The monkeys were taken from their birth mothers and paired with surrogates made from wire or cloth. They chose the soft cloth surrogate, even when the wire surrogate held a bottle of milk. The monkeys thrived on touch.

Having a skin condition like mine means people are scared of touching. Scared they may hurt me, and maybe scared of getting dirty or catching it. I see others touching things I've touched – they do so gingerly, as though they have pincers. That sometimes hurts, so I pretend I don't see, in case I make them feel uncomfortable. It is human nature, even for me, not to want to touch something that looks suspicious. And beauty product advertising is about smooth, touchable skin.

Touch validates people. It shows that someone cares. It shows that you're in fact a real human being – physical matter – and not just a concept that doesn't physically exist. Sometimes I wonder if we are all just stardust, and this world's not real, and then the cashier puts coins in my hand and I feel her fingers on my palm, fleetingly, and I am reminded, I am real. I exist.

I was thinking about touch at my grandfather's funeral as the celebrant read out the eulogy. I can't remember if I ever really held my grandparents' hands. I don't remember the feel of their silky, aged skin on mine. It made me sad that I don't remember, and even sadder if it's true that I never held their hands.

I went to the theatre with my friend. In the dark, he dispensed chocolates from a packet into my hand. One. Two. Three. Four. Five. It was innocent, his hand brushing my palm. And all the while I thought about how long it had been since someone touched my hand. The touch was less than 10 seconds, but it felt like a lifetime.

As my friend Mitch, Nigel Jones's brother, and I said goodbye for the second time that night – I had missed the train by a few seconds – he hugged me fiercely, said 'goodbye, darling' and kissed me on the cheek, his beard scratching me in a good way. We were only friends – but this touch stayed with me for so long I had to write about it in my notebook (OK, my iPhone notes function) the next day. That was the closest I've been to someone in a long time.

Skin hunger is strange. My skin is my existence – it defines me. I put cream over my whole body twice a day or more. Self touch is not the same as another's touch. And so few people are in contact with my skin. So, when someone does touch me, the sensation is accelerated. Yet I don't have a vivid memory of how my skin feels between touches. I have to concentrate really hard to remember. I lose so much skin, and it constantly renews. Is it because my skin constantly renews that I can't remember touch? Is it that my skin's renewal makes for a loss of its memory?

Some forms of touch do not satiate my skin hunger. When I was younger my parents would put cream on my body – in addition to hugs. Of course, it would be gentle and with love, but it was more of a carer-type of touch than a cuddle. And in hospital, the nurses and doctors would do my dressings and bath me too. Now I usually do what I can for myself in hospital, and the nurses just do my leg dressings. But this touch is different – it's vinyl-gloved, clinical and impersonal. I wonder if it is because of the barrier of my creams that the touch doesn't feel the same.

Other forms of touch do satisfy my skin hunger. A kiss on the cheek, a brush of the hand, a warm hug, naked bodies spooning. My mum's hands, they're soft and always warm. Our hands are alike; I remember comparing them when I was small. She doesn't mind when I get her clothes greasy or covered in skin.

I don't initiate touch much, and perhaps I should do it more. Although I don't feel lonely all the time, and certainly not depressed, my skin hunger makes me lonely. At this moment, I can't remember what intimate touch feels like. Someone give me a hug.

THIS SKIN, IT'S HUNGRY – 2013

you cling to me like a koala on my back,
warm and close,
arms encircling my paper bark trunk.
our limbs play, like intertwining branches,
tickling infinity,
delivering each other stars.
we doze, full of eucalyptus love,
concave like gum leaves,
i will store this memory
in deserted knots for the winter.

I wrote that poem many years ago, towards the end of a relationship. It was falling apart, but still, we clung together, him like a koala on my back – warm, close and sleepy. I knew we were coming to an end, and told myself those memories would be there when he wasn't. In the cold winter.

Storing the memory of touch for the winter. Like jars of bottled summer fruits, full of sunshine and bursts of flavour, mouthfuls transporting you back to the warm months. Only now, I think I've run out. My jars of peaches are low in stock. And the tree's knots are almost deserted.

The touch I encounter regularly is solo – a necessary oil-slick – and sometimes gloved and clinical, punctuated by medical terms such as erythrodermic and cellulitis.

I've shaken a lot of hands lately. Networking. But that's not satiating my skin hunger. I'm yearning for proper touch. And the irony of it all is I am surrounded by more people than ever, feeling loved and wanted, yet skin hunger is quite a lonely existence. It's empty and prickly and I wrap myself up in my blanket tighter each night.

A toddler on the tram clung to her bear, and I wondered why it's not OK for adults to carry around a toy, just to cling to something, to hold something close.

Touch is nurturing, regenerative. It's like the human equivalent of photosynthesis, allowing us to flourish. Sometimes standing out can black out the light, rendering a sense of the untouchable, consequently creating sensory deprivation. Without touch it's hard to flourish.

I try so hard to remember. It's two weeks or so since I've hugged someone hard. My friend gives the best bear hugs, and is generous with them too. It's getting harder as the space between touch grows longer. You can't bring out touch to evoke nostalgia. It's not like a smell or a meal, which can bring back a memory. Even a song that you share with a special person isn't the same as the hugs you share. Nothing ever compensates.

With everyone I meet, I am bursting with the expectation of tactile possibilities. I hope and I hope, hanging back awkwardly, unsure if I should initiate the first touch. This skin, it's hungry.

17

Carly in media land

I always wanted to be a dermatologist – until I found out it would take me until 2017 to qualify, and was told by my then dermatologist that I would probably be mistaken for a patient in my own consulting room. Plus I didn't fancy dissecting rats and human organs. My next choice was to be a writer.

And so I wrote – stories and essays and poems. I really enjoyed English at school – I was in advanced classes throughout high school, dedicated enough to take an early morning class in Year 12. I wrote a story about my dad's football fanaticism in Year 11 and was highly commended in the *Sydney Morning Herald* Young Writers Awards. I did work experience at Prime News, B104.9 Radio and *The Border Mail* in 1997 and 1998, though I never thought I'd pursue my dream of working in the media.

When I left school, my parents didn't want me to study away from home – my health was precarious and it would have been too expensive. Unfortunately, the local universities didn't offer journalism, so I did an eCommerce degree at La Trobe University in Wodonga. It was hard, I was uninterested in most subjects, and until I did first year accounting, I hadn't failed a subject in my life. In first year, I was so out of my depth that when my economics lecturer said we'd be making models, I thought we'd be making cute dioramas out of clay – not supply and demand models on the whiteboard. Fortunately, the HTML I learnt in the ecommerce subjects has been useful – at work and in blogging.

Throughout my undergraduate degree, I blogged – under pseudonyms. My blogs were never very good. In hindsight, they were similar to tweets – short and snappy thoughts, mostly about the guy who catfished me. They were on Diaryland then. Still, it was a way to practise writing. I wrote poetry too – moody and angsty, my scrawls filled many notebooks.

I wanted to quit eCommerce – or switch to Arts – in my first year, but my dad dissuaded me. I felt a lot of pressure not to disappoint him, because I was able to pursue higher education in a way that he and my mum hadn't been able to. So I endured my undergraduate degree just to get a stable job at the end – which happened. I did a degree I didn't enjoy and entered a graduate program I didn't enjoy (more accounting!) because it was what was expected of me.

And then I followed my dream. I commenced a Master of Communication two years after I started my government job. I studied at RMIT, taking six years to do my masters while working full-time and managing a chronic illness. Finally, I enjoyed studying – because I was doing subjects I was interested in, and because I had chosen this course. I loved the journalism and new media (social media wasn't a thing back then).

During my Masters, I started a blog – then called *Tune into Radio Carly* – to develop a portfolio. At first it was a diary, with posts about my thoughts on current events, as well as cooking, fashion, band reviews and what I'd been doing. And then I started to hone in on ichthyosis and appearance diversity, as well as disability.

I submitted a few blog posts to various publications – and I was accepted as a regular writer for some. It was while writing for a disability-focused government website that I met my best friend, Camille Condon, who also wrote for it. She wrote about the way strangers reacted to her disability – at the time, she carried a portable oxygen tank as she was on the waiting list for a lung transplant. I related to her story a lot – the stares, assumptions and the direct questions she received. I looked her up on Facebook and sent her a message. I discovered she was also a blogger, and a keen and talented seamstress and crafter. The first time we met was she was in hospital – I took her some chocolate and a craft magazine. We chatted for over an hour, and have been BFFs ever since. (Camille had a lung transplant in 2013 and she no longer has an oxygen tank.) Camille and I relate to the pressures of balancing work with being chronically ill – we constantly chat about the guilt we place on ourselves. She says:

> I always feel like I have to work harder and smarter to prove myself, and to make up for all of the time that I take off for medical appointments, hospital admissions, etc. I always feel guilty when I'm absent from work – whether it be for a medical appointment or even if I'm really ill and can't come into the office. I have the most understanding boss in the world, but that doesn't change the fact that I create my own guilt. I don't want to be seen as the person who is slacking off or taking 'sickies'.

I've been so thankful for her craft skills. She helped decorate my wedding, and made the bridesmaids' dresses for herself and Cassie, Adam's sister.

I also volunteered as a TV presenter for three seasons of *No Limits* on Channel 31 from 2010 to 2013. *No Limits* was a disability-led program on community TV. This gave me experience working with other disabled people, as well as interview skills, script development and speaking on the spot (because I couldn't read the autocue and sound natural). Most importantly, I saw firsthand the importance of disability-led storytelling and media production.

Once I found my feet with my current blog, around 2011, I set a goal to change the way people with ichthyosis, facial differences and disability are represented in the media. I chose to tell my story on my terms.

Writing my blog, and creating social media accounts, gave me confidence and built connections – initially with other bloggers, but also with readers, editors, and people who have hired me for work. I am confident that most freelance and consulting jobs that I've been asked to do have been because of my online presence. It's led to TV work on *You Can't Ask That* and *Cyberhate with Tara Moss*. I thanked a company for tweeting an article I'd written, and after a few more tweets, some emails and a meeting, they invited me to speak at their conference – in Bristol, England! That was my first proper speech. In 2012, with the financial support of the Royal Melbourne Hospital, I spoke at the Appearance Matters conference about living with a facial difference. I met with UK facial difference support group Changing Faces on that trip, and we've maintained a great relationship. Editors and festival producers have commissioned me for articles and projects. Speaking has been wonderful – I've been able to meet some smart, interesting people, travel and learn new ideas from the conversations

I take part in. At the time of writing this book, I do more speaking than writing. The opportunities have been amazing. I used to be told off for talking at school. But now I'm talking for a living.

I've learnt so much about disability politics, pride, history and activism by writing about it – especially through connecting with others in the disability community. Social media has allowed me to see many different perspectives, and support activists across the world in real time. I am so grateful for these friendships and working relationships. Writing and an online presence has helped me meet other people with my skin condition and facial differences – something I needed when I was little. Through my own writing, other people told me they've become more confident to tell their own stories. And that is an incredible privilege.

I've continued to speak up about ableist and discriminatory behaviour, and become less apologetic in doing so. As the Laura Hershey poem goes, I got proud through practising, and writing has played a big role in that.

> *Remember, you weren't the one*
> *Who made you ashamed,*
> *But you are the one*
> *Who can make you proud.*
> *Just practice,*
> *Practice until you get proud, and once you are proud,*
> *Keep practicing so you won't forget.*
> *You get proud*
> *By practicing.*

After years of showing up, writing on my blog and elsewhere, a publisher is paying me to write this memoir! I have been excited and hellishly scared all at once. My little blog, which is vulnerable, mouthy, personal and not favoured by brands for blog sponsorship, has meant I've got a track record of developing my writing and building an audience. And a publisher wanted my book – five publishers wanted it, actually. Turning down the other four was like leaving puppies behind.

The book deal didn't just happen – it took years of writing, putting my blog out there, meeting other bloggers and writers, pitching to media editors, battling tall poppy syndrome, navigating the tricky area of full-time work and not saying anything that could to jeopardise my safe job.

I've written pieces I'm not proud of. Like the blog I wrote about when my now husband first contacted me, and I felt like I was the object of his pity. (And then he read it and still wanted to meet me.) And like the blog I wrote about how I'm OK with writing for free – a few years before I worked out that accepting free work devalues all writers. That post is in the back of my mind as I continue to call out organisations who ask disabled people to work for free. But there are pieces I'm so glad I wrote – the one on parents who stunt their children's growth, the ones about the horrific murders of disabled people, the love letter to my body, and every piece that has helped someone with ichthyosis or another impairment, or a parent wanting to know that it's going to be OK for their child.

I know myself through my words. Writing gives me permission to show my vulnerabilities and my strength and to explore themes I hadn't heard of until I wrote about them. It allows me to speak of the past loneliness and bullying, and call out the present discrimination myself and others face.

In late 2016, I launched a podcast with one of my good friends, Jason-Scott Watkins, who I met through blogging. I found Jason's

I know myself
through my words.
Writing gives me
permission to show
my vulnerabilities
and my strength.

slow-cooked smoky baked beans recipe – I cooked it, tweeted him to thank him, and we met in person at a food truck opening where they served nothing but seafood and I had a temporary seafood allergy so had to drink cocktails instead – oops! We've laughed and eaten good food ever since. Jason and I have been podcast fans for years, and I think it was on my wedding day that we decided to make a podcast of our own. Our podcast is called *Refreshments Provided* and we talk about food, books, podcasts, films and other things we've been doing. It's a lot of fun – we swear, laugh a lot and hope our listeners are having as good a time listening to us as we have making it. It's great to do such a fun thing with Jason – I am thankful for his patience when I just turn up and talk and he does all the editing! And we have a wonderful podcast listener community where we continue the conversation from the podcast on Facebook.

My ultimate goal is to be asked on to radio or TV to talk about something not related to disability and appearance diversity. I'd love to show that I have opinions about many things and lead a full life. I would love not to have to provide a backstory about why I am qualified to talk about a subject when I appear in the media. I've never heard a white, middle-aged, non-disabled straight man do that!

In 2016, I was contacted by a TV producer – it was a more pleasant experience than the producer I mentioned in Chapter 1. She asked me if I was interested in appearing in Season 2 of *You Can't Ask That* on ABC TV, and said that my writer friend Robert Hoge had recommended me. *You Can't Ask That* is a TV show where people from marginalised backgrounds are asked curious and sometimes intrusive questions from anonymous viewers who send them in. I called her back immediately. 'YES, OF COURSE!' I said.

I was going overseas the following day, and wanted to lock things in before I left. I loved the first season, and really trusted the ABC with my story. We spoke for a while, and they asked me if I knew anyone who might be keen to appear on the show. I messaged a few friends with facial differences, passing on the producer's details but not giving away too much information. Two of them said yes – Ellen Fraser-Barbour and Belinda Downes.

Filming was done in the ABC studio in Melbourne. Although it was made by non-disabled people, I found the experience collaborative and kind. Some people filmed in pairs, but I did mine by myself. I was asked about 20 questions – none of which were a surprise to me. It was relaxed and funny, though when I saw the edit, I wished I had said some things a little differently.

While I know *You Can't Ask That* teaches viewers about our conditions, I also wanted to make the audience uncomfortable. I wanted to show them how tense, upsetting and shocking it can be when people like me are asked these confronting, intrusive questions. I want them to think twice about the appropriateness of asking.

The episodes went online before the season started, but I held off watching it until the date the facial difference episode went to air. I organised a live screening as a podcast episode. We had about 70 people come to my favourite sex bookshop to watch it, and afterwards had a Q&A. Ellen travelled from South Australia for the screening and we interviewed her for the podcast.

There is rarely a day I don't get recognised from *You Can't Ask That*. Often people tell me their children watched the show, or that they have learnt something. Some people have even stopped me for a selfie! Since the show aired, I feel like I get more questions about whether I was on *You Can't Ask That* than if I have been sunburnt!

With an increased media profile, and less time for writing for fun, I have been forced to be more discerning about what I write about online. This is mostly because of the growing audience and reactions I receive. When the really shit stuff happens, and I choose to write about it on my blog or on social media, I need to be mindful that it might create a bigger situation than I intended. For example, it might end up in the mainstream media, or to a lesser extent, it might be discussed at length on social media. This can be more overwhelming than the initial event.

I have received some pretty horrific abuse in my time writing online. One instance, on my blog, was a death threat from a person linked to a Nazi website in June 2017. The troll's comment was pretty horrific, vilifying all marginalised groups, and threatening me with a noose. In the end though, it wasn't the troll who upset me, but the lack of response from police. I was sent to local police from federal police, and back to federal police by local police.

I told the police that the only way I know how to act on this is to make it public through mainstream and social media. I can't make an official complaint because it's too hard. So I screenshot and share the abuse. I will continue to speak out because I feel safer knowing other people can see this trolling.

People tell me to get off social media if I want the trolling to stop – these people are often trolls themselves. I won't, because the internet is an outlet, a source of friendship and income. The good people and wonderful opportunities are the reasons I keep writing online. The media is full of highs and lows but overall it's where I want to be, and what I've worked for. I'm lucky that when things get tough, there's a wealth of support from others in the media.

In 2017, I took a serial online abuser to court – and had a personal safety order taken out against him. He was a man with ichthyosis.

Our online friendship started out pleasantly enough. He had finally found someone else with ichthyosis, and was elated at being able to relate to me, so there was a lot of discussion about skin.

I was generous with my time, experience and advice, and connected him with others, but I was also guarded. I felt his expectations of me were more than I had ever encountered before. He would share graphic details about how he wasn't coping. I referred him to dermatologists and psychologists. He pressured me to meet. 'If you care about ichthyosis and your work, you will meet me,' he once said. I met him to stop this pressure, taking my husband Adam with me. We met once more, him telling me to my face that he hated my work.

When I didn't respond the way he wanted, he would yell online. Then he would apologise, telling me how much I'd helped him, that I was his hero. The online abuse went on for a few years.

This man believed that he was entitled to my time, friendship and expertise, and when I didn't reciprocate contact, he believed I'd let him down. There was a pattern of abuse, apology, abuse and apology.

I felt a burden of expectation – that I should be friends with someone who abused me, because we had ichthyosis in common.

Doctors told me I should be his friend. Other people told me I shouldn't shut him out. But this person was not entitled to my time, friendship, collaboration and support just because we share a diagnosis, and especially not because of how he treated me. I wouldn't be friends with an abuser from any other part of my life. It came to a head when he tried to discredit my reputation and bring down the career I'd worked so hard for. While his words hurt and scared me, I knew they were untrue. On the day I was alerted to Facebook posts in which he tried to take down my reputation because I'm a terrible, terrible person, I decided to report this ongoing abuse to police and then the court.

I was scared, and didn't want to make trouble, but after enduring the abuse for several years, I wanted it to stop. I also wanted to do something for others who endure online abuse – it's increasingly prevalent. I wanted others to see that they can report this behaviour to authorities and it should be taken seriously.

As I gathered my evidence, I noted a few people who had stood by the abuse in Facebook groups and pages, and did nothing. The standard they walked past is the standard they accept. I unfriended many of these people, left those groups and cut ties with the major ichthyosis support organisations.

I went to court and the (female) magistrate heard me, saw my fears for my safety and reputation and granted a one-year order to keep me safe. I didn't say much in court, but I did speak to the public mediation officer prior, detailing the repetitive abusive behaviour. I was so grateful because, finally, online life was being recognised as real life.

I haven't written or spoken about this publicly before because I was scared of the repercussions. But this is my story and I shouldn't fear it. Plus, I feel proud of making that decision to keep myself and other women safe by seeking legal action. This particular abuse I endured was by someone I knew. It was therefore easier to take to police and the court than the abuse from unknowns.

I felt a sense of shame about having the court order, though. I had to reveal a really vulnerable yet assertive side of myself, often to strangers. I had to tell my new boss about it when I started work. I had to tell the mayor's assistant when I did a speech in the abuser's area. I had to tell the hospital.

Fortunately, this experience has been an anomaly. Most of the friends I have met through my media work and within the ichthyosis community have been wonderful, and so many people showed me support at the time of the court case. Adam, who doesn't often express his emotions, told me he was proud of me for facing the issue.

I collated a few media headlines about people with ichthyosis for a Media and Genetics class I teach at a university. They were all sensationalist, and all dehumanising.

The snakeskin woman
We're two rejects who found each other
16 people who are embracing their flaws in the most beautiful way
Mother gives birth to a 'plastic baby'
Teenager, cruelly dubbed Snake Girl, is forced to live as a recluse
Mum says her baby girl's skin is like 'petting a snake' due to rare
    skin condition
Mother of 'mermaid baby' with skin that sheds 10 times too fast
    has to spend four hours a day moisturising her daughter's skin
    and has broken two washing machines to keep her clothing clean

Imagine if the world saw you this way, because of the media you participated in. The media shapes the way we are seen. The headlines are sensationalist, dehumanising and degrading. To an average reader, a story about one person with ichthyosis is a story about everyone with ichthyosis. These headlines create more fear around people like me. I believe it's really important for people with ichthyosis to play a role in how ichthyosis and other impairments are seen, and that starts with being really careful and considerate when the media approach us. Even when we aren't the ones who write the hideous headlines, we also need to be responsible for how we – and our illness and disability community – are portrayed.

I receive emails from journalists and media makers asking me to tell my story about life with ichthyosis frequently. Most of these are for tabloid media, but some are for public media and well-respected publications and programs. I've said yes to a few and no to more. My friends with ichthyosis and other facial differences and impairments also receive media requests – some have taken up opportunities, and that's their choice.

As mentioned earlier, I've sold my story to two tabloid publications – *Pick Me Up* magazine and *New Idea* magazine. These were vastly different experiences – perhaps because the magazines are in the UK and Australia respectively. I regret *Pick Me Up* because I had no control. It was sensationalist, they spelt my dad's name wrong and they hounded me for the story. *New Idea* was far more respectful – even letting me write a follow-up article in third person. And I was paid well. I've been on radio many times, a couple of commercial TV programs and on many websites – and for the most part, I've had positive experiences.

I also write for a number of mainstream media publications – some of which could be classed as tabloid. But writing my story myself is different from being written about.

I blog to ensure I have control over the way my story is portrayed and how ichthyosis is represented. This has led to me writing for mainstream media publications and speaking on radio and TV and podcasts.

It's also led to me developing thick skin. I'd never give my story to anyone if I didn't have this resilience. I also have the benefit of a media degree and a little knowledge of how the media works to help me make a decision. I have media contacts and prefer to pitch my story myself. I prefer to write for publications that I read and respect, but sometimes I'll tell my story to those I don't, to help influence a new audience.

Tabloid journalists can be pushy. They can lurk in support groups, reading private discussions, and then they pounce – assuring you your story is in good hands and will help others. They can prey on people at their most vulnerable, drawing out private details and photos through sneakily winning trust. (I'm cynical!)

Rare medical conditions such as ichthyosis are not always portrayed in a positive way. Sensationalist, voyeuristic and othering language is used. Cameras zoom in on symptoms, dehumanising the subjects of the story.

Subjects of articles and programs are often portrayed as victim or hero. Commenters can be brutal. (And even when you write your own story, there's a risk of the sub-editors sensationalising a headline.)

I shared Sarah's story on my blog in February 2015. She had written it for me after we found each other on Instagram the previous year. Sarah lost an eye as a result of domestic violence. I took great care in publishing it. I had waited six months after receiving it, until she was safe from her ex-husband. I provided a trigger warning and links to support services. And an international tabloid wanted that story too. They asked me for her details and when I didn't pass them on, they tracked her down on Facebook. They pushed her when she was at her most vulnerable, convincing her to send graphic photos that she can no longer bear to look at. They didn't put a content warning or link to support groups. She didn't know or read the publication when she was approached, and tells me she'd never read it now. She regrets it and wishes she'd listened to my advice.

Two friends – one with a facial difference and one with ichthyosis – told me they sold their stories to media and regret it.

Jacki said:

> Terrible article, made-up scenarios and when I explicitly told them I didn't want it published after having a read through they said it was tough and was too late to pull it. I was distraught and there was nothing I could do. I was annoyed at myself too as I'm not naive when it comes to media, but at the same time wanted to set a positive example … can't win!

Rebekah told me:

> I sold my story to a magazine here in NZ. I wish I had the opportunity to proofread it first … they didn't really portray me the way I wanted them to. [I was portrayed] like I wanted everyone to feel sorry for me. I wanted to be

portrayed more as someone who is out in society making a worthwhile contribution and making most of every opportunity.

Telling your story to the media can be really positive and empowering. A friend with quadriplegia told me that when a newspaper covered her story, she felt listened to because the journalists were genuinely interested. Your story might help many others, and it can open up some amazing opportunities like further media appearances and getting in touch with others who have your condition. A close friend got a cookbook deal after appearing on a tabloid news program. And the media outlet might be really awesome – I loved working on Channel 31's *No Limits*, as they allowed people with disability to be in control of our stories.

It pays to do some research before saying yes to the media. Here are some questions to ask yourself and the media representative.

- Would you or do you already watch the show or read the publication?
- What else has the film company or publication made?
- How sensationalist is the publication or the program?
- Will the story be told by someone with the same medical condition or impairment as you?
- Will the title of the show be derogatory? (Think *Embarrassing Bodies* or *The Biggest Loser*.) What about the title of the article? (The *Pick Me Up* magazine article screamed I ALWAYS LOOK SUNBURNT!)

- What is the reach? Is it going to mainstream TV? A large publication? Is it tiny?
- Do you get paid? (You should!) Is it enough compensation to cover the instance that you'll be misrepresented?
- Can you tell your story to other publications or programs, or are you limited by an exclusivity clause?
- How much control will you have over the story and filming and editing? Will they let you see the final draft and allow you to suggest edits?
- What language do they use? Is it disability positive? Do they use person-first language ('person with disability') or do they see disability as part of the subject's identity ('disabled person')? Either is fine, but the former is the preferred usage by media outlets. Do they use language that portrays disability as tragedy ('suffers from', 'wheelchair bound')? Do they use euphemisms or made-up words like 'special needs' or 'diffability' to soften and often erase disability?
- Will the story be pitying? Will you be a victim or hero? (Neither is good.)
- Will it be inspiration porn?
- Will what you say as an interview subject represent the wider ichthyosis and disability community well?
- Are you using or approving derogatory language to describe yourself, or letting others speak badly of you – like some of the headlines above?
- Can you handle the attention of being in the media – good and bad? Is there someone to support you?
- How will this benefit you? How will this benefit others?

- Will they represent you well – alter or edit quotes or even photoshop your image?
- Have you got permission to tell your child's story, if that's what the media has asked for? What will be the long-term ramifications of doing so? Will your disclosure of your child's medical condition hamper future opportunities like employment, relationships or insurance?
- Could you tell your story somewhere else – to a more reputable publication?
- Could you tell your story yourself? (Maybe start a blog or start a YouTube channel.)

It's OK to say no, and it's OK to say yes to media, but only if you're 100 per cent comfortable with it. I'd be very careful about how ichthyosis is portrayed. It can be so exciting to be approached by the media, but you may be disappointed, even regretful if it goes wrong.

The media reports on ichthyosis and other impairments so poorly that I believe if we want to participate in the media, we have a responsibility to change it for the better.

With such poor reporting and representation of ichthyosis in the media, it takes a great deal of trust for me to let someone else tell my story. But every so often, there is a good outcome, and it helps that I am so aware and assertive of representation.

I agreed to let a friend, Mal Chambers, paint me for the Art Gallery of New South Wales 2018 Archibald Prize for portraiture. I was insistent that I be looking at the viewer and smiling in the painting – to welcome people and allay fears. I was so thrilled with the outcome. I look like me. I look confident and happy but still assertive.

The painting wasn't a finalist in the Archibald, but it was a finalist in the Black Swan Prize for Portraiture at the Art Galley of Western Australia. I am so thankful to Mal for painting me. I hope many other people with ichthyosis, facial differences and impairments will be painted in this way – because representation matters. And I hope it hangs in a gallery, for diversity and so kids with ichthyosis can see someone like them.

A few months after I posted about the painting on social media, I received a message from an older woman with ichthyosis. She hadn't heard of the name ichthyosis until she saw the painting and my description, and when she did, she went to the dermatologist to get an official diagnosis for her skin condition – ichthyosis. What a great outcome!

18

You're doing activism wrong!

This chapter contains ableist language, as examples only.

Through my work as a writer and activist, I meet an enormous number of people, mostly online, but increasingly in person. As my profile grows, so do people's expectations of me. (I'll detail those more a little later in the book, in the chapter on emotional labour.) And alarmingly, they can become aggressive if their expectations are not met.

In activism – especially as an opinion writer and with a social media presence – there's no room to make mistakes, or even for your views to evolve, or differ from that of your audience. You're pulled up by the people who want to learn from your work (in my case, the non-disabled people), and crucified by your own people (in my case, the disability community). Sometimes you're unfriended or seen as a traitor. Never mind the hard work you've done.

1 Proud mother. We were off to church. I was about four months old. 1982.

2 Me and Dad. The first Christmas morning in our house in Walla Walla. You can't see her very well, but I was clutching Baby, a doll who never left my side — until Baby 2 arrived.

3 'Hello. Is this the Human Rights Commission? I'd like to make a complaint about a breach of disability rights, please.' I call this look Mad Men Preschool Chic.

4 Time spent cooking with Mum was wonderful. She's a great cook, and as a result, I love cooking too. I would have been three.

5 This is the most superfluous outfit I've ever worn — goggles, floatie ring and flippers. I hated the water. My eyes are shut and face screwed up — I didn't love photos as a kid. 1984.

[ALL PHOTOS FINDLAY FAMILY COLLECTION.]

1 The dreaded bee net. I wore this to keep the flies away from my face and ears at preschool. Not my most fashionable moment.

2 First day of school. Lisa Jacqueline, the Cabbage Patch Kid, had now replaced Babies 1 and 2.

3 Tea party with Nanny and Mum, Christmas Day 1988.

4 Year 6 graduation. This outfit. Would wear again today. Can someone please make it in my size?

1 First day of high school. Mum bought me such a long dress, I could wear it until Year 10. [FINDLAY FAMILY COLLECTION.]

2 With Curdy, one of our curly-coated retrievers. I loved our dogs. [FINDLAY FAMILY COLLECTION.]

3 I did work experience at the *Border Mail* at the start of Year 11. I shadowed as a journalist, writing a story and calling the people who wrote letters to the editor. I also had this photo shoot — so very Anne of Green Gables. [BORDER MAIL.]

4 Year 11 school photo — 1998. I haven't aged a day, right?! [FINDLAY FAMILY COLLECTION.]

5 La Trobe University graduation, 2003, with Amber. Amber is the only person I know who talks as much and as fast as I do. [FINDLAY FAMILY COLLECTION.]

1 I was inducted into the Murray High School hall of fame in 2014. I gave a speech to the students — how I wished the people I went to school with could have heard it.
[FINDLAY FAMILY COLLECTION.]

2 Drinks out with Mum and Dad, 2015.
[FINDLAY FAMILY COLLECTION.]

3 Australian Ichthyosis meet, 2015. Such a proud moment.
[STASIA BARKER.]

1 Bridal party. Camille, Adam, Cassie and Jason-Scott. [FRESH PHOTOGRAPHY.]

2 Just married. Adam and me. [FRESH PHOTOGRAPHY.]

3 Bob Evans sang at our wedding! The perfect end to a perfect day. [LEONA TOOLEY.]

4 I'm just a girl standing in front of a boy, asking him to take my photo at the Notting Hill tube sign. European honeymoon, 2016. [ADAM MORROW.]

1 Performing in Quippings during the Emerging Writers Festival, 2017. I wore my less-formal wedding dress again that night, and felt so glamorous. [GENEVIEVE BAILEY.]

2 I do a podcast with Jason-Scott Watkins. It's called *Refreshments Provided*, and it's a chance for us to have a laugh. [CAMILLE CONDON.]

3 Speaking at the Albury-Wodonga International Day of People with Disability event, 2017. [ROGER FINDLAY.]

1 Behind the scenes at Access to Fashion, Melbourne Fashion Week, 2018. [ANNIE NOLAN.]

2 Another proud moment. Surrounded by the models who participated in Access to Fashion — a history-making event at Melbourne Fashion Week. [IAN STUBBER.]

3 Don't forget your disabled sisters. Speaking at the Women's March, Melbourne, 2018. [WADE BUCHAN.]

1 It was an honour to be painted by Mal Chambers, a family friend, in 2018. This portrait was entered in the Archibald Prize and the Black Swan Prize. It was a finalist in the Black Swan, hanging in the Art Gallery of Western Australia. Little Carly could never have imagined this! [MAL CHAMBERS.]

2 No filter. 2018. [CARLY FINDLAY.]

A lot of my work is online. For the most part, the interaction I have with others is lovely. I've met amazing people. And I wouldn't keep doing it if it was entirely awful. But everyone wants a say. Even on smallish platforms like mine – and it happens to many of my friends too. (Imagine being a moderator for a highly subscribed social media platform!)

We can't be one thing and think another – we have to be everything to everyone. I talked to a writer who was terrified of anyone ever finding out she bought a house – because she has written about anti-capitalism. But she needs a roof over her head, right? Another high-profile friend was raising money for charity on social media – but most times she posted, people called her out, suggesting her clothing choices were unethical and excluded the plus-sized market.

The very wise Pip Lincolne, a writer, crafter and tea lover, once wrote on her blog that 'it's OK to be a cake cheat' – meaning it's OK to be inconsistent.

> When you're a human being, sometimes things can be a little bit complicated, wouldn't you agree? You can endeavour to be a vegetarian, but sometimes not be. You can try to run every day, but sometimes stay in bed instead. You can vow to not eat bread and then eat a sandwich. People are trying their best. And that's if you are just a regular-yet-excellent human. If you are an online writer, like me, you are pretty much a switcheroo/slip-up-eroo machine. Granted, I am really a super-consistent and conscientious type gal, but that doesn't mean that I don't fall prey to the old chop and change/whoops manoeuvre. And I think lots of other online writers might be a little bit the same.

People hold each other to ridiculously high standards on social media. They're waiting to trip us up. Looking for something to criticise. They forget the other things we do in our lives to make the world a better place.

Some of the comments left on my social media posts are exhausting. If I disappoint someone, they will let me know. That the balloons I posed with for a photo will ruin the ocean. That I am cruel to animals because my breakfast contained eggs. That I went to see two white women speak at a book launch. *Oh, and remember the time a stranger on FB told me she is offended that I am happy with my body because I am a size 10?!* She said she can't support my appearance diversity work because I'm size-ist. I can love my body, but not in that way, thank you very much. I need a lie-down.

The outrage is often disproportionate to the issue – like the backlash Muslim writer Yassmin Abdel-Magied received after her seven-word Anzac Day tweet in 2017. She wrote, *LEST. WE. FORGET. (Manus, Nauru, Syria, Palestine …).* Between 25 April and August 2017, the media wrote 64,000 words about her, and she was ostracised to the point where her local work diminished and she moved overseas.

I have been guilty of commenting on social media posts in a self-righteous way in the past. There have been things that I could have done better. I wanted people to know that their behaviour contributed to ableism, inspiration porn and discrimination. For the most part, I tried to be gentle, sandwiching criticism with praise and suggestions for how they could do better. But then I called out an article by the mum of a disabled child. She wrote about how she grieved over her child, who was alive and leading a fulfilled life. *How would your child feel if they read this?* I asked. I was too quick to post; I hadn't seen that the author was in fact a mum I had been in touch with for years – and that most of her previous work had been good. My post made her question her role as a writer, and she removed her articles from that (problematic) website. I offered my apologies and gave her my number should she want to call. I think we are OK now, but it taught me a good lesson in not being too hasty and being kinder when I comment publicly – or even refraining from saying anything at all.

Most times, the activism I've been involved in creates some sort of meaningful change and is recognised by more than just the community being fought for. In 2016, friends and I protested *Me Before You* – a film based on a novel – which has the key message that disability is a worse fate than death. Spoiler alert: the story was about a rich man who acquired a disability, got a super-hot girlfriend and still thought disability was a worse fate than death, so he killed himself. The book and film portray disability as a tragedy. Many readers and viewers will get their perspective of disability from this without ever interacting with an actually disabled person. They won't see the barriers and discrimination actually disabled people face in our everyday lives. They won't know about the low employment rate and poverty experienced by so many disabled people. And they won't see that a person with a disability can have a joyous, pride-filled life.

The able gaze is narrow. People are fascinated by how we move, eat, think, have sex, and can be loved, but they look away quickly. While watching the film, I paid attention to the audience's reactions. The audience laughed at the severity of Will's disability symptoms – spasms and mannerisms, and any scenes that hinted at love and sex. (Was that funny for them? Awkward? A bit gross? Can a disabled person even have sex or be found attractive?)

The saddest thing for me during the film was hearing the audience laugh at how inaccessible a racetrack was for Will's wheelchair. It sunk into the muddy grass. Help was called. This inaccessibility is every day for disabled people. And the audience laughed.

Our protest was picked up by many news outlets in Australia, making people think more deeply about the messaging of this film — and prompting serious discussion around the ethics of assisted dying and the danger it might be to disabled people.

The problem with disability representation in movies like *Me Before You* is that viewers get a sense that disability is only like this — tragic and restrictive. And roles are so often given to non-disabled people. But disabled people represent approximately 20 per cent of the Australian population, and we lead diverse lives. Many of us don't see disability as a tragedy. So it's time disability was reflected accurately in film and television. We need to be invited into acting schools, authentically cast in films and television programs, and to play characters that are more than our disability.

I also took part in #CrippingTheMighty — an online protest about a troubling disability website that thrives on inspiration porn, parent stories over stories by actually disabled people, and not paying writers. We took to Twitter to talk about how good media about disability is done. This led to many new relationships, and showcased many disabled writers.

But sometimes the disability community can turn. We are often fighting for the same human rights and change, yet we shout over each other, trying to be right. And other activists can be frightening. I think some activists are so used to fighting the system that they fight each other, so they lose out on the cause they're fighting for. My friend Anna says, 'While the chickens fought over the highest perch, the fox got in.'

Sarah Blahovec, an American activist and writer, wrote a great piece, published in the Huffington Post, that speaks to any of us who feel we don't always do disability activism right. Often, if we aren't the right type of disabled, or our views differ from the most dominant activists, we are looked down upon. And there is no room to make a mistake. Sarah writes:

> Nearly every single disability activist I have talked to has expressed discomfort with sharing their opinions or differences due to these swift and severe callouts. And unfortunately, many of us who have felt the sting of these unforgiving responses have also perpetuated callouts against others. I know I may have been too harsh with people who simply have a different opinion or may not know that what they said is wrong, and it's something I'm actively trying to catch and correct. Because of this intensity, the climate within the disability community has felt like there's no room to make mistakes. It feels like expressing a thought comes with the extreme risk of anxiety-inducing backlash, and nobody is safe. Some of us have decided to try to keep our mouths shut and heads down so that we don't say something wrong. Making a mistake feels like failing as an activist.

It has happened to me – and this hurt more than when strangers have criticised or harassed me online, because I value the opinions of my community, and the sense of belonging I have within it.

There are so many ways to do activism – whatever works for you. But don't put down others who do it differently.

When I embarked on this book, the people I was most fearful of letting down were other disabled people – those who think similarly to me, and who do similar work. And as I wrote, and got more speaking work, I felt increasingly on the outer from the disability community. Some people in the community told me I had to choose between activism and mainstream work. My work, including this book, was questioned and ridiculed. And I was slowly pushed out of a friendship and activist circle – which I was acutely aware of, though it was always denied by the people involved. I spoke up about how I felt. It was denied, or put back on me as bad behaviour or whining. And now I realise that was gaslighting.

As people dropped away, I worried what they hinted at was true – that I'd sold out by working with a mainstream publisher and a speaking agent. I wondered whether individual success and personal branding could sit comfortably next to creating collective change (which I'm sure this book will assist with in the long term, but at the time, I had *so* much self-doubt). I worried because people were whispering, and shouting too. I was concerned mainstream success was letting down the wider disability community.

But here's the thing. Disability activists fight for mainstream representation and to be paid. I'm achieving both. And so their fight is now levelled at me. It's lateral violence. But I've always been somewhat mainstream – even when I spent a few years loving Triple J – and I hope that I'll reach a new audience to shift perspectives of self and other. I agree critique is important, and I engage in it too. But when critique is the only contact between 'friends', it's not friendship. The friendliness has definitely left the friendship.

Besides, mainstream participation didn't happen overnight. It took years and years of work, rejections, and more work. There are words and words and words of evidence. So if I'm not what an activist should look like in certain people's eyes, that's OK.

The fear of doing the wrong thing by our community might hold us back from making meaningful individual and systemic change. I think it's time activists were given space to grow and make mistakes – and do things differently from other activists. Surely it is better to progress something with imperfect politics than not do anything at all for fear of not being 100 per cent right? If our intentions are good, and we look to others for guidance and ideas, I think we should progress the best we can.

And I hope that my friendships can survive different ways of doing activism. I'll always cheer other disability activists on – because we have to support each other, especially when we endure ableism and discrimination from non-disabled people. We are all fighting the good fight, not ready to make nice with those who deny us human rights. But let's be nice to our fellow activists while we fight.

I contort myself to fit into a non-disabled world – sometimes enduring the everyday ableism because I need to work. I want to be professional, and while I don't want to shake disability from my identity, I don't want to be too high-maintenance. I remain polite during difficult media interviews, and stay silent when people encroach on my bodily space and privacy because I worry that I will be viewed as so difficult I won't be asked back.

And I run the risk of losing non-disabled friends through activism too. As gently as I try to educate about ableism (such as disability slurs like the R-word), their discomfort means they distance themselves from me. It's often over social media, so I am sure if we talked face to face, it would be different. When disabled people call out ableism, it would be really great if the people we're calling out took a moment to listen and reflect, before reacting quickly and cutting us off. So much of our work is done carefully and considerately – the emotional labour is big and the risk of isolation or another pile-on is even bigger. When I try to educate people about ableism, I would love for them to acknowledge the hurt caused, to listen, and even to say thanks. The hurt compounds when they tell us not to be offended, or that their language has evolved from medical terms (like 'retard' and 'moron'). If we are offended by ableism, we shouldn't have to switch off/shut down the media. I don't want to go into a comedy show frightened of how the comedian might mock disabled people.

I'm tired of being seen as a sensitive snowflake, 'PC gone bananas', or the fun police. I'm more tired of people *not* taking a step back and listening, and working on how they can do better. Is that too much to ask?

I've never wanted to speak on behalf of anyone – this is my story – but I know that some people do look to me as an authority. I sometimes feel this responsibility is far too big for me, and want to ensure many other voices are heard too.

The more media opportunities that are given to disabled people, the more the public can see that we aren't a homogeneous entity, that we deserve respect, and that activism can be done differently by different members of the disability community. (And some disabled people don't want to do media or have a profile at all, and that is OK.)

Activism takes place in many ways. Activism can be quiet or loud, in public or private. It can be supporting someone in court, appearing in the media or just one on one with a friend, telling them that using the R-word is problematic. It can involve taking part in advertising campaigns, going to protests, writing a social media post or tackling the comments sections to help change the conversation. There are so many ways to do activism – whatever works for you. But don't put down others who do it differently.

I can either be stifled by fear and do nothing at all to create change, or do activism my own way, and create something I needed when I was younger. I want to see my work alongside many other disabled people's. There's room for all of us.

19

Becoming disabled

You can't advocate for yourself if you won't admit what you are.

Lindy West, Shrill

I didn't always consider myself disabled. Nor chronically ill. My life with ichthyosis just was. While I was born with ichthyosis and my parents received disability support from the government, I wasn't – to my mind – disabled like those 'other people'. Having red skin and trips to hospital was just part of my life. I was encouraged just to get on with it, not to dwell, and reminded that there were children in hospital with much more serious illnesses than mine.

To me, disability wasn't me. It was the tragedy that I saw on the TV – stories of pity and inspiration porn.

A girl in my primary school class had cerebral palsy. She was tall and strong, and had beautiful shiny hair. She walked differently from the other kids – like a foal finding its feet, her knees often bloody from falls. Her speech was slow and loud. She had an integration aide at school – I didn't have one, which to me meant that she was much more disabled than I was. The only thing we had in common, I thought, was the way kids (and adults) teased us. If I ever joined the kids who mocked her speech, I'm deeply sorry, and wish I never saw her as the other. I saw her as the other because her body and speech was so different from mine and my peers at school. I didn't know it then but I created a sense of hierarchy between us.

One Christmas Day, she came to our house, because her parents had left her at home. They didn't include her in their Christmas celebrations – they'd often leave her behind when they attended religious and social events. And she cried. Were they ashamed, or did they think she was she too much work? I wonder.

I met with her recently, after not seeing her for many years – and sought permission to write about her – and I brought up this memory. I prefaced it by saying, 'It might be upsetting to talk about, for you and for me.' And she knew what I was about to say before I spoke.

I'll never forget the howl of her aloneness.

I didn't have any disabled people as role models when I grew up – I only understood disability as a deficit. The few disabled people I saw were Paralympians – and of course then the Paralympics weren't broadcast continuously on TV, they just got a small item on the news every four years. And because I hated sport I didn't take notice. I'm sure if I'd seen a disabled newsreader, or fashion model or cook, I would have been more interested.

I believe it was internalised ableism that prevented me from seeing myself as disabled. I saw disability as a bad thing. I saw it as something that made families want to exclude their children. And those children's bodies were different from mine – my limbs worked. I didn't need help at school. I was mentally cognisant. Disabled kids went to special schools. They were the subjects of heartwarming stories on *60 Minutes*. They weren't me.

And I didn't have a chronic illness, either, because I wasn't bed-bound or coughing a lot – my narrow, ignorant definition of chronic illness.

My parents never saw me as disabled, and didn't allow me to think of myself that way. Through my work, though, they've come to see that social barriers are disabling for me, and that identifying myself as disabled has enabled me to grow stronger.

When I moved to Melbourne, I started writing more about my experience with ichthyosis on my blog, and dipped my toe in disability media by writing for a government disability website. I also auditioned for a presenter role on Channel 31's *No Limits*, where I did three seasons and produced and presented on two further shows the following year. I felt a sense of community with the cast and crew, and I also came to understand disability-led media. And all of the writing I was doing on my blog helped me get to know myself. I came to know that disability wasn't a bad thing.

To recognise internalised ableism is difficult. To my schoolmate, whose voice I might have mocked in an attempt to fit in with the other kids, to those with ichthyosis who I doubted, to those who I tried to talk out of having a disability – trying to compliment them, questioning whether they should identify as being disabled – I'm sorry. And to me – I'm sorry for denying disability as part of my identity for so long.

It took finding other disabled people for me to realise that I was also disabled. You can't be what you can't see, and growing up I didn't have a tribe. My life changed when I found that tribe. The people I hang with now – writers, performers, disabled, queer, trans – are the people I needed to hang with when I was young. They show me what's possible, make me feel OK to be the other and enable me to practise my pride.

In 2013, I got involved in Quippings, an LGBTI-friendly disability performance troupe, co-founded by Kath Duncan, a disabled artist and academic. My first Quippings experience – before I was a performer – was in the audience after The Other Film Festival in September 2012. New York actress Christine DeZinno Bruno was performing, and so were some of the Quippings team. It was full of disability pride and sexual content. I admit to being a little shell-shocked – my mind was opened to butt plugs for the first time. Four months later, I received a message from Kath, butt plug educator, asking me to fill in for a performer that night. *Shit*, I thought. *I might have to talk about butt plugs. At a sex bookshop! But I don't know anything about butt plugs!* Kath assured me I didn't have to. *Phew!* So I read out 'Untouched', part of the 'Skin Hunger' chapter in this book. It received roaring applause. And then, I guess, I became a performer. I've been a part of the troupe ever since. We've performed at the Malthouse Theatre and Spiegeltent, and a few other Melbourne venues.

As we toasted the end of our 2015 Melbourne Fringe Festival shows, we talked about what Quippings means to us. All of us said that through it, we've found our people. People who understand disability issues and aren't afraid to speak about them. We're not afraid to laugh at our disabilities – in a way that takes back our power. We invite the public gaze – literally in our Fringe show, beckoning audience members to look at us, and laughing and pointing at them just as the public has done to us. We satirise the disability sector. It's such a safe space – body positive and sex positive. This isn't disability as many people assume it to be. We remove negative connotations. We don't want pity; we are empowered. We are so proud.

I've lost a lot of friends. The closeness of the disability community – be it in proximity or across social media – means deaths have shaken me, and often mobilised me to be a better activist. These deaths are a reminder that while disabled people have a resolute strength, sometimes they just can't lead a long life. Survivor guilt comes with the grief – how unfair that they have passed and I am still here.

Friends from hospital died when I was a child and teen – Nigel Jones and Kate O'Connor. People I mentored at ChIPS died. And most recently, Megan Barron (a woman in her early twenties who had a very severe skin condition – her disability politics were very similar to mine); Madeleine Sobb (a Melbourne activist friend who had just graduated university and had such a bright future); Stephanie Moore Turner (the first woman with Harlequin ichthyosis to have not one but two babies); Zak Bohling (a polite and funny teenager with ichthyosis who I was so lucky to get to know at the ichthyosis meet); 17-year-old Savanna Addis who died just before she was about to take part in the fashion parade I'd organised, and, of course, Stella Young.

Some of these people I never met, some had different impairments from me – but the grief is raw. We are a small community of people with rare, severe diseases. No matter what type of impairment we have, whether it's severe and obvious like Harlequin ichthyosis or Netherton syndrome, or one of the milder or less obvious types of ichthyosis, the impact of losing one of our own is colossal. Our bonds are strong. We are family. Steph and Zak showed the world what good, full lives people with ichthyosis can lead. Their deaths do not mean they're in a better place – they're needed in this world, right now.

When we lose our own, we are doubly reminded of how fragile life is.

When I describe myself as disabled, some people perceive this as a negative. 'Disability' is a bad word. 'Disability doesn't belong to you. You're not like those people,' they tell me. But I am like those people – and I am proud of that. And I know if I had recognised that I was disabled when I was younger, I could have received the help I needed – as I have done through self-advocacy as an adult. It might have meant having a choice in the uniform I wore, so I didn't endure summer-long infections due to school dresses that left my legs bare. Or my parents could have asked for a year-long medical certificate, so Mum wouldn't have had to constantly write notes to excuse me from sport – and I could have been allowed to sit inside where I wouldn't overheat. Not seeing or being with anyone disabled as a child – and being told that I was 'not disabled like them' – taught me that not being disabled was an accomplishment. I still see this among people with ichthyosis today – they are proud not to be disabled. (Granted some of them have different types and experiences from me. Perhaps the social barriers they face have been less disabling than mine.) Throwaway lines like 'Don't dis my ability' or 'It's just a skin condition; at least I'm not mentally or physically disabled' are used as place markers in the disability hierarchy. Their only connection to disability might be receiving 'Disability' – a support pension from the government – or an access plan at school. Disability as a government definition, for support purposes, but definitely not disability as part of identity.

I've even been told 'I don't see your disability' – meant as a compliment. But it's not. Overlooking disability denies disabled people of our identity.

When you say, 'I don't see your disability,' you think disability is below me.

When you say, 'I don't see your disability,' you don't think I'm disabled like 'them'.

When you say, 'I don't see your disability,' you don't see that you and I have different experiences of disability.

When you say, 'I don't see your disability,' I see your perceptions are shaped by inspiration porn and negative stereotypes.

When you say, 'I don't see your disability,' you forget I have specific needs to ensure I'm comfortable.

When you say, 'I don't see your disability,' I feel you're in denial.

When you say, 'I don't see your disability,' you believe disability is a tragedy.

When you say, 'I don't see your disability,' my type of disability doesn't fit into your narrow definition.

When you say, 'I don't see your disability,' you regard disability as a slur.

When you say, 'I don't see your disability,' it is silencing.

When you say, 'I don't see your disability,' you don't acknowledge the richness of disability culture.

When you say, 'I don't see your disability,' you don't see that I am unapologetically proud of my disability.

When you say, 'I don't see your disability,' and avoid describing my face as red, you think I'm not comfortable with the reality of my appearance.

When you say, 'I don't see your disability,' you erase my identity.

I don't want you to use euphemisms when referring to disability. Say the word.

I don't want you to stare, point, ridicule and ask questions before you've said hello, but I don't mind if you talk about my disability politely after you've got to know me.

I want you to see my disability as a part of me. Because when you say, 'I don't see your disability,' you invalidate who I am.

Sometimes people compliment me when my skin looks paler than usual. It's as though I'm five shades closer to a white complexion. What they're not seeing (or feeling) is the pain in other parts of my body, and the itching. And while these compliments are well meaning – and who doesn't want to be told they look great? – I can't help wondering whether looking paler is seen as the path to being normal. Normal. What's that?

It's as though the path to 'normal' is the path I should want to take. When people tell me that I'm normal just like everyone else or that I'm doing things normal people do, they don't understand their good intentions are quite othering. 'Looking past' my face or coming to some sort of epiphany that I'm really quite 'normal' is naive and shallow. It's as though someone thinks they've done a good deed for not lumping me in the other category – the one where people are not 'normal'.

For me, becoming disabled has meant a richer life, involvement in the arts, a writing career and wonderful friends. Above all, it's meant coming to a place of pride.

For me, disability pride isn't about loving all the parts of ichthyosis. Honestly – painful, scaly, weepy and bright red skin can be very annoying some days. Ichthyosis can get in the way of living life. And it's not about loving the barriers either. Pride is defying society's low expectations. It's accepting my ichthyosis, even when people tell me I should want a cure. It's seeing ichthyosis and disability as part of my identity even after being worn down by ableism. It's feeling a sense of community.

Jenny Morris, former disability policy researcher, wrote a book called *Pride Against Prejudice*, which played an integral part in my changing the way I saw myself and developing disability pride. She wrote about how society's negative assumptions about disabled people shape the way we see ourselves, and that it is these external factors that are oppressive and anger-inducing, not our impairments. Jenny Morris's book showed me that we can develop pride in the face of prejudice.

There are many ways you can practise disability pride. I think the quickest way is to surround yourself with other disabled people who also see disability as a part of their identity and who also express their pride. Connect with others online (the Disability Visibility Project on Facebook and Twitter is a good place to start) or in your local community. Start up a group if you can't find one in your town. You can also make art, alone or with others. I took part in the creation of a disability pride mural on a Melbourne wall in September 2018. It was dreamt up and organised by street artist Larissa MacFarlane. Larissa's aims were to 'celebrate the culture of Melbourne's disabled community, challenge narrow stereotypes of disability, reclaim public space and make a stand that joins with the international Disability Pride movement'. It was wonderful to create paste-ups and to see the finished mural, but it was the community spirit – coming together – that meant so much. Larissa says, 'I am the strongest when I am with my community.'

You can also practise ways to respond to ableism and discrimination, and also establish self-care methods to ensure you are looking after yourself. For me, self-care often means taking time away from disability activism.

Pride is having the courage to look the world in the eye when the world won't look me in the eye, or looks too much. It's not wanting to cover up my face, or lessen the redness with harsh drugs. It's being happy with myself – after wanting to change for many years.

Now that I identify as being disabled, I am better able to advocate for myself (and others). In the past, it was rare that I spoke up about being sore or cold or hot or affected by cigarette smoke or wind, because I didn't want to be seen as being difficult. I didn't want to be a princess. So I put up with it. I didn't act on my limitations because I didn't want to be defeated or look lazy. For years, I walked to and from primary school in 40-degree heat. I know. But with maturity came speaking up and acknowledging I might have to do things differently, or not at all.

I've gone from putting up with discomfort and pain to speaking up (politely) to change things. This usually involves requests for chairs! I ask for a seat on the train if I'm very sore. Sometimes I carry a chair around at a party so I don't have to stand. I ask for a seat at concerts. And I often ask for heaters to be turned on or to move out of the sun in the summer. Most recently, I've made the choice to only drive at night if absolutely necessary, because my eyes get dry and cannot handle the light. It's sometimes not easy to recognise these limitations, and even harder to make others aware of them. If people aren't aware of my skin, explaining my limitations can be a coming out process.

I am no longer scared or embarrassed to ask for what I need, or to put ointment on when I am dry, or ask for my employers to assist me. Identifying as disabled and developing pride has helped me with this.

When you put 'disability' in speech marks, or make air quotes when referring to mine, you are silently adding 'so called' to it.

People tell me, 'But you don't look disabled!' because my disability doesn't fit many people's idea of what disability looks like. I don't use a wheelchair. I'm not blind. I don't have a cognitive impairment. To the uninformed, I just look like I forgot to put sunscreen on. And skin conditions are only cosmetic, right? So how do I make others understand that I am, in fact, disabled?

One night, I went to dinner and a concert with a friend. I was so sore. I caught the tram, which was full. Two women, a mother and daughter as it turned out, were sitting in the disability access seats — the ones below the sign asking commuters to give up the seat for anyone pregnant, disabled and elderly. I asked them for a seat. They refused, asking if I had a disability. I said yes. They wouldn't move.

A lovely woman called Kate gave me her seat, saying she saw me on *You Can't Ask That.* I said, yes, I was on that show, where I talked about why I identify as disabled.

I offered the two women who refused me a seat a card so they could see my work, but the older woman told me I did not need a seat, and how rude I was, and how she had a real disability. They continued to quibble. They said I need an identity card to prove that I have a disability. The older woman showed me a card that looked like a concession card — which doesn't prove someone has a disability.

I told them to fuck off.

And then the daughter came up to me to tell me I didn't have a real disability and didn't need a seat, I just had a bit of inflamed skin, and that I'd antagonised her mother. She called Kate a dumb blonde.

For a second I wondered how I could prove my pain. Should I remove my stockings to show them how dry and raw my legs were? Was there a loose bit of skin that I could peel? Could I make myself bleed on cue, to show how fragile my skin is?

I got off the tram and cried. Kate got off with me, ensured I was OK and called me an Uber. We hugged and I gave her my card, asking her to contact me so I could buy her a drink. I posted about it on Facebook, and she got in touch. We're friends now. I am so thankful for the Kates, who stand up and say this isn't OK, who give up their seats and do not doubt anyone who asks for a seat.

We should not have to prove our need for a seat. Real disabilities come in all forms.

I hate being the angry disabled person – anger can set the tone for how people perceive all disabled people. All I did was ask for a seat. I am not proud of my bad language, and as a writer, I wish I was more articulate in the moment. I wish I had said that disability comes in all forms and that a skin condition isn't just cosmetic, it's painful. I wish I had said that I know people who have died from ichthyosis. I wish I could have said that while the older woman may have been disabled, she needs to stop being so offended when someone who doesn't fit the traditional appearance of disability asks her for a seat. And I wish I said that if I hadn't needed a seat, I wouldn't have asked for one.

This wasn't the first time a disabled person had got angry and denied me a seat. If you're disabled and are asked for a seat, you don't need to give it up. You can just say you're unable to. I will never question whether you are disabled or not, and I'm sure others wouldn't either. But to question the validity of the person asking for a seat is wrong. We rarely do ask – for fear of reactions like this one. Had this woman refused her seat politely, and said, 'I'm unable to as I have a disability too,' and not questioned and then denied mine, it wouldn't have come to this.

I don't write about these encounters for sympathy, or for attention seeking. I do it to show the everyday ableism that people like me endure.

When I told the tram story on Facebook, others told me their stories – that they are too scared to ask for seats because they worry they'll be turned down. People with invisible disabilities told me they have to prove they are disabled, and that commuters pretend not to notice requests for seats.

The need to prove and perform disability may come from the media and government narrative that disabled people are welfare cheats – that the fault lies with us. Often when we ask for a hand up, it's assumed we are asking for a hand-out.

But disabled people live in a world that hasn't been designed for us.

The social model of disability – where the environment and people's attitudes are seen as the disabling factor, rather than our bodies – means that our impairments are compounded by ignorant, ableist and discriminatory acts like being refused a seat on the tram, not being able to access a building for a job interview or medical support, or Auslan interpreters not being provided at a conference. Me being denied a seat on that tram exacerbated my pain that day.

Andrew Pulrang, disability blogger and activist, defines the point at which we can call ourselves disabled:

> I've thought about it a lot, and here is the definition of disability that makes the most sense to me. It's a personal definition, not a legal or bureaucratic one:
>
> If you have a physical or mental condition that you have to think about and plan around every day, then you are disabled.
>
> This definition encompasses any physical, mental, cognitive, and sensory impairments. I personally don't include temporary impairments, impairments that are seamlessly adapted (like glasses for nearsightedness), or ordinary variations in personality, talent, and physical makeup.

And that's what it comes down to. I call myself disabled because I am always aware of how my skin feels, I am often sore, and I have

Disability is complex. It doesn't look typical. And often the physical and attitudinal barriers are more disabling than the diagnosis.

to plan my day so that I am comfortable. I need a few reasonable adjustments, and sometimes I position myself to avoid difficult situations.

If I go out after work, I have to make sure there's enough time to dash home to have a shower, or pack some Chux cloths so I can wash in an accessible bathroom. When I travel overseas, I write to the airlines to request accommodations like extra legroom, and I book into airport lounges so I can shower between flights. I budget for medication expenses – I don't get any financial support from the government, as there is little support for disabled people who work. When I am sore, particularly on my face, I am reluctant to look at people in the eye because I don't want them to see how ugly I feel.

It doesn't matter if I identify as having a disability and others with the same condition don't. I don't receive the disability support pension. I work 20 hours a week in a part-time job and another 20 freelancing. I don't use a wheelchair. I am not neurodiverse. I do have a parking permit but am afraid to use it because I might be shouted at. And I don't resent or question those who do receive pensions and permits (they're definitely not privileges nor anything to be ashamed about). But the very questioning of my identity as a disabled person is damaging.

Disability is complex. It doesn't look typical. And often the physical and attitudinal barriers are more disabling than the diagnosis.

Every week I encounter someone who is not comfortable with me and others using the terms 'disabled' and 'disability'. They're even more uncomfortable with disability being a proud part of disabled people's identity. It's almost always non-disabled people who have a problem. I wonder if they'd tell people of colour not to call themselves black?

If you're non-disabled, and a disabled person tells you their experience, take the time to listen. Don't try to get us to see it another way, or reject disability as identity, or tell us how negative the word 'disability' is. Don't dismiss disability pride and tell us our lives are tragic. Don't justify your bad behaviour.

Don't ask us to school you further than we can stretch. If you're genuinely interested, read widely. Read the work of disabled people who write and speak on disability and other topics. And don't expect a pat on the head for engaging with disabled people.

Sometimes when disabled people talk about microaggressions, discrimination or exclusion faced, people tell us how we should feel (which isn't the way we ARE feeling) and justify the behaviour of those who made us feel this way.

This isn't the time to play devil's advocate. It's the time to listen and acknowledge our feelings, and not diminish our experience. It's the time to realise that disability is part of our culture and that it isn't a bad thing.

I identify as a proud disabled woman.

It is true that I can do a lot of things. So can many other disabled people – those with all types of impairments. And I don't want to have this part of my identity erased because someone else isn't comfortable with disability.

This dismissal of disability as part of my identity empties my cup. It took years to get here.

20

How to be a good non-disabled feminist

Inclusive, diverse, intersectionality. These are all buzzwords right now. But so often disability is forgotten when these words are used.

In 2017, I was removed from a Facebook group for being too political about seeing disability as part of my identity. (I've since been removed from more, for the same reason. I'm doing something right!) I had answered a question from one of the group's founders – should her daughter make a dramatic change to her hair, which was a huge part of the daughter's identity.

My answer, of course based on my personal experience, was polite, encouraging and empathetic. I said that as someone with a disability and visible difference, I'm always so proud of a young person who chooses to make themselves stand out in some way. I said that telling someone they might regret changing the way they look (or regret looking different from their peers) is limiting. I added that long hair is often the mark of a feminine woman (and thought back to when I planned my wedding and found very few photos of short-haired brides on Pinterest). I ended my comment by saying how my scalp became very patchy when I was a teen (and sometimes still is) because of my skin condition, and I was so self-conscious about what others thought of me. I said how I loved seeing girls and young women make the choice to have short hair.

A week after that post, I was removed from the group, and unfriended by one of the founders. I questioned her, and was told they didn't think the group was for me, as I was too political about my disability, which made people uncomfortable. My voice – a disabled viewpoint – was shut down.

The Facebook group is run by a couple of women, for women. Just like me, the members like champagne and fashion, and occasionally complain about their husbands not picking up the slack around the house. Many of us want to do good in the world – improving it for future generations. Some group founders and members went to the Women's March, wearing their pussy hats. They call themselves feminists. Yet they excluded a disabled voice from the discussion. I wondered if other women were removed? White, middle class, Jewish, married, mothers, heterosexual, black, gay women? I checked – my friends and others who expressed a similar view to me are still in the group.

This might seem like just a social media fallout, a minor disagreement between two women. But I believe it symbolises more. This microaggression reminded me that the exclusion of disabled people still happens. Excluded from employment, from buildings, placed in group homes and segregated schools. Excluded from female relationships because our disability politics and pride are too confronting. Excluded from feminism.

Another example: A few days before the Sydney and Melbourne Women's Marches in 2017, I was contacted by two different organisers, asking how to make the march more accessible. I gave them suggestions, including asking a woman with disability to speak, but I was disappointed that accessibility appeared to be an afterthought.

Disability was left off the agenda at Women's Marches around the world, and accessibility was hard to come by. American disability activist Emily Ladau wrote for American opinion website *The Establishment* in January 2017: 'Disability can intersect with every identity. Every. Single. One. But I shouldn't have to be explaining this – especially not to people who deem themselves leaders in social justice.'

Side note: I was invited to speak at the Women's March in 2018 and I spoke about these issues. The squeaky wheel gets the grease, right?

These two examples show, yet again, that disability is the forgotten part of diversity.

Here's what I want to tell the non-disabled feminist:

Disability is part of my identity, just like gender, race, sexuality and religion. It cannot be separated. I am a proud disabled woman and I will speak about it. I will make you uncomfortable with my politics and pride. The personal is political. You will not silence this part of my identity.

You can't be a good feminist if you are not intersectional. That means you must include, listen to and value people with disability in your conversations, policies, writings, conferences and protests. It hurts when we're excluded. Even from Facebook groups.

Progressive, inclusive and diverse people still use ableist slurs. I've seen prominent activists from marginalised communities use the R-word and derivatives of, and not realise the impact. The way people talk about Donald Trump – calling him a moron, mocking his speech and diagnosing him with a mental illness or intellectual disability is ableist. It suggests people with those impairments are like him; it paints disabled people as less than. And to those who defend the use of slurs like the R-word – it's *never* used as a compliment.

You can't fight discrimination with discrimination.

Stop consuming media about disability that is not made by us. It's often othering, exploitative and oversharing. Headlines on tabloid articles about people with ichthyosis – the same skin condition I have – scream 'Snakeskin Woman', 'Alligator Boy' and 'Mermaid Baby'. Everyone raved over *The Greatest Showman*, but it's ableist and exploitative. Hugh Jackman's character PT Barnum ran a freak show for fuck's sake. And audiences' hearts were warmed. Were you even really watching?

Disabled people are making our own media, we are our own voices, we are all over your social media. So get to know us.

Don't make disability and accessibility an afterthought. Make sure we are on your panels and behind the megaphones at your marches. Plan and budget for accessible events from the start. It will keep the cost down and your disabled attendees will not be exasperated having to chase this up.

Pay us to provide lived experience and advice. I recently experienced yet another refusal of payment for me to talk. The reason floored me – I was told by a disability worker that they couldn't justify my fee because the disabled people they asked me to talk to did not have the intellectual capacity to understand a

I am a proud disabled woman and I will speak about it. I will make you uncomfortable with my politics and pride.

formal speech. Just digest that for a moment. They didn't want to pay me because they thought other disabled people wouldn't understand me. The low expectations this worker had of their clients was disgusting. If I was paid, I'd want to donate my speaker fee back to the disabled people at the day centre so they could spend it on attending personal development sessions like disability pride performances and buying books by disabled writers.

Invite us to be involved in the media. Centre our voices. If you're writing a story on disabled people, don't forget to talk to us. Ask us on *Q&A*, *The Project*, *The Drum*, *Insight*. Even *The Bachelor* or *The Bachelorette*.

Nothing about us without us.

Include statistics about people with disability when talking about and preventing violence.

Remember us and ours in your activism.

You support black lives matter. You champion marriage equality. You want fair pay for fair work. You want to close the refugee camps. You're calling for a halt to climate change. You want violence against women to stop. You want equal representation in the media. You attend the Women's Marches. So do I.

Don't forget to include, listen to and value your disabled sisters in your feminist movements.

Are you really inclusive, diverse and intersectional, or are you just reciting buzzwords?

21

Access to fashion and beauty

It was an ordinary Thursday at work. Deadlines to meet and senior staff to reassure. Busy-busy. A colleague was leaving – she had become a good friend to us all. I took a phone call, talking to someone in another office about a new recruit. I looked up and noticed my team had gone – I was the only team member left in the area. They returned after a short time, cheerful and peering though the preview screen on a camera. They'd been to take farewell photos for the colleague who was leaving. And they didn't include me.

I couldn't be sure, but I suspected they excluded me because they were embarrassed or ashamed to have me in the photos. That, or they simply couldn't wait for me to finish the phone call. I asked them why I wasn't included. There was a lot of stammering. No one was willing to say they didn't want me in the photo, but some of my colleagues looked sheepish. My heart sank – I wasn't as close to or valued by my colleagues as I'd thought.

Society assumes that people with facial differences and disability are not happy with our appearance. That we should feel ashamed. We should want to and try to change how we look. We should seek a cure, or at least something to cover up that unsightly blemish.

Why should we want to get a fabulous haircut or buy some great clothes when we've got this hideous face? How can we possibly be happy when we're so far removed from any magazine cover, let alone the model on page 87 of that magazine?

So what would you say if I said I was happy with myself when I look in the mirror? I'm tired of other people's negative self-talk – and criticism of others' appearance. And it worries me that society expects us to conform to the beauty ideal.

Having ichthyosis and a facial difference has meant I haven't worried about makeup – through default, mostly. I can't wear it, although as a teenager I spent many Saturday nights slathering on my mum's Clinique foundation, trying to cover my redness. To cover up with makeup not only hurts my face (and looks like I am trying to put glitter on lizard skin), but it sends a signal to the world that I am not comfortable with my natural face. To wear makeup is to give in to those who suggest that I should look less red, less confronting.

It concerns me that there is such a quick fix for faces. The pressure on women (and men) to look youthful, hairless and perfectly groomed at all times goes beyond using makeup. Newspaper headlines scream, 'A lunchtime facelift has never been easier!' I can't believe that you can pop to the beautician in your lunch break for eyebrow threading, botox and microdermabrasion (something a lot of strangers assume I get, because of the redness microdermabrasion causes, I think). Women become reliant on these procedures for confidence. While travelling, I met a woman who said she couldn't go to work without her fake eyelashes. I don't even have eyelashes, and my workplace isn't poorer for it.

Women say they get beauty enhancements for themselves, but when they can't face the world with their natural face, is it for themselves or for other people? Their appearance mimics other women's – both uber-celebrities and Instagram starlets. No one looks individual anymore, everyone is homogenous. Digital alteration means people often don't look like their online photo in real life. A face becomes so removed from their original appearance – both actually and digitally. When does it stop?

The media and the beauty industry praise women for going makeup-free – because it's brave – and I roll my eyes. Women aren't brave for looking natural. And what does applauding makeup-free women say, when people stare at or look away from those of us with facial differences?

The people who are applauded for going makeup-free (like Alicia Keys in 2016, and Kylie Jenner's selfies with her newborn baby in 2018), or participate in no-makeup challenges, almost always meet conventional beauty standards. They've got a beauty privilege. They have media platforms. And they are almost always glamorous.

Google 'celebrities without makeup', and headlines describe their photos as 'shocking', 'unrecognisable' and 'caught out'. So embarrassing! How can an everyday woman afford to be seen not wearing makeup?

I flicked through the latest *Cosmo* to research this chapter, and couldn't see a fresh-faced woman on any page. Magazines and websites tell women how they should look, with countless pages of makeup advertisements – and airbrushing of every face. It's an industry cashing in on women's insecurities.

I gave up this type of magazine years ago, because they didn't represent my appearance or my values. I never saw myself in them.

Going makeup-free shouldn't be considered scary or brave. Looking your natural self is not brave. And worrying that people might be staring at your makeup-free face is a waste of time.

It's time the myth that beauty is a face full of makeup stops. Offices, magazines and the world need to welcome diverse, bare faces.

When people are insecure about their own appearance – when they can't go to the shops without makeup, or have to ensure a photograph of them has a flattering filter – it shows they're judgemental about others' appearances too.

I don't pretend to know what it's like to be fat, but I can relate to writer Rebecca Shaw's words on fatness because of how people talk about their own appearances so self-consciously, if not disparagingly. Bec spoke on ABC's *Ladies, We Need to Talk* podcast about the way thin people talk about being fat as the worst thing in the world. She said that this reflects on how they must feel about fat people: 'If they hate themselves, they must hate you much more,' Bec says.

For the ABC website, she wrote about friends' fear of being fat, and how they put their insecurities about their bodies ahead of their friendship:

> All the while my tenuous belief that even though I was fat
> I was still worthy of love and respect was worn down with
> each remark about their own bodies … They were taught

to hate fatness more than they hated hurting me. They were taught to be scared.

For some people, being ugly is the worst thing in the world. Having a pimple makes them want to cover up and hide away. When I hear friends make self-deprecating remarks about giant pimples or an embarrassing rash – especially when I'm sore – I want to remind them they actually haven't grown two heads, and it's unlikely their face will be the subject of stares and comments from strangers.

The way women talk about their own and others' appearances says a lot about how they might judge people with facial differences. I was in the lunchroom one workday, in an old job a few years ago. Some female colleagues were chatting about their weekend. The conversation moved to the appearance of a woman they had seen when out for drinks on Friday night.

'She turned around and I saw her face. I thought, you'd be so much more attractive if you just had a different face.'

I asked them what they would say about someone with a facial difference? They said they would never ridicule someone with a facial difference. But I wondered why they remembered this woman's appearance so vividly – three days after their night out – and why they thought it was OK to discuss it, let alone suggest she change the way she looks to meet their expectations of attractiveness? I don't think they even considered that at their table was a woman who was probably the subject of these conversations every day.

Another time, I was at a wedding with my parents. We were surrounded by pretty young things wearing gorgeous dresses. I'd glammed up for the occasion too – fashion is life so I was feeling fabulous.

I talked in hushed tones with Mum, discussing how beautifully some of the girls were dressed. It turned out some of those beautifully dressed girls were talking in hushed tones about me too.

Later in the night, after a few wines, I went to the toilet and got talking to a girl. We talked through the toilet walls, small talk – about the food, the great wedding, and that our shoes were killing us.

Then, out under the fluorescent lights as we washed our hands, the girl turned to me, looked closely, and said, 'So what happened?' What happened to my face? she meant.

'I was born this way,' I told her.

'And what happened?' she asked again. Drunk people can be hard to reason with.

'I was born like this; that's what happened,' I told her. Again.

She asked me if it was a skin condition. I said yes, and I told her the name. Drunk people are also quite honest. 'I thought it was a skin condition,' she said. And then she added, 'The people I'm with were arguing about whether it was a burn or sunburn all day.'

Right. So while I was complimenting some of those girls, they were discussing my appearance.

There's a microaggression that exists only on social media: tagging and untagging people with facial differences and other impairments to both see – and not be seen with – them.

The first instance: tagging a friend in to gawk. This is the virtual equivalent of whispering and pointing. A person sees my photo on social media – and tags in their friends to have a look. Rarely do they say anything, they just call on friends to see a funny-looking face. This happens to me occasionally – if I am featured on someone else's social media or if I use a hashtag that is unusual for me, like the time I was at the football and used a football-related hashtag. If people call their friends to have a look at me on my social media posts, I ask how I can help them. Otherwise, I just leave it – but it can still sting.

The second instance: when people say what they're really thinking when they upload a photo of me. You know, make a big deal about the way I look, in an othering way. A bit like the time my former colleague asked her partner if I was as red as she'd described when she introduced me to him. That was pre-social media. An example of the social media equivalent is the time an acquaintance wanted to catch up for lunch. Lunch was pleasant. We had the obligatory selfie. I uploaded it to my Facebook with a call for my followers to 'go show her some love'. I was saddened to see the photo she uploaded included a comment about how great it was to meet with me, and that she wasn't even worried about people staring at me. This was on a public social media page! When I addressed it, she said she hoped I was not upset or annoyed. I don't know if she wanted a cookie for being OK with the stares I endure, or if she forgot that her thoughts were aired in public.

Some people don't want to be seen with me on social media at all – so they either avoid photos with me altogether, or untag me in their photos. It's the 'you can't sit with us' mentality – embarrassment at being seen with someone with a facial difference. One friend was so concerned about their social media follower count, they deleted a photo of us from their account. My face might have been the cause of lost followers. I was sad that my friend seemed to think a photo with me in it was not worthy of social media inclusion because it might affect their image. Of course, they defended their actions by saying the picture was removed because they were self-conscious about their own appearance.

But no amount of justification made me feel better. As someone with a facial difference, I can't help think that I was the reason. I wondered how many other people's photos they've removed – people who don't have facial difference.

I know these microaggressions too well.

Maybe, just maybe, if people with beauty privilege were nicer when talking about themselves, and embraced their natural face, it would lead to a little more inclusion of those with facial differences. And perhaps one day, I can bottle the confidence that I have in my own appearance, to replace all the potions designed to plump and smooth women's faces. I wish everyone could feel this way.

My hospital file is thick. That's what happens when you live with a rare, severe illness requiring many inpatient stays and outpatient appointments. The file is more than a medical report, though. While it's filled with doctors' notes and medical photography, it's like a scrapbook – with pages of articles I've written, and locks of my hair. My hospital file has come with me from the children's hospital to the adult hospital. A few years ago, the head dermatologist – who I've been seeing since I was six years old – flicked through the pages from my childhood. He told me that when I was a little girl, I wanted to become a doctor and have long hair like Rapunzel. My childhood dreams have not come true. I'm living a great life, but I'm not a doctor, nor can I hang my tresses out the window for my prince to climb.

Ichthyosis has meant my hair has never been long. And it will never rival my hospital file for thickness. I have brittle hair, prone to breaking off at the root. My scalp is scaly.

My hair as a newborn was thick and straight – much different from my mum's African 'fro. And then it fell out when I was a few months old. It grew back curly, and patchy. At preschool and primary school, Mum would scrape my hair into ringlet pigtails. I never wanted a haircut because my hair took so long to grow.

At high school I discovered hair clips, which broke my hair, and mousse for curly hair, which gave me round but crunchy curls. All the girls were dying their hair with supermarket rinses – reds and burgundies. I tried henna, but it was very messy, and the white scales on my scalp ended up redder than my very dark brown hair.

When I was around 15, the hair just above the nape of my neck fell out. Like an undercut. Except I never wanted an undercut – they were so 1994. After a holiday to the Great Ocean Road, where we stayed in cabin accommodation, my scalp became more itchy than usual. Maybe I picked up an allergy from the pillows. I scratched and scratched, and the hair on the back of my head broke off. My scalp bled, my skin peeled, my hair didn't grow. I also had lots of bald patches over my head, including at the front of my head. I would clip the wispy strands over the bald spots to hide them.

Dermatologists did not know the cause, nor what to do – it could have been a fungal infection, but was probably just my unpredictable skin condition playing up. It went on for two and a half years – the less I scratched it the better it became. But it was so hard not to scratch.

The hair loss came at a time when I was at my least confident. I just wanted to fit in and not look any more different than I already did. I wanted to use Clearasil and shave my legs and wear skimpy clothing – even though it was impractical to do any of those things.

I was so self-conscious. I hoped no one would notice. Mum used to brush the sparse hair over the bald patch at the back. When my hair did grow a bit, I would flatten it and tie it back, doing a side part to cover the bald bits at the front. I hated it.

Going to the hairdresser (and nail salon) has also been a challenge. I need to explain to each new hairdresser that I am not contagious, and to be gentle with the comb. Sometimes I see overt fear, like at the nail salon, the day before my wedding. The staff thought I was contagious and made me go out and buy gloves for them to wear. The other customers looked at me to check out the contagious specimen and I left in tears. I just wanted a relaxed mani-pedi before the wedding – instead I felt like an outcast.

Other times, I experience microaggressions that are more difficult to pinpoint. When I'm sitting in the chair, I look at how the other hairdressers are treating the customers around me. They're talking to them, really taking care with the cutting and colouring. Meanwhile, the hairdressers barely speak to me, and barely touch my hair. I leave feeling like the cut and style is half-hearted. It's as if they assume that because I have a facial difference, I don't want to have amazing hair, or be treated like the other customers. But I want bouncy curls that put a bounce in my step, a new style occasionally, and to walk out of the hairdresser feeling fabulous.

Fortunately, I've had some fantastic experiences too – especially with the hairdresser who made my hair so lovely for my wedding. And I have recently found a hairdresser who specialises in curly hair – going to him is a treat.

For the past 15 years, my hair has been the best it's ever been. While it's not long, it's thicker and healthier. It's curly so it looks full. Sometimes I get bald patches when the comb nicks my scalp, but these grow back much more quickly than when I was younger. I stopped using supermarket and salon shampoo, switching to sulfate-free products, and I condition more than I wash my hair. I comb the scale from my scalp every second or third day, which gives it a rest from the gentle trauma of skin agitation. And I wear hats – not only to protect me from the sun, but to keep me warm. We lose so much heat from our heads.

It's rare to see actors and models with short hair. I used to see long hair as a sign of femininity – and so because my hair has always been short, it was hard to feel feminine. It didn't help that sometimes, when people stared at or commented about my skin, they'd ask why that boy had a red face. They couldn't see past my red skin *and* they thought I was a boy.

As I looked for wedding inspiration on Pinterest, I saw that short hairstyles were lacking. But I pored over pictures of Keri Russell in her short-haired phase, and pinned some beautiful photos of women wearing floral and pearl hairpieces over their short curls.

The way the media and advertising portray people with scaly scalps can be damaging – have you seen dandruff shampoo commercials? They do nothing for our self-esteem, screaming, 'OMG skin flakes on shoulders – avoid me at all costs!' People with flakes in their hair and on their shoulders are depicted as dirty, unsuccessful and to be avoided. The ads suggest our lives are doomed. This isn't the case. Newsflash: people can be successful, happy and find love with flakes in their scalp and on their shoulders.

Conditions like mine can't be treated with anti-dandruff shampoo. People with dandruff and other scaly scalp conditions shouldn't be socially penalised for our appearance.

Now I'm in my late-thirties, I am at peace with my hair and my scalp. I'm still not Rapunzel and that's OK. I love my curls, I love it short (because it makes me feel tall) and I loved wearing a sparkly accessory in my hair on my wedding day. That dream of being Rapunzel is long gone – I've learnt to manage my hair and scalp the best I can, and realised that others' perceptions of short hair and a scaly scalp do not detract from the person I am.

One of the most common questions I see in ichthyosis support groups is, 'How do you stop skin showing on clothes? Do you avoid black?'

For me, the short answer is that I no longer worry what others think of the skin on my clothes. I wear what makes me happy and comfortable. I wear black. I wear other dark clothing – and fabrics like velvet and lace. Skin flakes show. The world doesn't end.

Sometimes when I've spoken out in the media, people comment on my pretty dress rather than reading the words I've written. Fashion is my life, but I'm starting to think it stands in the way of me getting a message across. As a result of the 'great dress' comments below my articles, some of my good friends in the disability community named me 'Fashion Angel' – a nod to both my love of fashion and the commenters who have missed my point.

I've loved fashion from a young age, but I didn't become adventurous with it until I developed body confidence.

For more than half of my life, I avoided wearing dark clothes because of the skin that was left behind. I was self-conscious of what people would think. When I was younger, I'd avoid sleeveless dresses and short skirts. I'd avoid black tops because my skin could show up on my shoulders. And while this wasn't due to societal pressure, I wouldn't wear jeans much because they'd scrape my legs, making my skin powdery and raw.

But then I began to dress for me – wearing the colours I wanted to wear – and if that included black, so be it. I wear soft dresses and leggings if I am sore. I love fashion, and I'm so glad I've found ways to work around ichthyosis. Now I have body confidence, I wear whatever I want.

I often get asked why I cover up so much. Am I hiding my skin condition? Am I cold when it's really hot? Am I sure I'm not hot? Am I really sure – it's boiling outside!

I don't go out of my way to hide my ichthyosis. I am very proud of who I am. However, I do cover up to be comfortable.

Wearing layers helps to protect me from the sun, the cold and from the scratches and bumps I encounter from living life. Sometimes I wear sleeves that don't quite fully cover my arms, and I end up with small cuts just from doing deskwork!

Getting dressed can be tricky – what clothes will keep me warm, not show too much ointment and look good? I need that trifecta.

I pat myself dry before getting dressed. I have a base layer wardrobe – long-sleeved tees and stockings or leggings. They're mostly black or charcoal grey. And then I have fun with the top layers – dresses, skirts, tops and pants.

When I'm really sore, I wear soft clothes. Pyjamas. All the time. If I have to leave the house, I wear clothes that feel like pyjamas – like silky pants or a T-shirt dress. I don't wear denim when I'm sore as it scratches. I also avoid stockings on super sore days – taking them off rips my skin and makes it bleed. (Sometimes I take my stockings off in the shower if I'm having one of these days.)

And I try to make sure my clothes are breathable by choosing natural fabrics like cotton and merino wool, which I wear directly against my skin.

As I've grown older, I've also learnt to wear quality, comfortable shoes – if my feet are sore, my whole body hurts. Last year I got a foot infection from wearing cheap, poor-quality shoes – the non-waterproof upper and sole meant my feet got wet. As soon as I switched to leather, my feet felt better.

I avoid plain-coloured silk, satin and shiny fabrics because it gets so oily. Once, I wore a silky dress (I think it was polyester) and it got so oily on a car trip that I looked like I'd wet myself! I took a detour to a shopping centre and bought a new outfit.

I hate trying on clothes as my skin rubs against them and I leave skin behind. Sometimes I've bought something just because I've left too much skin behind.

My skin definitely improved when I stopped going to school. I put this down to not having to wear a uniform anymore. I think one of the reasons I was often sore was because I had to have bare legs in the summer. I might have been able to wear stockings or leggings under my dress, but I didn't want to stand out any more than I already did. I was uncomfortable for the sake of fitting in. In hindsight, that was so silly. As I've aged, it's comfort over conformity all the time.

Now I love pretty dresses layered over basics, and colour. Lots of colour. I now use my face as an accessory too – it's a colour that I work with in my style palette. Choosing clothes brings me so much joy.

I have never been as confident showing off my outfits as I have in my thirties. I hardly have any photos of me as a teenager –

maybe that's because of the pre-digital age, but I think that I just didn't feel confident in front of the camera. I didn't think people like me were allowed to show that they enjoyed fashion or took pride in themselves.

And then, with blogging and Instagram, my confidence grew. Because people did enjoy what I wore. And I get lots of inspiration from other fashionistas participating in #everydaystyle – a social media movement started by fashion blogger Nikki Parkinson. Nikki encourages people to share daily photos of their outfits, to show off our everyday style. I don't take part in #everydaystyle every day, but I do try to put up one or two posts a week. Sometimes it's what I wore to work, other times what I wore to dinner.

While it might seem narcissistic to take photos of what I wear, it's given me lots of confidence. People are seeing the style; they're liking my style. Generally, they're not asking why I look the way I do. Instead, they're asking where I got my dress or shoes. Their comments lift me up.

I've also been involved in fashion groups on Facebook. They're all uplifting and supportive, and there are no negative comments on appearance. I've made true friends in these groups; they're such a nice distraction from activism on social media. One fashion group moderator messaged to tell me she is always there to protect me against online abuse, should it occur in that group – and I felt so safe and loved.

Dressing well makes me feel good about myself. Sometimes, when I am feeling really sore and not wanting to face the world, putting on my favourite dress helps me get through the day.

Other fashionistas with disability have inspired me – with dressing for going out of the house, and also confirming that it's OK to wear pretty pyjamas.

Michelle Roger started the social media hashtag #UpAndDressed. It showcases disabled and chronically ill people who are up and dressed, even while in pain and desperately unwell. Dressing in fabulous clothes helps Michelle feel good, just as it helps me. Michelle writes:

> I was getting to a point where I got bad medical news and my body was playing up all the time. I'd had enough. I looked in the mirror one day, I was in my PJs – not even in my nice PJs – and thought, I feel what I look like. I looked sick. I am the daggy flannelette PJs where the elastic has gone and they're a bit threadbare. That's what I felt like. And I thought, stuff that. I looked in my cupboard, which is chockers full of nice stuff, and thought, why aren't I wearing them? And so I started wearing them. To hold myself accountable, I started putting them on Instagram. It captures a moment, says 'screw you body'. I did it for 17 days straight till I got sick and had to go back to bed. And even then, I put on my nice PJs.

Michelle also has a section of her wardrobe called 'PJ alternatives' – clothes to make her feel super dressed up even when she is sick. Her PJ alternatives are beautiful stretchy floral dresses and scarves. Similar to Michelle, I have a few pieces of clothing that I can wear out of the house when I'm sore. A soft draped pant can be worn with a floaty top and blazer for work, as can a long-sleeved, soft swing dress and leggings.

Karolyn Gehrig, an American queer disabled artist and writer, runs #HospitalGlam – a social media movement for chronically ill and disabled people, correcting the power imbalance between patient and doctor while in a clinical setting.

Karolyn describes #HospitalGlam on her website:

> #HospitalGlam is a movement for and by people with invisible disabilities that started by appropriating fashion imagery and reinserting it into medical environments using bodies that don't outwardly present as sick or disabled. #HospitalGlam is about contextualising ourselves inside an often alienating medical environment in order to assert our rights as patients and better our treatment. By taking #HospitalGlam photos and posting them on social media, patients increase awareness of invisible illnesses in their communities and with doctors.

She tells me that it's about 'turning the space into your own workspace prior to the doctor's entrance, which reinforces your bodily autonomy. This small action has a big psychological payoff, and makes the space feel more comfortable, and like it is yours. When you have that, it's easier to be open with doctors and speak to them like they are a colleague with whom you are working on the task of achieving better health, with different skill sets.'

Initiatives like #UpAndDressed and #HospitalGlam allow people who are less able to get out of the house because of their illnesses and disability to partake in strong and empowering online communities. They change the perceptions of chronically ill and disabled people – showing that not only do we purchase and enjoy fashion, but we can create our own narratives around what it looks like to be chronically ill and disabled.

I no longer worry what others think of the skin on my clothes ... skin flakes show. The world doesn't end.

I share my style on social media because I love the community it creates. It also means that I – and others – can show brands and wider society that disabled people do indeed love clothing. Getting disability fashion into mainstream advertising is something that is needed. And there are brands committed to featuring disabled models.

Seeing models like Robyn Lambird, Julius Malaquias, Kelly Knox, Jason Clymo, Mama Cax, Jillian Mercado, Madeline Stuart, Angel Dixon and Jamie Brewer on the catwalk is progress. Mannequins depicting disabilities in stores, and clothes to accommodate non-normative bodies and movement restrictions will be further progress. The fashion world can't be complacent, thinking one model with a disability in one fashion show is enough. More designers and retailers need to include people with disabilities. And this needs to translate from the catwalk to the shopping strip – with proper access to stores and disability awareness training for staff.

In September 2018, I organised and participated in Access to Fashion – an event that was part of the curated program at Melbourne Fashion Week, the first of its kind. The event comprised a fashion parade and discussion panel featuring a diverse range of disabled people. We had a hard time narrowing down 25 models from over 90 applicants. I put together a wonderful project team including a director, stylist company, media manager and videographer and more, crowd-funded the event and put the word out to media. So many people were excited to support the event, evidenced by the designers, volunteers, sponsors and donors and media involved. The event sold out in 12 days, even before we had selected the models.

Melbourne designers lent their clothing to Access to Fashion – and one model designed her own outfit, a blue and black lace steampunk dress. It was so cool.

Access to Fashion was held on the first day of Spring. It was wonderful to see the excitement in the green room as models waited to walk the catwalk. Many had not participated in this type of event before, but some were already forging a career in modelling. Everyone was so happy – there was not a sad-looking model on the catwalk!

I wanted Access to Fashion to be a statement to the fashion industry – that we are 20 per cent of the population, deserve access, and are buying and enjoying fashion. But more so, I wanted it to be a chance to come together to celebrate ourselves and each other, to practise pride, and to have fun.

Seventeen-year-old Savanna Addis was one of the people selected to model, but tragically died just before the event. Her family chose Access to Fashion as one of the causes for mourners to support, and we are so grateful to them for that. In her application to model, Savanna said:

> I believe that fashion has the power to change society's perception of disabled people. Image is very powerful and what we choose to wear has a big impact on how we are perceived. I want disabled people to know that they don't have to be intimidated by fashion and they should feel confident enough within themselves to explore their unique style. I believe that personal style is a huge part of a person's identity. It is an important tool of self-expression and can be very empowering. I also believe that fashion and style is a particularly important tool for the disabled community because it is often the second thing people notice about us after our disability.

History was made that day at Melbourne Fashion Week. It was a dream I'd had for a few years and I made it happen. I was pretty proud.

Let's shake things up and normalise disability. Let's ensure this access and inclusion is on the ready-to-wear rack in all stores. We need to see disabled people feeling great in fashion on the runways, in catalogues and on social media.

22

Adam

As much as I believe in love, I don't think being loved romantically is the pinnacle of 'normal' for disabled people. It's about the moment you love yourself. I wouldn't have the romance I have if I didn't have self-love. As clichéd as it seems, I met my now husband when I didn't have time for a partner. I found career success, fantastic friends, knew that the disability community was my tribe, and had a strong sense of self-love and identity. And then I met him.

The first date with Adam – my now husband – was at a Mexican cafe in Lygon Street. I wasn't getting my hopes up – our conversations online hadn't been that exciting, and I'd been hurt so many times in the past. I got to the restaurant and smiled at a well-dressed, dark-haired man. He greeted me warmly. And then a shorter man, with floppy dark hair, kind eyes, a big smile, said, 'Hello Carly.' He was wearing shorts. That was Adam. I had thought the cafe's doorman was my date. What kind of man turns up to a date in shorts? I wondered. He did. Our date was dull. I thought he wasn't interested, because he's not much of a talker. Still, he persisted. And Adam has worn shorts almost every day since we've been together. And he often reminds me that I thought the doorman was my date!

Adam and I met online in 2013 on OkCupid – a free dating service. (Neither of us were so committed to looking for love that we'd pay for a dating service.)

While my profile was on OkCupid, I wasn't actively looking for anyone. I had responded to a few messages and been on one date that year before Adam messaged me. My writing career had just taken off, I didn't have time, and I really wasn't looking to be brought down by men telling me they weren't expecting me to be so red, or 'I'm not that into you'. Internet dating had been, for the most part, horrendous for me.

Adam wrote to me on a weeknight. A short message with lots of Xs and Os. He was polite, but didn't really say anything. I'm a conversationalist, always wanting to know more. He wasn't going to give me more. Later, I'd find out he's extremely quiet and shy, and my words outweigh his by about a million per day.

He said I had a nice smile, and told me a little about what he did for work. He knew who I was already. This was the year that I took the taxi company to the Human Rights Commission, and I had been in the media. He already knew about my skin – the disclosure of which was something I found very hard to navigate during my dating periods. He wrote:

> I was hesitant, but since I've got to know you, you seem like a very nice person. I can see why some people would be turned away, but not me, I see your inner beauty. It took me a while to send the first message but I'm glad

I did as I can see that you are a wonderful person inside
and out.

I admit that his honesty stung, though not as much as the guy who told me about visiting sex workers while we ate pasta, and then told me he hates Darren Hayes. That was too much.

After this online interaction with Adam, I wrote a blog about it. I was pretty assertive, and quite unfair. I broke my rule about not blogging about people in my personal life without their permission. I wrote that I felt like I was his heroic moment. That he looked past my face, when I wanted him to see it. I wrote that I felt he pitied me, and I don't want that.

While I am political about disability, because the personal is political, in hindsight I realise this wasn't the moment to be political in such a public place. I should have processed my feelings privately. He wasn't the guy who dumped me in the supermarket car park because of the way I looked, or the unreliable guy who kissed me then said he just wanted to be friends, or the guy who would message me like I was his personal counsellor. I should never have expected him to be down with disability politics in his first message. His kindness and willingness to really get to know me should have been enough.

Adam read my blog, and still wanted to meet me. Still. I was such a bitch. We met, and after several mediocre dates, a dumping – again that was me (complete bitch) – and then some pretty awesome dates, we married in March 2016. We had a brilliant party with our loved ones. Adam came down the aisle on his bike and I wore two different wedding dresses. We laughed and cried, and ate really good food. Our first (and only) dance was to Bob Evans – live! Who would have thought, on that first date, we'd end up married?

Adam was the guy who really wanted to give me a chance. He sent me a love song – Ellie Goulding's *How Long Will I Love You?* – which was later played at our wedding. And he came with me to see Bob Evans three times in our first three weeks of dating and did not complain once. He's the guy who loves cheese as much as I do. He's the guy who wants to see me and touch me first thing in the morning, when my skin's at its worst, when I don't even want to look at myself.

In addition to blogging about him without his permission (I ran this chapter by him, don't worry), it turns out that my expectations – because of my experiences – were unfair on him.

For so many disabled women and men, finding love is hard. There's constant rejection. And when interest comes, we are expected to settle. We even tell ourselves it's OK to settle. We should be grateful for any attention that comes our way. Society assumes that we will only date other disabled people – I can't tell you the number of times people have asked me, or my mum, if Adam has my condition too, waving their hands around their face in the international language of 'I don't know what to say about your face'.

But disabled people are also choosy. We are allowed to be. I didn't click with Adam initially, and I did feel a little internal pressure that because he was OK with my skin, I should be keener. It took work for both of us.

I overlooked the loving potential because I'm often on the defensive – fending off stares and low expectations.

But Adam has done so much to understand. When we first started going out, he switched to low allergy skin care products so he could hug me without my skin being irritated. (Now we're an old married couple, I'm lucky if his beard doesn't scratch off my face.)

He's involved in my disability community. Lately, we've been looking at houses, and the first thing he checks is if they are accessible for our disabled friends. Even if the house has cardboard patching up the walls, is heavy with cigarette smoke and $200K out of our price range, he'll focus on whether a power chair could get in the toilet, or whether he could install a ramp out the front so our friends won't need to enter at the back.

He wants to take my soreness away all the time, looking more forlorn than I am when I'm very unwell.

He loves my cooking, telling me he'd eat my mac and cheese every night if I would cook it every night. And he's funny. So funny. He loves to dance when only I am watching. He has a boyish joy about him. And he loves my boobs. 'Don't worry, Carly's boobs, you'll always have me to talk to,' he said one night.

His proudest moment was organising for Clem Ford to bring me some green tea when I was in hospital in 2016, because he was working and couldn't be there. Then she turned up with a gift bag of amazing stuff from all of our feminist friends, and he beamed over the phone saying, 'I helped organise that.'

He picks up on inspiration porn and exploitation. He's attended protests with me – even supplying the gaffer tape for my friends and me to tape posters to the backs of toilet doors. He gets it.

It was hard settling into a new relationship – learning quirks and not doing a poo for three days because your partner's staying over for the weekend. When I began my relationship with Adam, I had to see ichthyosis, chronic illness and facial difference in layperson's terms – from the perspective of someone who had been raised with good values and had a polite demeanour, yet never encountered such visible difference or chronic illness. Until he met me, he knew nothing about ichthyosis or appearance diversity.

But I commend him. He does an amazing job with such a high-maintenance partner. He asks a lot of questions, is never rude and is very patient. And he's so gentle with me. He wants to spend every moment with me, ichthyosis and all. I ask him often, 'Are we real?' He pinches me gently and says, 'Yes, we are.'

One thing that I've noticed since being with him is that this skin condition is deceiving. While I look the same most days – and while my face looks relatively calm, there's the painful skin that is not so obvious. While I say I'm sore, he might not always see the difference, except perhaps in the way I walk or my need for rest. I ask him if a sore spot looks inflamed and he says, 'It just looks normal to me.' But he can feel when I'm sore, because my body becomes so hot – trying to expel the heat to reduce inflammation.

In the early days, I felt like he just didn't understand that I can't just bounce back from a day of regular activities. I need to lie down after a shower to calm the pain, I need to do nothing for a while – I'm not lazy. I didn't want to be seen as a burden on him. Now he's used to it, moving off from the couch for me to lie down or leaving me to nap in the afternoon.

Adam says he wished he knew more about the everyday minutiae of ichthyosis before he met me – though he had access to the information on the internet, he says he couldn't be bothered reading the mumbo-jumbo. He needed to see it for himself.

I shed so much skin. Initially I would brush it off his clothes, embarrassed to leave my mark on him. I'd worry about the skin in my bed. I'd worry about my peeling face in the morning or how my skin would fall onto him. I'd worry about my cream and how oily it made his clothes. He's said countless times that it doesn't bother him. He finds my skin flakes in his pocket and smiles that he's carrying me with him wherever he goes.

These little things my skin does, which I take for granted, amaze him. And his acceptance of them – the aspects of the condition that so many have found yucky – amazes me. I feel so, so lucky to have found him.

He holds my hand right, pulling me closer while we are waiting to cross the road, and steering me away from those who stare. As I previously mentioned, I don't see them staring much anymore, but I know he's trying to stop me seeing. He looks back at those staring, angry for me. I see that.

He noticed the stares a lot when we first got together, but now he has shaken off those stares like I have. He had never really noticed how much disabled people were stared at before he met me. I asked him how it feels to him when people stare and make comments. Always the optimist, he says, 'They're just looking at your beauty.'

He never speaks up on my behalf, because he knows that I can. But he is always miffed when I tell him about acts of discrimination and abuse that happen when he's not around – and thankful for those who do stand up and speak up for me.

It's been an adjustment for both of us. This isn't just adjusting to space, music tastes or bad habits. It is an adjustment in which compromise can play no part. It's adjusting to a medical reality that can often be severe, unpredictable and embarrassing for me. My ichthyosis can be frustrating, upsetting and an inconvenience, and for so long, my skin's nuances have been private. I guess it's a unique challenge like every relationship has. I've said to him ...

'I'm not telling you it's going to be easy, I'm telling you it's going to be worth it.'

He looks at me adoringly, whatever face I've got on. In the morning, his beautiful face beams at my just woken up face – taut with yesterday's skin. I'm feeling my least beautiful and he looks at me like I'm a supermodel. When my new face is on and I'm feeling good about myself, he'll say, 'You've got something on your face. It's beautiful.' And my heart melts. Every time.

I never thought someone could stare at me lovingly when I have skin hanging off my face – when I'm the scaly lady that you never see in public or online. He's seen all of it. My wincing and asking for Panadol after a shower, me delicately tearing the stockings off my legs, leaving perfectly straight wounds and tiny drops of blood dotting them like rubies. He's seen me cry in pain and wants me to be better again.

I don't need anyone but myself to make me feel happy with my appearance. But it is amazing knowing and seeing how someone else sees me. It's such a joy to love and to be loved. And I love how it shows. This isn't vanity. It's seeing myself as my love sees me. When I see a photo he's taken, I see the beauty he sees in me. How wonderful that a camera can capture that – I thought only a human could, not a machine. I thought that beauty was fleeting, merely dandelion fluff that could never be caught.

One weekend early in our relationship, we were laughing about something. I told him to 'just be normal'. And then I apologised. 'Sorry, here I am telling you to be normal when I hate that term.' And I joked again that I am not normal enough. He told me to stop using *that word*, because I hate it. He gets it.

He recalls funny experiences that happen to me – the time the man suggested that I needed sunscreen by waving his hands around his face after he saw me, and denied he was talking about me when Adam called him on it; the waiter who told me urgently that I must avoid eating soy sauce because it will turn me black; and the group of tourists who took off their glasses to get a better look at me – Adam put on his sunglasses and stepped up to get a closer look at them.

He has a nickname for me – born while watching *The Great British Bake Off*. It's Flaky Strudel. 'I love you, my flaky strudel,' he says. And I say that as long as we have each other we will always have heat. Cue bursts of laughter.

And that's it. It's about being comfortable enough to have a big laugh about my situation. Our situation. Because that's how we rise above the hard stuff.

So, you've got a new partner and a disability or chronic illness …

Communicate. Be up front about your condition. Tell them when you're in pain, and when you're doing well.

Don't expect your new partner to know everything about your condition straightaway. It's a learning process.

Invite them to a doctor's appointment.

Believe them when they say that aspects of your condition that you're self-conscious or embarrassed about do not bother them.

Have a laugh; see the funny side.

Thank them when they're taking care of you.

Back to skin hunger – I told you in Chapter 16 that the story wasn't finished.

NEW TOUCH – 2014

I've been experiencing new touch. I'm far from experiencing skin hunger now. I can't even remember what it's like to yearn for touch, after doing so for years. It's like this frequent touch has erased all loneliness.

He holds me so tight I might burst. My love is so willing and eager to touch me – day and night. Sometimes I've pushed him away, because I'm not in the mood – and then I feel guilty because of just how unreserved he is, and remember how much I wanted this touch.

He has been touching my face. He makes my ear tickle – until now, I only knew what it feels like to have skin removed from outside and in my ear. That's clinical touch, never pleasurable. (Except for the surgical removal of skin – that feels amazing! I joked to him that having my ears cleaned out at the hospital feels so good that we might have to introduce a surgical ear vacuum into the bedroom.)

He feels the contrast of an oily face in the day and a dry, rough and flaky face in the morning. There are a few hours in the evening when my face is at an equilibrium – relaxed enough to be paler and supple, when the cream has soaked in. He caresses my face with the same tenderness – no matter how my skin feels or looks. He says I'm most beautiful in the morning before a shower. I still don't believe him.

If only we could see ourselves as our partners do, hey?

I'm so glad Adam has taken my hand and helped me overcome my own reservations about being touched.

MY SKIN HUNGER HAS BEEN
SATISFIED – 2014

I've written a lot about how my skin was hungry. Hungry for moisture, but also hungry for touch. For so long I yearned to be touched – dreaming of the times to come, remembering how long it had been since.

And now, I am touched, often.

My boy, he wants to touch me, and he doesn't hold back for fear he might hurt me, or that much of me will end up on him (inevitable with ichthyosis).

He can't get close enough, asking me to stop what I'm doing for a hug, holding my hand when we walk and drawing me close when we stop to wait for traffic to pass.

My skin hunger being satisfied has changed my life. At times my skin feels as smooth as his. I don't wake up as scaly as I used to and I haven't had an infection for months. Touch really does soothe it. Loving touch is healing. It's more than pleasurable, it's life-giving.

I'm a marsupial in the warm pouch of his arms.

I fall asleep on his chest, my ear hearing that his heart beats fastest when I'm close.

He's the big spoon and I'm the little one, my body shining with warmth.

His touch is a salve – as critical to my needs as my cream is.

Some have said I'm glowing since I've found this love. I think he's my sunshine, making me glow, and grow.

My skin hunger is satisfied and it's most wonderful. I'm thriving.

23

Letter to my unborn child

I wrote this for the Amazing Babes spoken word event at the Emerging Writers Festival in 2015. About 10 women read letters to the women they admire – from TV icons to pop stars. I wrote a letter to my future child. Gosh, I was nervous about reading it out. I cried when I read it to Adam (and so did he). And I choked up on stage. And I was scared about publishing it. Because these issues aren't discussed enough. And people fling judgement around – even people in my own community. I don't think they realise how their judgement creates fear about discussing issues like this one.

But I got brave after a good response from the Amazing Babes audience and I pitched it to *Daily Life*. It was edited and published. And the response was wonderful. People told me how much they related, told me their own stories of deciding to have a family, and said that Adam and I will make loving parents if we decide to have children. People said they cried. Even my editor. And I cried again. Here is the unedited version – longer and funnier than you may have previously read.

This is a letter to my unborn daughter – an amazing babe. The hardest letter I've ever written and read.

Before my husband Adam thinks I'm telling you before he hears the news, before you tut-tut at me for drinking wine, and before you tweet to the world that Carly Findlay is having a baby, I'll set things straight. I'm not pregnant. Nope. Not yet. That's just a food baby under my dress.

I'm not even certain that I want my life changed drastically by a baby. But I'm getting clucky. I'm mid-thirties. My friends are having babies. I gush over animal hoodies and denim pinafores – I've been browsing the baby section of H&M. I want to squeeze chubby cheeks and blow raspberries on tummies and tickle wriggly toes.

In 2015, I hosted an event for adults and children affected by the same condition as me. Adam was king of the kids – entertaining them, making them laugh and making play dough hearts for me.

As I was chatting to a panel of doctors, the sight of Adam distracted me. The photographer was taking a photo of a 10-month-old baby, and Adam was behind the photographer, making the baby laugh. Oh, my ovaries. He will make a wonderful father.

Amazing babe, I'm wondering so many things. I wonder what you'll look like? How will I handle changing nappies and wiping your nose when I can't look in the toilet after someone else has left their poo unflushed? What will your hair be like when mine is African and Adam's is Asian? Will I hold back from sharing your photo on social media? Will having a baby make me a mummy blogger? (I wonder if brands will be more willing to work with me then?)

Will I be a stay-at-home mum and a writer, or will Adam be a stay-at-home dad? I wonder if you'll be an only child like me or have a sibling like Adam? Will it hurt when you come out? How will we even afford it? Will I have to go to weekend sport when I hate sport, and can your dad take you to swimming lessons because I can't swim? How can I give up soft cheese for nine months?

All these thoughts and you're just a twinkle in my eye.

When I grew up, the kids at school told me I'd never have sex. They assumed that my appearance and skin was a deterrent to all boys. And for a long time, and after dating a few losers, I assumed I'd be single forever. But then I met the beautiful Adam. And now we're married. I can't believe it! This wedding, as well as being the best party I never thought I'd throw, was the middle finger to those high school bitches.

And with marriage comes the possibility of having children – something else I never thought would be on my horizon. Amazing babe, you might be in my life one day.

You've inspired me and you're not even born yet. You've inspired me to think about disability and genetics and the value of a life.

After doctors congratulate me on my marriage, they talk family planning. I am confident that with my medical team, Adam and I will have all the support we need to make informed decisions.

For me, it's not simply going on or going off contraception. It's about genetics. A gamble. An informed choice. And it's made me think about being pro-choice. I am pro-choice – a woman's body is her own and if she is not in the right space to bring a child into the world, for whatever reason, I respect her choice. I also believe that any life, even a life with a disability – including my genetic skin condition – deserves to live and be loved.

And then there's this. I know the heaving pain that this condition brings. I know the social challenges, the isolation and the discrimination. It gets better but it never ends. Could I put my little one through that?

There's also my health to consider. It is possible for women with ichthyosis to have a baby – I have friends who've recently become mums. But what if I get too sick to be a good mum? How could I care for a tiny baby *and* myself when my skin is sore? What if you have the same condition as me?

So many thoughts. And you're just an amazing babe in my mind. This isn't even something I feel I can discuss in my own illness community because views about pre-selection, abortion and religion are so staunch, and genetic testing isn't often considered until after the baby is born.

Amazing babe. If you are born with ichthyosis, know that you will be as loved as if you were born without. I know this condition so well. It will get better, but it will be hard. And you'll have a supportive community around you. And my mum, the most amazing babe, has taught me so much. She's going to make such a wonderful grandmother. You'll be spoilt!

And there are so many new developments in the treatment and management of ichthyosis that weren't around when I was little. Play therapy, assistance in school, cooling vests and creams. Society is so much more diverse now, and there are anti-bullying programs in schools. Progress.

And maybe you'll be our adopted child – Adam and I can give you the life that your birth parents couldn't. You'll be loved no less than if you had my smile and Adam's nose.

You might get some comments about your mum looking different from your friends' mums. I hope that you teach them about diversity and inclusion through leading by example, and you don't get too tired explaining my appearance.

Amazing babe, before I'd even typed these thoughts into my computer, before Adam had the chance to smile at me during a folate commercial on TV (he does it all the time now), before we'd even been engaged for four months, I was faced with The Talk. The one where I'd have to tell someone my thoughts about having children. The one where I had to tell someone my views on ichthyosis, genetics and pre-selection and abortion and ...

I hadn't even processed the idea of having children myself.

What should have been an exciting conversation – preferably with Adam or my own mother or my geneticist – was one that left me in tears and shaking. Words were spat at me. Words about me being a burden and potentially being an irresponsible mother because I have a rare, severe, genetic illness. And some arbitrary statistics were thrown around about the likelihood of me passing on this condition to my unplanned, unborn child. It wasn't said but I could hear what the person was thinking – that I'd knowingly cause physical and social pain to a baby by passing on my ichthyosis.

It did not matter to this person that I have a wonderful team of specialists or that I know more about the condition than they will ever know. It did not matter that my parents had no family support when I was born, but they did their very best. It didn't even matter that my partner is 100 per cent committed to me – and that not even he and I had discussed having children at the time. It didn't matter how much this conversation hurt me and that I will never be able to feel comfortable around that person again. Disability was positioned as a tragedy – my disability and your potential disability – and I could not reason otherwise.

These judgements about reproduction are passed my way all too often.

A quick Google search does not provide accurate details of the chance of me passing on my condition. With Adam's 'normal' skin, and me having the condition, there's less of a chance than my own parents had. A discussion with my geneticist confirmed low odds – and she also said I should not be denied the right to be a mother. When you have a disability, your appearance, body and ability is up for discussion by everyone. Stares and comments, questions and assumptions, judgement and sometimes discrimination. I never thought I'd be discussing my reproductive choices with anyone other than my partner and my medical team. People assume that through disability, we will make 'irresponsible' choices, and those people will vocalise their judgement.

I know what people think when children with disabilities are born to disabled parents. I see it in the media. Headlines scream, 'Disfigured Dad Decides to Keep Baby with Same Disfiguring Condition, Despite Cruel Comments and Push by Others to Abort' – and commenters unfairly weigh in on a right to life. Friends say they don't mind the sex of the baby, as long as it's healthy. This implies they don't want a baby that is disabled, even when they claim to be good disability allies. Doctors force sterilisations and abortions on people with physical and intellectual disabilities. When I was in Year 7, a fellow student told me that if I was born to her mother, she'd have given me up. I've been shamed because I'm an only child, and told that it would have been fairer on me if my parents had given me a sibling – preferably one with ichthyosis. A person with my skin condition told me it was child abuse for people with the condition to have children. And as mentioned, I was forced to discuss my preferences re having children.

It was then that I experienced a small part of what my parents might have felt during apartheid. That my colour – my condition – will make me an unfit mother.

This is why I write. To raise expectations. I have to do that every day of my life.

But disability is not the worst thing that could happen. Disability is not the worst thing that could happen because you will be loved, supported and planned for. You will be warm and your tummy will be full and you'll have lots of books to read. You will have a wonderful life – I'm proof that you can.

Amazing babe, you will be so planned. I'll even draw up a spreadsheet for you – and I don't make spreadsheets willingly.

Disability will not be the worst thing to happen to you as my child, or for me as your mother. The worst thing that could happen is other people's closed-mindedness.

Amazing babe, I don't even know if you'll exist. But it doesn't mean I haven't been thinking of you.

24

The mouths of babes

It was a balmy December night. We were at a dumpling house in the city, both out with our mums.

You were about seven years old, and had a party dress on. I bet this was a lovely night with your parents. Maybe you were celebrating the end of school? Or your mum or dad got a promotion at work? I was having a quiet drink to celebrate my birthday.

You sat at the table next to me. Your mum sat on the bench seat beside me, and you sat across from her. Your dad came later. Once you saw me, you became scared. I saw your mouth drop, your body recoil. I know that fright – I've seen it a lot. My smile didn't put you at ease.

You reached for a scarf – I think it was your mum's, because chartreuse doesn't seem like a kid's colour – and quickly covered your eyes with it. You kept the scarf over your face for as long as I was there. Sometimes you peeked from under it, but mostly it covered your mouth and eyes, and you sat with your back to me.

I know the scarf wasn't to cover your eyes or mouth for physical comfort reasons. There were no fumes in the air. You weren't coughing. And you weren't using it before you saw me. You were hiding because you were scared of me.

Sometimes I position myself facing away from people so I don't have to deal with this. It breaks my heart to see kids look at me and decide not to sit next to me, or stare, or make a fuss. It's easier to turn my back on a crowd.

I think your mum talked to you about the way you hid from me. I didn't want to eavesdrop, but I could tell she was embarrassed, trying to address the topic of my face while I was sitting next to her.

I just wished your mum had said, out loud, that there was no need to be scared. She could have gently invited me to tell you about myself (and understood if I didn't want to explain). I hate it when parents tell their kids that I've been silly in the sun, or badly burnt. Let me tell my own story. I hate it even more when parents say nothing at all when their kids' behaviour makes me feel sad and uncomfortable.

I wanted to say something too, but I didn't know if it was my place. And it's not my job to make strangers feel comfortable about my appearance. If I spoke to you or raised my voice, even to say that's not OK, you might have been more scared. I didn't want to make your experience of seeing a person with a facial difference worse than it already was.

Even though I'm probably almost 30 years older than you, it doesn't mean I'm not hurt. It took me back to kids at school, who would also cover their eyes, saying my red face was like a bright traffic light. I'm glad that my mum was there, because I needed her then just as much as I needed her when I was your age. It also hurt because I don't want to be scary.

Your parents need to talk to you about appearance diversity at home – how everyone looks different, but some people are born with or acquire facial differences and impairments. How difference isn't to be feared. Your schools need to be teaching diversity and inclusion on the curriculum, next to English and maths.

What made you scared of my face? Is it the way villains are portrayed in fairytales, where the evil people often have facial disfigurements? Is it because the people you see in magazines and on TV all have smooth skin and pretty faces? I hope you can play with toys and watch and read about characters that look like me (and others with facial differences and disabilities), because representation matters.

It's really important for kids like you to have exposure to all sorts of faces and for parents and teachers to reassure you that you shouldn't be scared. Exposure to different faces in artwork, photographs and even fabric prints can help you get used to encountering different-looking faces in real life. I think if it wasn't for 'scary face' depicted as evil, I wouldn't encounter as many children who hide from my face. Even funny, scary faces can belong to kind, smart and caring people.

I didn't have a good time at dinner that night. I suspect you didn't either. I had to make a stranger comfortable with my presence, and you spent half an hour hiding away. It was hard work for both of us.

When I left the dumpling house, I wrote my feelings down, and I talked to my mum. I wanted to curl up in her lap like I did when I was little, but instead we sighed into our wines back at her hotel.

This is my every day, for the rest of my life. I'm used to it, but that doesn't mean I deal with it well every time it happens. I hope the next time you see someone with a face that you're not used to seeing, you can just smile, shrug and eat your dinner happily. My face looks different and that's OK.

I'm often asked how to talk to children about disability and appearance diversity.

Encountering children often fills me with dread. As I said above, it brings back memories of being at school. I want to avoid children's direct honesty. Even more so, I don't want to be the scary person they see. Children are curious, but they can be cruel too – even if unintentionally. And adults can feel hurt just as much as children.

I once stayed with a family that had known me my whole life. They should have been prepared. For two days, I endured two children – aged six and eight – not looking at me. Being afraid. Not speaking to me unless prompted by their parents. It was tiring.

Their cuteness waned fast. I spent much of the time being polite, smiling my discomfort away, trying to make conversation. I asked the children's parents if I should explain about my skin. No, they told me. Then I asked them straight out, in front of their parents, if they wanted to ask me anything about my face. No. No. And still no conversation. In the end I told them, 'I'm not talking to you if you're not talking to me.'

Their parents put this behaviour down to shyness, but I've seen the reactions of enough children to know they were not shy. What made it worse was that someone else who the children had just met for the first time was also staying over. The children were not 'shy' with that person.

I had hoped that this family would prepare the children for my visit. I had hoped (especially in this age of social media) they would have been shown my photo and encouraged to ask polite questions. I had hoped that they were a little more appreciative of appearance diversity. It was a difficult stay. I found it especially difficult to raise this issue with the children's parents – I was a guest in their home.

I was on the train one day and a little kid saw me and threw an absolute whopper of a tantrum. He screamed that he didn't want to look at me or sit next to me. He kicked the inside of the train, hit his dad, and said how yucky I looked. It was really embarrassing because people were looking at me to see what the boy didn't want to look at. And I had to say something, because his father wasn't saying anything. I said to the boy that he was very rude. I told his dad that I write about what it's like to look different, including how to educate kids about diversity, and gave him my card, suggesting he talk to his kid so this doesn't happen again. The dad thanked me and got off at a stop I presume wasn't his, because the kid – mid-tantrum – said it wasn't the right stop. The dad was so embarrassed. And so was I.

Not all my experiences have been bad. I have a great memory of a time at my government job – my manager had her then seven-year-old nephew and his parents in at work one day. I'd heard lots about him, especially his intelligence and confidence, and was excited to meet him. (I expect he and his parents had heard a bit about me too.) We chatted for about 15 minutes – about lots of things like school and what he is going to do when he's 18. I could see him looking at me, curious. I smiled, and continued our conversation – about everything but my skin. When he left, he said, 'Bye, Carly', waved his hand around his face, and said, 'I hope your face will get better soon.' It was such an emotional moment for me – he was clearly concerned and very thoughtful. I didn't want to break his heart by saying it won't get 'better'. And so I said, 'Thank you.'

I've had some great questions from children when I've done talks at schools. I spoke to a group of eight- to 12-year-old children about diversity when I was in Scotland. I stayed in a tiny town in Ardrishaig, about two and a half hours drive from Glasgow. The friends I stayed with have a primary school–aged son, and they suggested to the Principal that I talk to the class. The school was tiny too.

I opened up the talk with a question about whether any of them know people who look different. Half of the class raised their hands – saying they've got family members and friends who have a range of disabilities, and some children's parents worked in disability care.

The class was doing a module on diversity – studying Scottish discrimination law and inclusion rules, and creating an accessible sporting venue. So cool! The best statement from a child was, 'You should be someone's friend no matter what they look like.' It was wonderful and I'm so hopeful for the future. This session proved that diversity and inclusion would be a great addition to the school curriculum.

And it's always lovely when my friends' kids are well adjusted around my face. I bumped into a good friend of mine at the local supermarket recently. Her beautiful kids – aged two and three – smiled at me from the trolley, saying 'Hi, Carly' through chubby-cheeked mouthfuls of biscuit. Her kids have never been wary around me. They've spoken to me, given me cuddles and laughed with me like my difference doesn't bother them. I sent her a quick text telling her that her kids have never seen me as different – and I am so thankful for that. She should be proud.

So what would be my advice for preparing children to meet a person with a visible difference?

Tell your child that everyone is different – in all aspects of diversity. People come in all colours and sizes and have lots of different skills. Talk to your child regularly about diversity at home. I am a strong believer that the responsibility to teach diversity lies with the parents.

Don't make something up as an answer for your child. But what about when a kid asks you – their parent – and you don't know what to say? One thing I'm big on is telling the truth. You don't need to give a complicated explanation or even expect me to explain to your kid. You don't even have to know the answers.

A participant in one of my training sessions told me she would tell her child I'd been sunburnt if they asked about my face, because they were too young to understand an honest answer (or an 'I don't know').

No.

Don't assume.

Don't tell them lies or push the blame or irresponsibility of letting myself get sunburnt onto me. (There's so much focus on how sunburn is bad!) Tell them everyone's face is different. That's the truth. Everyone's face is different. (And that was the answer I gave her in person.) I hate a parent telling their child I've 'been stupid in the sun'. I'd prefer them to say, 'I don't know honey, maybe this woman would like to tell us about why she's got a red face?'

I understand that it can be embarrassing if your child asks questions about someone's visible difference. The shrieking, the repeated whys, the candidness. And it can be hard for people with visible differences to answer these questions, especially if they're not confident. Don't be offended if a person with a visible difference, or their parent, finds an innocent question hurtful.

Sometimes I wonder if parents want me to speak up if their child doesn't ask me about my skin directly. Most of the time I smile at a curious child and then I say, 'Everyone is different. I was born this way – like you were born with your blue eyes.' Most of the time they understand and move on.

While I'm usually happy to explain with honesty and candidness, there may be times that I just don't want to answer. I might be sore or having a busy day, or have been inundated with questions already. If I don't want to explain, please accept that.

I don't want to parent your child. I am happy to answer questions, and I realise children can learn just as much from a stranger as they can from their parents. But I will speak up if your child is being rude or cruel, or pointing, staring for an extended period of time or laughing.

It's up to you as parents to have that ongoing discussion about diversity and the need to treat people – no matter how they look – with respect. Because when you're in a situation like the one I had on the train, or in the dumpling restaurant, or in the house with that family, you'd wish you had.

Before your child meets a person with a visible difference, show them a picture. Tell them your friend may do things a little differently from them – like using a wheelchair because they are unable to walk, or put cream on their face, or use a device that helps them to see, hear or talk. Tell them it's OK to ask questions. Tell them it's not OK to be rude.

Ask your friend with a visible difference about their condition before you introduce them to your child. Ask your friend if they are OK to explain their visible difference.

Don't provide an excuse if they are rude or scared.

If you encounter a stranger with a visible difference, encourage your child to say hello and preface any questions with, 'I hope you don't mind me asking.'

Don't be offended if I don't want to explain my visible difference. Just like when adults approach me, children approaching me – and making a noisy scene – can be tiring too. It's a fine balance.

Sometimes I set out to be an appearance activist, other times I just find myself being one by going about my daily life.

25

Who does awareness raising benefit?

The calendar year is filled with awareness months for impairments and illnesses. I can't keep up. May is Ichthyosis Awareness Month.

While I did a lot for Ichthyosis Awareness Month for many years — including running dozens of blog posts by people with ichthyosis and their family members — since 2013, I haven't felt like participating anymore, because awareness for awareness's sake is of little benefit to the community it purports to serve.

I feel it's not on us with the condition to create more awareness. People know we are here. It's not on us to educate at every opportunity, nor to be kind to those who are not kind to us when they see our visibly different faces and bodies.

Despite awareness raising, adults with ichthyosis find it hard to get employment — because employers are scared of how our

Awareness for awareness's sake is of little benefit to the community it purports to serve.

skin looks, and they underestimate our abilities. Others and I still experience exclusion, rudeness, stares and discrimination on a daily basis – despite awareness raising. We are expected to be teachable moments during every difficult encounter – even by people in the ichthyosis community. I'm bloody tired.

In recent times, a cleaner ran away after seeing my face, a woman laughed at me several times, not believing I was born like this, I was refused a seat on the tram, taxi drivers have been scared, I was told what a shame it is that I look like this, and there have been countless other times when I just wanted to get on with my day and not have to deal with stares and comments and ridicule.

These people were all 'aware' of my presence. I educated them as much as I wanted to in the heat of the moment.

I've been asked to take part by changing my social media profile pictures. I don't feel that changing my profile picture to a logo will help those ignorant and rude people I encounter on the street to treat me any better.

I still read stories of young kids being treated with disgust, exclusion, and heightened curiosity – people demanding to know what is 'wrong' with them. Things have not changed since I was their age. I do think it's important to connect with other people with ichthyosis – to provide advice, and to make each other feel less alone. That I will continue to do, and encourage others to do too.

But making other people more 'aware' by making them feel more comfortable with our visibly different appearance is tiring. I'd rather celebrate difference – talk about pride, think about the broader issues of disability politics – than furiously raise 'awareness'. I feel it's important we do things for us, rather than to make our ichthyosis more bearable for others.

And despite myself and hundreds of others raising awareness, there is still hate speech on Reddit, and stolen photos of people with ichthyosis posted on YouTube and Facebook – dripping with ridicule and exploitation.

We still have to explain why we look like this, tell people we aren't contagious, and receive stares, comments and ridicule regularly. One friend, a parent of a little boy with ichthyosis, experienced swarms of concerned people at an event asking why they let their child get so sunburnt, and even calling the police. Another friend endured a nurse calling child protection because they thought she wasn't looking after her child properly. Both these friends continually raise awareness.

Anyway, despite awareness raising, there's little acceptance. While I am proud that I've helped to change perceptions of people with ichthyosis (and other facial differences and disabilities), I'm also jaded. Will these awareness months ever be about us looking inwards and finding self-acceptance, rather than looking outwards to make others accept us?

In the name of 'raising awareness', parents share well-meaning yet undignified photos and videos of their children with ichthyosis. The content should be kept private. I've seen some pretty horrific images and videos on public Facebook pages and highly populated Facebook groups, including nudity, piles of skin, a baby still in its colloidal membrane and a screaming child in the bath. They've made me cry. This stuff belongs in the home, never to be photographed, and never on social media so others can say they've learnt something new.

Disabled people are not often afforded dignity throughout their lives. So it's crucial that it's demonstrated from the start – in the home – where children know that they can feel safe and have their privacy respected. Often medical treatment – including bathing, removing scale from the scalp and body, putting creams and dressings on – can be painful, messy and bloody. No one else needs to see this.

I wonder what will happen when the child's peers find the photos and videos on the internet. How much further ridicule will they endure? A friend with ichthyosis, similar in age to me, told me that she couldn't have coped if photos of her as a child were made public. She told me:

> My parents have some baby pics of me that were taken for a university treatment team I had when I was a baby. I was all red and raw. Had they been accessible to everyone (like internet-ish) and my peers stumbled across it during middle or high school, it would have ended me. Literally, I most likely would have killed myself because the teasing would have been unbearable. I was already depressed and suicidal in fifth or sixth grade because of my skin. I couldn't imagine as a pre-teen, teen, or even an adult having other people broadcast my skincare routine. If I even WANT people to see how hard it is to keep myself comfortable and look presentable, I would show them myself.

I wouldn't have coped either if my classmates, already teasing me and avoiding me at school, had found medicalised photos of me.

I know parents do this to raise awareness with the best intentions. But private groups of hundreds of people or more aren't private.

And a public Facebook profile certainly isn't. As well as the risk of sexual predators, there's the risk of hate speech and image misuse. When a video of a baby with ichthyosis is viewed tens of thousands of times and is shared thousands of times, I guarantee that not all of the shares and comments will be positive.

I've been shouted down and blocked for speaking up for privacy and dignity. I've lost a lot of friends for wanting to protect other people's privacy. Activism can be a lonely and isolating road.

I wonder whether those adults without ichthyosis, who are doing the oversharing, would like their images shared in this way, images of private acts like bathing or period stains on bedsheets, in the name of awareness raising. It hurts. It hurts me and it hurts all of us.

Despite awareness raising, there are still uninformed, sensationalist media claims that ichthyosis is caused by marriage between relatives. Documentaries with titles like *Snakeskin Woman* don't respect their subjects, and heighten fear and stigma around the condition. No official ichthyosis support organisation has spoken up to say this language is abhorrent or raised awareness with journalists about how to write about us. I do it a lot – I'm the angry woman calling out language.

Snakeskin Woman was a documentary about a friend. She rejected the label 'snakeskin woman' in the show, but the title was still used. Parents of children with ichthyosis said it was awareness raising, no matter how the name tarnished the ichthyosis community. It still invited viewers to gawk, and incited fear by likening us to snakes. Sometimes 'Mermaid Baby' is used, which is much cuter – although it still dehumanises us.

Raising awareness can be an echo chamber. The majority of people raising awareness are those with the condition, or our family members. The shit that happens to us constantly makes us tired, and so sometimes, even we don't want to raise more awareness. I'm not sure if it's awareness fatigue, apathy or the inability to handle another issue that isn't ours, but even those with the condition don't speak up when members of the ichthyosis community face injustice.

We need to move past raising awareness. People know we're here. We leave trails of skin like breadcrumbs. We need to get to acceptance – acceptance of our condition by others, and by ourselves.

Next May, and every Ichthyosis Awareness Month after, I hope for more than awareness raising and tokenism.

I hope individuals and companies take committed action to tangibly improve the lives of people with ichthyosis.

I hope that support groups employ people with ichthyosis.

I believe ichthyosis charities especially need to focus on supporting the everyday, rather than cures – offering advice about education support, helping with addressing online and offline bullying, and coaching for job seeking.

I hope more of us can meet in real life.

I hope more parents can listen to adults with ichthyosis and really respect and value our experience and advice (and so I'm thankful for the many who already do).

I hope the new generation of children with ichthyosis learn to love themselves, speak out about their experiences, and not feel the need to conform to a beauty ideal. Above all, I hope the ableism myself and so many others have endured stops at us, and these beautiful kids never have to experience it – because society is more aware and accepting.

And on a personal note, I hope the pain of my ichthyosis subsides a little so I don't spend so much time in bed. This isn't me slacking off. I've done a lot – through writing and speaking. And I live it. I exist as a teaching moment, whether I like it or not.

Raising awareness about ichthyosis is a start. But it's up to those without the condition to remove their prejudices and judgements about our appearance and medical needs so they can accept and include us. Over to you.

Awareness raising is based on the medical and charity models of disability – our bodies are seen as the problem, something to be fixed, and we are seen as objects of pity and charity who need to rely on other people's goodwill to live life. And so it's often non-disabled people who are in charge of these campaigns, exploiting us.

Sometimes the awareness and fundraising initiatives around disability are a complete contradiction to their cause, have no correlation, or even make light of the issue. They don't align with disability rights. And they quite often don't even involve the voice of the people they're raising awareness and funds for. I've seen absurd and downright offensive awareness and fundraising activities – like Odd Socks Day to raise money for mental health support (they use the tagline 'because anyone can have an odd day'), and parents slathering themselves in ointment to experience what their child with ichthyosis experiences (why not ask the child?). There is a Parkinson's Walk in the Park ('Parkinson's is no bloody walk in the park,' my friend Elisha Friday Wright says). Then there are the simulations for non-disabled people ('disability drag' as another friend calls it), like wearing nappies and using walkers to empathise with residents in aged care homes, or being locked in a glass box, supposedly to emulate the experience of autism. These simulations often replace actually interacting with disabled people.

There are also awareness campaigns that do nothing for awareness – like asking people to post their underwear colour or a heart emoji on their Facebook profile for breast cancer awareness. (I think it's more productive to share guides to checking your breasts, or links to breast cancer support organisations, or even checking in with friends who've had cancer when a high-profile person dies from the disease.)

The campaign #selfiesforsmiles encourages people to send in selfies so a dental company can donate money to an organisation that performs facial surgery on children with cleft lip and palate. I find it strange the company is using faces with beauty privilege to promote a facial difference cause. They're making it more comfortable by using people with beauty privilege, and are promoting the idea that an appearance cure is necessary. It screams the opposite to awareness – it promotes the idea that we need to change our faces to be accepted by ourselves and others.

Loud Shirt Day supposedly supports deaf children, however only those who choose to hear and speak – not those who sign. People wear loud shirts, have a laugh and raise money for an organisation that helps kids to hear. The people participating in Loud Shirt Day have hearing privilege. They are overlooking Deaf culture and think a cure is best. All the proceeds go towards the medical model industry that is already heavily funded and supported. The same status is not given to Auslan (Australian Sign Language).

Drisana Levitzke-Gray, Young Australian of the Year 2015 and Deaf activist, says:

> Loud Shirt Day is all about hearing and speaking. Auslan and Deaf community barely get any funding, if any, and we're the ones who support families and their children when they come to us linguistically and cognitively delayed due to not having full access to language from birth.

There should not be any prejudicial bias. It all comes down to what is best for the Deaf children, and best means giving them everything – starting with Auslan.

September seems to create punny fundraising initiatives. From Steptember – to help children with cerebral palsy to walk, to Liptember – to kiss the blues goodbye. If only it was so easy.

Often actually disabled people are excluded from awareness campaigns and charities – through inaccessibility, a lack of paid staff and board positions, or just because we make potential donors uncomfortable.

Sonia Marcon, a performer and writer, tells me:

> When I was first diagnosed with Multiple Sclerosis (MS), I saw that the MS society of WA was putting on a production of *Les Miserables* to raise money and awareness of MS. I contacted them because the year before, I had been in a production of *Les Miserables* where I played one of the leads (Eponine) and I wanted to find out if I could audition for the show. I said that it would be great publicity to have someone in the show who has the condition the show is there for. I was told that all the main characters

were pre-cast with performers from the Eastern states. I was also told that the production will not cast someone with MS. I asked them why, and they said that the show is to raise awareness of MS not to offer parts to people with MS. I said that I didn't want a part, I just wanted to audition for a chorus member or something. They said no and that was that.

It was particularly hard because the MS hadn't progressed as much as it has now, so I would have been completely able to do the show. I was still coming to terms with what the MS was possibly going to do in the future, and being told 'no you can't do that' by the MS Society was a real head fuck.

And then there are rubber wristbands. While money from purchases of the wristbands goes to charities, the wristbands don't do as much. It's really hard to see a diagnosis imprinted onto rubber on someone's wrist — and it's out of context too.

Championing rights is much better. I love seeing what some of the mums in the ichthyosis community are doing to change the world for their children and others.

Laurie, a friend in the USA, has been calling and emailing US senators, campaigning for adequate healthcare in the USA since the Trump administration proposed cuts to Medicaid and changes to the *Americans with Disabilities Act of 1990*. She is one of the few ichthyosis parents I've noticed openly campaigning alongside the actually disabled activists. I know she's tired, but I'm so thankful and hopeful because of her work.

Silje in Norway has a young daughter, Marion, with ichthyosis. She's worried about costly changes to prescriptions, and so, in late 2017, she started telling her story on Facebook to show the politicians how this will affect her family. She has also been contacting a lot of politicians on a more private level, and contacted doctors, newspapers and TV stations too.

Silje is making a real difference – not just for Marion but countless other chronically ill and disabled children in Norway.

Allies like Laurie and Siljie are sticking their necks out with us, shouldering the burden. I appreciate them sharing the activism load. They're good allies.

It can be hard speaking out about the problems with awareness and fundraising activities because it's seen as biting the hand that feeds us. We're told we should be grateful for prominence, grateful that we are being helped – even if it's not on our own terms. But we can question the campaigns and try to influence them. We can push for the awareness to benefit us, rather than make non-disabled people comfortable.

How do we move from awareness to acceptance and inclusion?

- Encourage and celebrate pride
- Put looking for a cure on hold
- Tell your story on your own terms
- Participate in patient-led media
- Consult with actually disabled people
- Encourage connections with others
- Don't erase our disability.

26

Scary face – Big-screen baddies and Halloween

Stacey, a friend of mine who has a cleft palate, says:

> I dislike it when horror movie characters are depicted as having facial abnormalities because of 'inbreeding'. I've lost count of the amount of times I've seen clefts and other facial anomalies depicted as being something that only happens to inbred weirdos, and that really bothers me because it's not at all true.

Disability and facial difference representation in popular culture still has a long way to go. Have a think about why you are afraid of facial difference – why you look away at the ugly. Did it start with reading and watching fairytales and action films about heroes and villains? Did it start with the dress-up box?

When I was a small child, about three years old, I had a Snow White doll and a wicked stepmother doll. Snow White, of course, was beautiful – pale skin, ebony hair and a yellow and blue silk (probably highly flammable nylon) dress with puffed sleeves. The wicked stepmother had a disfigured face. She was yellow, wrinkled and contorted, with a pronounced nose – complete with a wart on the tip – and long, sharpened fingernails. I remember being scared of her – hiding my face when my parents brought her to me, playing with her less than I did with Snow White, and even speaking badly to and of her. I stored her with her face down, not wanting to scare my other dolls. She was a plastic doll, for goodness sake, but because she looked different, she scared me. Her wickedness was depicted by her appearance. And, ironically, I didn't know any better.

Sometimes when a small child sees me, they are scared, and vocalise or gesticulate their fears. They tell their parents they're scared or hide behind their parents' legs. Honestly, this saddens me – I don't want to scare anyone. I think that it's because they've not seen people with visible differences before, but I also believe it's because they have seen masks and screen characters who are depicted as evil. Think Freddy Kruger and Two-Face from Batman. Does this evil come about because the characters are lashing out over the misfortune of looking different and the associated social reactions?

I went to see *Wonder Woman* in 2017. I really enjoyed it – loved Diana's strength, resilience, no-bullshit attitude and her belief in love. The costumes were amazing. But you know what saddened me? That the villain – Doctor Poison – had a facial difference. (Spoiler: she took her mask off to reveal a scarred face.) There was no backstory about why she had a facial difference. She was evil, intent on killing people using chemical warfare – and so the filmmakers gave her a facial difference.

I am tired of the trope that beauty equals good and facial differences equal evil.

I have blogged about the issues with facial difference in Disney's *Beauty and the Beast*. 'But it's just a movie; stop ruining the childhood magic,' people cried. Oh yes they did! But when I raised the issue of Doctor Poison on Facebook and Instagram, there wasn't the same outcry. Perhaps people are thinking more broadly – because of exposure and discussion about facial difference. When people tell me they are thinking more about representation because of my work, it makes me happy.

I hope *You Can't Ask That* has helped too. I think it's definitely allayed people's fears around facial differences. Since *You Can't Ask That*, I've seen a lot of Ellen, one of the participants with a facial difference. Our friendship is cemented by the experiences of stares and being othered, and also our love of fashion. We've been recognised in the street, and it's such a thrill. People's responses have been so positive – they aren't frightened at all.

A character like Doctor Poison, with evil depicted by a facial difference, is the reason a child hides behind their parents when they see me. A character like Two-Face is why the cleaner was scared of my face and ran away. A character like Freddy Kruger is the reason Ellen and I were sent violent tweets, first saying *Jesus Christ what's wrong with your face?* and then a photo of a man holding a gun to his head, with the caption *here you should watch this.*

In my lifetime, I want to see a character with a facial difference as someone who puts people at ease, not instils fear. I want to see a person with a facial difference save the world, not destroy it.

Representation matters. If we're going to talk about how empowering *Wonder Woman* was, why can't we have a character with a facial difference who is empowering too?

Halloween, on 31 October, is a celebration steeped in supernatural and superstitious traditions. On this primarily US celebration – which is creeping into Australian culture – some people costume up in scary face.

They wear scary face masks and characterise themselves as well-known evil characters with facial disfigurements. Most of the scary face masks depict evil, and are designed to shock. Halloween masks change Halloween goers' faces into scarred, burned, contorted, eyeless, skinless characters.

But what about the people who live with visible differences for their whole life? Our faces are not costumes, and nor should our faces be appropriated in them. Children celebrate Halloween, and through masks and costumes they are given a negative message about facial difference from an early age.

While I might be raining on the candy wrapper–littered parade, I wonder why scary face is still tolerated. Sure, Halloween is a bit of fun, with trick or treating and a chance to dress up, but what message does dressing up as scary face give about people living with facial difference? That people with disfigurements are to be feared, and mocked on this holiday? And why should people with disfigurements be mocked?

In my lifetime,
I want to see a
character with a
facial difference
save the world,
not destroy it.
Representation
matters.

James Partridge, founder and former CEO of Changing Faces, the leading UK charity supporting and representing people with facial difference, has spoken about the impact of disfigured screen characters. He also writes about Halloween masks on his blog:

> The ghoulish and scary face masks that are sold in the annual mini retail boom around Halloween – none of them are branded as 'let's pick on people with scars, eye patches and asymmetry'. They don't need to. Everyone accepts – unwittingly perhaps? – that this is the time of year when children dress up to scare the wits out of others … and if the face masks are extreme, they simply reflect the idea that skulls and skeletons are ghostly and scary.
>
> Is this OK?
>
> Every year, Changing Faces has a problem with Halloween. We debate it but always end up concluding that whilst it is tiresome to have facial disfigurement associated with evil (again), we don't want to be kill-joys – and actually some children with disfigurements find the whole event rather fun too, able to indulge themselves behind a mask without worrying.

Perhaps for some with visible differences, Halloween is a chance to hide behind a mask, to temporarily change our appearance. I have a young friend with a facial difference, Corbin, who enjoys dressing up for Halloween and Comic-Con. I've seen some gorgeous pictures of him getting into the spirit of things – with face paint, armour and zombie poses. His mum Roni tells me, 'I have been approached at Comic-Cons and asked where Corbin got his mask. I always wondered what they thought he was dressing up as.'

Another young friend with ichthyosis loves trick or treating, but a few people have asked him whether he's painted his face. (A question I sometimes get: 'I see you've painted your face tonight – a fancy dress party?')

As a child, I hated wearing a mask because of how it scratched my skin and left me feeling dry. But at times, I did want to have a different face. I wonder if there are children with visible differences who celebrate Halloween who wear masks depicting beauty, rather than scary face. Princesses and princes, characters they admire and appearances they aspire to?

Maybe scary face isn't harming anyone – though to me it seems so similar to black face and cultural misrepresentation, and stereotyping of people with visible differences. I'd like to see scary face ruled out as a Halloween costume. Maybe we can complain to costume manufacturers and distributors, requesting them to remove such masks from sale, explaining the offensive portrayal. Halloween revellers need to choose their costumes more cautiously. I know – the fun police strikes again – but there are so many ways to dress up at Halloween without being offensive. Personally, if I celebrated Halloween, I'd go in a unicorn onesie.

27

That radio interview

You might have heard a difficult interview I did with a well-known radio host on ABC Melbourne early in 2018. I was invited on the program after performing at the Wheeler Centre, where I spoke about how to be a good non-disabled feminist – similar to the material in the chapter of the same name in this book. Before that interview, I had a strong relationship with the ABC – as a regular guest on radio, doing the occasional TV appearance and writing opinion pieces for the ABC website.

The radio host is a powerful, middle-class, middle-aged, non-disabled white man, who has his own radio show every day. He had a regular co-host with him – a female writer and broadcaster. There was a power imbalance – two older, non-disabled, white and experienced broadcasters and me. I felt nervous before the interview. But I was reassured that it would be fine, that the host was lovely, and at worst, he'd call me a 'snowflake' in jest.

I arrived in the waiting area, met the host briefly, and then he went to the bathroom. The co-host asked me how to pronounce ichthyosis. I do not recall any briefing about what could and couldn't be asked. I trusted that this seasoned broadcaster would be professional.

Just before 10 o'clock, I was taken into the studio where I'd been many times as a guest before. I asked his co-host if the sit-stand desk could be lowered. It was a half-hour interview and my legs were not up to standing for the whole time. The producer did so, but when the host returned to the studio, he asked who had lowered his desk. I told him it was me. He seemed inconvenienced by it.

I was asked to speak about microaggressions – the exclusionary and discriminatory ways I'm often treated. Unfortunately, his interview demonstrated the microaggressions very clearly. He began by describing my appearance: 'I've never met you before. You look like you are a burns victim.' He later added, 'It can't be good at Halloween.'

Was this a case of him not extending past his own experience? And even if he had never met me, was it really appropriate for him to describe my appearance on live radio – had he ever done that to another guest?

He asked me what was the most offensive question I've been asked – and I said that it was whether I can have sex. I tried to move on, but he said, 'Hang on, what's the answer?'

I laughed off the question, stunned he had asked it, a bit lost for words – and I didn't want to prolong the awkwardness. He spoke flippantly about former ABC staff member Stella Young's death. 'And then she went and died on us,' he said.

And he insisted that people praying for me have the best intentions and that I should welcome them, despite me not wanting prayers. He said, 'I don't believe in Jesus. But if someone wants to pray for me, that's fine. Thank you very much. I'll take that as their version as giving me good wishes …'

I remained cool and calm — answering his questions clearly and politely. But I was uncomfortable. *Did he just say that?! No! He did it again! Maybe it will improve … it's OK, I'm used to these comments.*

A caller rang in, telling him that she had never heard him describe another guest's appearance as he had mine. I was thankful someone had picked up on it.

At the end of the interview, I thanked him and the producers, smiling, with little time to process what had happened.

After the interview, I bumped into two of my music idols in the ABC foyer — Tim Rogers and Julia Zemiro — and told them what had just happened. When summarising the interview for them, it dawned on me just how inappropriate it was. Then I went back to work, just down the road at Melbourne Fringe. When I told my colleagues what had happened, they all gasped and fell silent. No! He didn't!

At the end of my workday, I checked my Twitter and a friend had live-tweeted the interview, summarising what had been said, and her feelings about the host's ableism and intrusion. Her tweets went viral, with many people in the media and the general public weighing in. I didn't create the social media storm — others did. That evening, after debriefing by telephone with the co-host — who told me she was mystified and disappointed by aspects of the conversation — I blogged briefly, sharing the audio file the producers sent me, and writing that this interview was demonstrative of the microaggressions and intrusions I face. I tweeted the link to my blog, and shared it in a few Facebook groups, not anticipating the reaction.

That night, I was a trending topic on Twitter and Facebook. And the next day, it was all over the media – running into the following week, even. My phone didn't stop ringing or buzzing.

The host apologised on-air the day after the interview, apparently his first apology in 21 years.

On advice from my agent, I chose to do two media interviews – in *The Age* and on *The Project* – and the story was covered by many other outlets. In my interview on *The Project*, I welcomed a personal conversation with the radio host, but that didn't happen. I only received an apology from a senior manager and heard his apology on air.

And I was careful in how I responded to the social media outrage. I didn't share any news story apart from *The Project*, I expressed my love for the ABC, and didn't berate the host, instead offering gentle education like sharing a video I made (ironically, for the ABC) offering tips for journalists covering disability.

So many people reached out to see if I was OK, and to offer praise on how I handled it – from Yassmin Abdel Magied, who has experienced her fair share of media storms, to comedian Hannah Gadsby, a number of ABC staff and even Andrew Denton, one of my favourite interviewers. Lisa Wilkinson called me 'grace personified'. Strangers in the street congratulated me. My workplace was wonderful, asking how they could support me. A lot of people had heard the interview.

I also had a revelation – because I hadn't seen such a reaction before. It's rare that non-disabled people call out ableism and discrimination – usually it's left up to disabled people to fight. But the public had my back. Perhaps the work that I and so many other disabled people are doing to highlight disability rights issues is becoming a part of the public consciousness. They recognised ableism and spoke out against it. I was thankful.

But I worried that I didn't speak up enough. While I didn't read many online comments, and resorted to stopping comments on my own blog, I noted that some people questioned why I let the interview continue.

Why didn't I tell him it was inappropriate? Partly because I didn't quite believe what was happening – the interviewer has had an extensive media career, speaking to all sorts of different people, and I assumed he would realise what was appropriate, or not.

I also feel a lot of pressure on live radio, even if I know the subject well. You have to think on your feet, take questions, and I suspect for women especially, not be too shrill.

Why didn't I walk out of the interview? That would have caused a bigger scene. Imagine how much more media attention there would have been if I had stormed out. And it might have hampered future media opportunities – not just with the ABC.

I wanted to, and still want to, be calm and professional. So I remained composed, I continued the interview even when I was uncomfortable, I thanked the host and his producer afterwards and left on good terms. Because that's who I am.

Also, I didn't realise quite how bad it was during the interview because these comments happen all the time. The things he said to me are things I have encountered before. For me it was a regular experience – but in an amplified medium, with an audience. People got to hear it firsthand.

I also believe in the power of letting people show who they are when they carry out ableism. It demonstrates how ableist they are, no matter how well meaning, no matter the intention. I could be the bigger person.

During the media storm, some disability activists suggested I talk about wider disability issues in the media while I had the chance, to shift the focus from me. Disabled people get so little media time – we're all clamouring to be heard – so I understand why there was this pressure. I did my best, but I only had four and a half minutes on live TV.

The media around this radio interview was overwhelmingly positive. And I was grateful for the tone of the coverage. I didn't read the Facebook comments, and this did wonders to keep me calm.

But I would have loved to see disabled writers commissioned to report on the story. It would have been refreshing to read an article by a disabled writer with a different view.

The thing I was most worried about was that this situation would hamper my future with the ABC. And I felt it did. I wasn't invited back to ABC Melbourne as a guest for three months – when a friend was filling in as a host. My pitches for interviews were ignored, despite having been a regular guest for over six months prior to the interview. They unfollowed me on Twitter. I have since been asked to work with other areas of the ABC, on both a paid and unpaid basis, but my relationship with ABC Melbourne seems fractured. I was left feeling punished, a liability.

I can't contort myself to fit into a non-disabled world. While I can't leave my identity or appearance behind in my work, I also expect to be treated with the same level of respect as other people in the media.

I feel that non-disabled people expect us to be compliant, to be nice and educative. I feel the burden of making them comfortable with the other, rather than them making us comfortable. The message seems to be that disabled people should never get too loud about ableism. We must be grateful for what we are given. As Ruby Hamad wrote in her brilliant *Guardian* essay: 'Whether angry or calm, shouting or pleading, we are still perceived as the aggressors.'

When I am invited to participate in the media, and the hosts perpetuate the behaviour I speak about, it is exhausting and disrespectful. I'd also *love* to do media where I don't have to give a description of what I look like in order for me to qualify to talk about that topic. I don't see people who are specialists in other areas do this. Having someone describe my appearance, as they see it, is never comfortable; neither is expecting me to, instead of taking me for my qualifications and expertise.

If the media reference the work I do, and say they value it, they could at least try to show that I have taught them something about disability pride or ableism or discrimination or identity or microaggressions. They need to demonstrate their commitment to inclusion and diversity by giving us the chance to call them in or out when they've let us down.

This was not the only uncomfortable interview or speech I've done. I've experienced intrusion, condescension and ableism before. This is the nature of my work now, this is the price of performing awareness and education for an audience.

Many articles have been written about this radio host since that interview, and in every one of them, I've been mentioned. It makes me uncomfortable – my name being used as clickbait every time he's in the news. There's more to me than that interview.

I get the feeling that disabled people are sometimes brought into the media and corporate organisational settings as a token gesture. We are expected to say that they are doing a great job, and when we don't, we are seen as troublemakers. I am worn out, because I know they aren't even listening. I wonder if it's better to help influence the mindset of the public, or talk to my own people. Can I do both?

If I've taught the media anything, I want to see that they are willing to change. I want them to invite me back even when I've been assertive. And I want the chance to talk to my own people through the media – because I know firsthand how alone they might feel.

I hope I talk to this host again one day. Off air, and then perhaps on air. I hope I can talk about why the interview was so inappropriate, that it held a magnifying glass to the microaggressions I face on a regular basis. And I hope I can talk to him about the importance of the reporting guidelines developed by People with Disability Australia. If he and the ABC give me that chance, it will show the power imbalance is truly shifting.

28

Emotional labour

There is a moment in comedian Hannah Gadsby's show *Nanette* when she says she identifies as 'tired'. I laughed so much at this, because it's true for me too. In this book, I've written a lot about being tired, exhausted and overwhelmed. And ultimately, I think that comes down to the emotional labour attached to being disabled.

Emotional labour is the work it takes to explain what it feels like to be marginalised – the discrimination, the microaggressions, and even just helping people understand disability rights, culture and pride. That's my job, right?

When I write or speak about disability rights issues, and my own experiences, the audience often wants and expects me to give them more – more time, more information, more support. Of course, I want to help, but like everyone else, I have my limits.

I often endure the expectation to perform emotional labour when I write about the discrimination that happens to me. People ask me for advice so *they* can do better. But I don't want to be asked for *further* advice about how you should respond to people who look different, when I've just experienced a discriminatory incident. It can be exhausting.

Emotional labour can also be the result of well-intentioned requests – the media and the general public wanting to do better. They ask for resources on reporting disability, or quotes for articles, advice for how to talk to their kids about disability or links to things myself and others have written.

Sometimes people want me to make a complaint about offensive media or an issue, because they don't think they can do it themselves. They'll tag me on social media, asking me to respond. But it's not the job of a marginalised person to constantly make complaints, explain discrimination or tell people how to do better, or to congratulate privileged people for recognising and responding to discrimination.

When you see problematic or hurtful media about ichthyosis or disability in general, make a complaint. I hope you recognise this shit because of what I write about, and please don't let me be the one to always do the work. That's your role in being a good ally.

And there's also the assumption that I'll be available at all times – because social media is 24/7 and the news cycle never stops, and if I am unable to respond for whatever reason, I've let someone down. Late one Friday night I received a Facebook message from a woman in Europe. She asked me how she should react to someone with a facial difference – her mother always told her to look away but she wondered if she should talk to the person. I read the message, went to sleep and had a full Saturday of life admin, filing the message away in my mind to respond to when I got a moment. Late that Saturday night I received another message from this woman. It was rude and demanding and said my non-response had shaped the way she will interact with people with facial differences from here on. She told me she'll just continue to look away when she sees someone with a facial difference. And because I didn't answer the way she wanted, immediately and then with a pat on the head for asking the brave, life-improving question, she was rude to me. (On the up side, I collected another anecdote for this book!)

But I am not an on-call etiquette advice line. My number is allowed to be busy. And I can't be held responsible for how others choose to interact with disabled people. That's up to them.

My work might wear me down eventually. I continually tell my story, sometimes reliving my trauma. I'm not sure how much longer I can endure the emotional labour of performing my own story. These situations make me think about the work I do – I know there is great power in telling my own story, but there is also great emotional labour. When can I stop telling my own story and start telling a bigger story when I write and speak to an audience? It can be overwhelming to live what I write, and write what I live. The emotional labour of producing ichthyosis-related media on top of living with ichthyosis itself is heavy.

Emotional labour is also the damage – or fear of damage – to relationships when I talk about disability discrimination with friends and sometimes strangers. So often when I mention the use of disability slurs like the R-word, it ends in defensiveness on their end, and me being dropped as a friend.

Why is it more important to defend yourself from accusations of ableism than to listen to my story of experiencing it? How do

Why it is more important to defend yourself from accusations of ableism than to listen to my story of experiencing it?

we have proper conversations in which non-disabled people who use ableist slurs listen and reflect on how to do better? Is that too much to ask?

Emotional labour is getting up the courage to tell a child that them being scared of my face makes me sad – it could either end in a tantrum and me being told off by their parent, or an apology and a lovely conversation between us. These encounters often result in all the emotions – sadness, hesitancy, courage, happiness and tiredness, and are a reminder I'm working all the time.

Emotional labour is managing others' reactions to my appearance – while I'm trying to keep it together. When someone else – a fully grown adult – is scared of my face, and shows it, I feel like I have to make them comfortable. That is overwhelming. Impossible at times. I'm too busy managing other people's fragility to process my own.

My friend Namila Benson, a broadcaster, educator, writer and proud PNG black woman, talks about code switching – the need to lessen our identity to make it palatable for others. I do this often, by not speaking out, or being measured in my responses, for fear of the reaction or rejection. For example, I didn't feel comfortable speaking out more about what happened with ABC Melbourne, because I worried about losing media opportunities and creating further tension with the radio host. I've done this with other media outlets – stayed silent and avoided confrontation, and even played down my identity a little, as they have the power. This is emotional labour too.

And then there are the invalidations. The emotional labour of explaining disability, and writing about my experiences only to have them invalidated, can be exhausting. People question whether the discrimination or microaggressions actually happened, or excuse the behaviour, citing good intentions.

Living with ichthyosis every day, it becomes really easy to pick up on tones, comments, stares, and so on. Receiving pushback after talking about these encounters is often as damaging as the actual encounter. Disabled people need advocates, not devil's advocates, when we tell our stories. We should be treated as reliable witnesses. Please don't play devil's advocate in order to justify ableism and discrimination.

The emotional labour that I perform, on top of living with ichthyosis and experiencing discrimination, is huge and tiresome. I need to schedule time out.

29

The ichthyosis community – finding my tribe

It is critical for disabled people to find a sense of community … Our strength comes from the relationships with other disabled people that we create, whether these are online or in person, and the lifelong mentorship that these relationships foster.'

Alaina Leary, *The New York Times*

Adam and I packed the car early one Saturday morning in May 2015. The weather was cool – perfect for people with skin conditions. My parents were going to meet me there. I was jiggly with excitement. This was the first time a large group of people with ichthyosis had met in Australia. And I'd created it. I was so proud.

It's so important to connect with others who relate. Meeting people with ichthyosis has changed my life. Meeting people with other types of facial differences has been wonderful too. There is power in connection and seeing ourselves in others.

As mentioned, I never saw anyone like me in ads or on the TV when I grew up. In my late teens, there was a program called *Medical Incredible* that featured two girls with ichthyosis. But that was it. Seeing someone with ichthyosis on TV or in an ad would have been brilliant, but meeting someone in person would have been so much better. But the condition is so rare, and I grew up in such a very small, isolated town – pre-internet of course – that there was no chance of meeting anyone. It was only likely in the rare instance a doctor put my family in touch with another family via letter writing, or if I bumped into someone in a medical setting, like the woman I met at a conference in my teens, the one who was chasing a cure. Now, with the internet, that's changed of course.

The ichthyosis meet, which was held at the Melbourne Zoo, was one of the best days of my life. I know it changed people's lives, too.

Seventy-five people attended – 25 of those have ichthyosis. Some of the attendees had never met anyone else with the condition before. This event was life-changing – for the attendees and for me. It was the best day of my life next to my wedding!

I coordinated crowdfunding, promoted the event, booked the venue, sourced sponsors to provide gifts for goodie bags, and kept the attendees informed about the event in the lead-up. I asked doctors to do a panel discussion, although this wasn't a medical event – it had a social focus. Most attendees had never met another person with ichthyosis before. Advice was exchanged, and strong friendships were formed. We had dinner afterwards, and lots of laughs were had across all ages. It was such an amazing day. I am so proud. I created the event I'd wanted and needed as a child.

I first met Jeff Gridley, a young man with ichthyosis, in 2007. He was only the second person with ichthyosis I had met, apart from woman at the conference when I was a teen. Jeff has a different type of ichthyosis from mine, although we have similar issues with our eyes. He's a bit older than me and lives in Brisbane. I met him briefly, before seeing Darren Hayes in concert. I kept my distance – perhaps back then I wasn't ready to see ichthyosis as big a part of my identity as I do now. I regret not seeing the meeting as life-changing at the time. Upon reflection, Jeff was my first real-life role model, someone who showed me what was truly possible career-wise. I think his deteriorating eyesight scared me though; I worried that my eyes would also deteriorate like his. (Some people with ichthyosis have ectropian eyelids, where the lower lids don't have enough elasticity to hold in tears, and eyes dry out, becoming scratched. It can lead to blindness.) I felt a sense of curiosity when meeting Jeff – could it be the way a stranger feels when they meet me?

Jeff wanted me to connect with a young family, though back then I lacked the confidence. I have since met that family – their teenage girl with ichthyosis is a delight. I regret not reaching out earlier. And Jeff has become an excellent friend and ally who I talk to online regularly. He's compassionate and committed to making a difference to society – a long-term Cub Scout leader like my husband. And he's given me lots of advice – from how to respond to discrimination to what to do when I burn myself at work (run it under cold water and get to the hospital as quickly as possible, FYI).

Jack was the next person I met. I met his family while I was in London in 2012. He was four then. Looking at his face was like looking into a mirror. We've met a couple of times since. His parents, Danny and Julie, have done a lot to raise money for ichthyosis research in the UK, and we've become firm friends and supporters of each other's work.

And since then I've connected with hundreds of people with ichthyosis – from tiny babies to women in their sixties. I regard so many people with ichthyosis as my close friends – because we are so rare, opportunities to meet each other arise, and I count that as good luck. I've also become close to a handful of parents – online and in person. While some ask me for advice, many of our friendships transcend ichthyosis. We talk about all sorts of things – not just skin. I want to give them hope for their child in the future.

In 2014, my friend Friday and I coordinated a fundraiser for Tina, who lives in India. Tina does it tough with her ichthyosis – it's much different from my life in Australia. It's medically, socially and financially challenging. She has been excluded from her community her whole life, and three-quarters of her wage goes towards her medical costs. The heat in India is particularly difficult for her condition. People are afraid to shake her hand, and when she was a child, mothers wouldn't let her play with their children because they thought she had leprosy. Tina's mother raised her alone, while working as a medical missionary. Tina spent a long time caring for her mother, which placed greater financial strain on her. When her mother died in 2014, Tina really struggled. We raised $1100 for Tina. This bought her a cooling vest and also some medical supplies and treatments.

In 2015, I did a social media–based ointment/fundraising drive for a baby with ichthyosis in the Philippines. His family can't access advanced medical treatment. Tight skin stopped blood-flow and fused his hands and feet. He's blind. He didn't have enough ointment to last him a month. With his mother's permission, I asked people to send creams or money for me to purchase them. I mailed three boxes of ointment. I posted photos of him and his family receiving the parcels on social media so people could see how they helped. This boy's health improved. He is now a chubbier, happier little boy.

In September 2017, a mother of a child with ichthyosis reached out, asking to meet with me fairly urgently. She was new to Australia, and had little local family support. She and her son met my husband and me at the Collingwood Children's Farm. We looked at the animals and talked about life with ichthyosis. Her child is filled with joy and energy. I told her how important it is to instil pride in her child, to listen to him when he's in pain/hot/cold/itchy, and that it does get better. We also talked about the importance of connecting with others who have ichthyosis – so her child has people to look up to and empathise with and to see what's possible. I organised for another parent to send her a cooling vest for her son. And I put her in touch with a lot of other parents. She immediately felt like she had a new family around her.

I am so thankful to my online communities for supporting these people.

When I've met others with ichthyosis, especially women with Netherton syndrome or Harlequin ichthyosis, it's like we're sisters. We finish each other's sentences and laugh and gasp at the similar experiences we've had.

My friends with ichthyosis look very similar to me – like they are my family members. I've got a few doppelgängers. They span generations – some are 20, 30 years older than me, and others are toddlers. Genetic similarities thread through strangers across the world, giving us a sense of knowing and belonging, even though we might not know each other.

Sometimes, of course, this can be irritating. Once, when I was at a party, a friend introduced me to her friend, whose eyes immediately lit up. She thought she 'recognised' me. She told me she'd seen me on a friend's Facebook that week, and was adamant I'd been in Brisbane. I hadn't. She finally found the photo – her friend was indeed with a female with a red face. But it wasn't me. Her friend had met my friend Lucia (who was *nine* at the time), who also has ichthyosis (the same variation as me).

I got a little frustrated and told her that I knew she didn't mean harm, but I think there can a problem with people without disabilities seeing one person with a disability or facial difference and thinking they've seen them all. I also told her that my little friend was nine, and I was 33! (My beauty regime of paraffin and natural facial peels leaves me looking super youthful!) She understood where I was coming from and apologised.

I am mistaken for others with ichthyosis a lot. Sometimes people stop me to tell me they've seen me on *Embarrassing Bodies* or *Medical Incredible*. That wasn't me, I tell them. But yes, they've seen me and my sister, and how much I scrub my skin. And they ask me when I moved to Australia, because the show's subjects were English. And I tell them again, that wasn't me – I'm an only child and am Australian. They shrug and tell me, 'But you look just like them.' Yes. Yes; I do.

Professor Ingrid Winship, Professor of Adult Clinical Genetics at the University of Melbourne and Royal Melbourne Hospital, explains that the reason patients with genetic conditions look similar is a complex one. She told me:

> The DNA instructions that cause the health issues may also have an influence on the development of our facial structures. We are able to recognise faces from an early age, and it is possible that it is the relationship of facial features, i.e. how widely spaced one's eyes are or the shape of the chin, which people with some genetic conditions have in common, that create a 'pattern' that is easily recognised. A child with Harlequin ichthyosis, for example, may look more like another child with Harlequin ichthyosis than their own sibling.

My new friend from the party can be forgiven for mistaking two people with ichthyosis. The genetic explanation has taught me not to be so defensive when encountering these doppelgänger questions.

When I've met others with ichthyosis, it's like looking into a mirror, despite any age difference. We have similar face structures and hairlines, a slight build, and I've been told our pinky fingers and toenails are curled. It's like we are one family. Parents of children affected by the condition tell me about the cute instances of their child seeing another child with ichthyosis and thinking it's themselves. It must be such a relief for them to see others like them out there. It has been a relief for me.

Professor Winship continues:

> Being a bit technical, there is a recognised genetic effect called pleiotropy – that a change in one single gene can cause multiple effects on the body's health and appearance.

This is seen in Marfan syndrome, where the eye, the heart and the skeleton may all be affected by a single genetic change.

This similarity of appearance is an interesting phenomenon. I can't speak for others with ichthyosis, but I think it's pretty amazing that I have a whole 'family' out there that truly shares some of my experiences of what it's like to look different.

Often, when people with ichthyosis (or parents of children with the condition) come across my blog or social media profile, they are overwhelmed. I might be the first person they've ever found, or they might be surprised to find someone who looks just like them and experiences similar pain and social barriers. It can be such a privilege to be the person who guides them through a hard time, but it can be overwhelming too. There's a huge sense of responsibility.

Their reactions can vary – from relief, to shock, to telling me their whole life story, or disclosing graphic photos of painful, infected skin and more.

Parents have sent me photos of their children's genitals – in desperation to find answers. I've asked them how they'd feel if their genitals were shared with strangers? Other people have told me it's a 'sick joke' to find someone who looks just like them. Most people have simply been relieved to finally find someone they can relate to after a long (or short) time of feeling so alone.

Most often, though, they're grateful to connect with a person who knows what it's like to grow up with ichthyosis. It's really important to listen to our experiences – and also realise that what works for one person might not work for another. My friend Kaysie, mum to Lincoln, told me she appreciates my perspective as an adult:

> I've learnt so much from you regarding ichthyosis these last two years. I remember reading ALL of your blogs late into the night while Lincoln was in the Neonatal Intensive Care Unit. I learn so much from the ichthyosis adults, more from you guys than the doctors.

Meeting and seeing others with ichthyosis can be affirming, but it can also be confronting. Seeing someone who looks just like you, if you thought you didn't look that severe, might be hard to deal with. You might have spent your whole life – consciously or unconsciously – rejecting your diagnosis. I imagine if you've spent your whole life rejecting ichthyosis as part of your identity, and not seeing yourself in others, seeing someone who looks just like you could bring up all sorts of denial and discomfort. It's understandable to feel this way – but don't discount a friendship with someone because you're still coming to terms with your appearance or medical condition.

Support groups can be wonderful as they allow us to connect with other people who share similar medical and social experiences. But one-upmanship exists. Illness one-upmanship is one of the reasons I am not too keen on support groups for specific illnesses, because there is so much comparison about who has it worse.

I've been one-upped, several times. I've been told that my pain looks nothing compared to someone else's. I was offended by this.

Pain is relative. How do you know what my pain feels like? How can you assess that yours is worse than mine?

Once, someone posted in our ichthyosis Facebook community that other people with ichthyosis had doubted the severity of her condition, sending her nasty messages about her appearance, because it doesn't look ichthyosis-y enough. What? As with most chronic illnesses and disabilities, there are different variations of ichthyosis.

I wonder whether being around others with chronic illness and disabilities perpetuates one-upmanship, especially when those people are online. In 'support groups' (which aren't half as supportive as the title suggests) there is a race to the rarest. And I wonder if this hierarchy is perpetuated when some people with ichthyosis don't have a broad political view about disability, when they might not be aware of the social model, or reject it as party of our identities.

There are no wins in having it worse.

Medical shaming – the act of shaming people about their medical treatments – can also exist in support groups. It can occur when people don't think your way of treating your medical condition is right – to the extent of alarming you. Medical shaming feels harder when it comes from within your own community. And it concerns me that much of this medical shaming comes from people relatively new to ichthyosis. Newish parents. New spouses, hoping to cure their partner, because *love*. Many have no scientific knowledge or qualifications – jumping on science, cosmetic and sales jargon, making unfounded claims about products' success. Some people try to sell natural skincare products over prescribed ones, claiming petroleum is cancer-causing (it's not). Others spout false history, claiming ichthyosis was caused by 'unclean' Europeans who ate dirty meat and were involved in the sex industry in the 1500s–1700s. Talk about fear-mongering. And a few try to sell expensive and unproven products that I and other adults with ichthyosis have managed without all our lives. It's very opportunistic.

New parents have told me that when they encounter these salespeople, they feel guilty and worried they're not doing the right thing. I worry they target vulnerable new parents and families in developing countries where the priority is just getting clean water and basic ointments to stay alive. They don't need and can't afford a luxury item.

Just as you ask me to respect your religion, please respect my medical choices. This sort of advice, fear-mongering and guilting is not compassionate. It is divisive and dangerous. It's bullying. I worry about the impact it will have on new parents looking for information. I won't tolerate medical shaming from a well-meaning, yet unqualified and opportunistic, stranger.

My advice to people who feel overwhelmed in support groups is not to compare yourself to others. Everyone experiences impairments differently. What works for one person might not work for others. Don't rush out and buy an expensive bubble bath – learn from others who have managed our skin without expensive baths. And I encourage you to gain some confidence by drawing on the confidence of others. So often the people with the least obvious and severe types of ichthyosis are the most self-conscious – but those of us with severe ichthyosis who cannot hide it exude confidence, because we cannot easily pass as not having ichthyosis.

30

Letter to my little self

Dear all the little ones born with ichthyosis or a visible difference, and dear little me,

I want you to know that it will be OK. Life will be OK. Wonderful even.

There's a long journey ahead of you, with your daily care regime, specialist appointments and therapy. It will be hard – people will stare, say mean things and exclude you. I hope the children you grow up with are a little more aware and tolerant of diversity than when I was at school.

As you get a little older, it will get a lot easier. You find your tribe. It might be at school, or it might be in after school sports or a club. Or it might take a little more time – like when you get a part-time job after school or start college. You'll find friends who will love you for your entire being. The way you look won't matter to them, but they'll also be so considerate of it. When you're in the trenches, they'll be by your side, just like your family.

Your family will always have your back. Sometimes it will be hard for them to see you in pain – medically and emotionally – but that's because they love you. They'll be the ones to see the real you – how much skin you shed, how much cream you get on every single thing you touch, and praise you like you've just won a gold medal at the Olympics when you reach every milestone. They'll love and fight for you.

The love that you're surrounded with is so powerful. Take that love and show others the same. If you see someone who hasn't got many friends or looks a little different, bring them into your life.

Work hard at school and then at university or college, if that's what you choose to do after school. Sometimes we feel the need to prove ourselves when we look different. Don't put too much pressure on yourself – stress might make your skin sore.

You can be anything you want to be. I wanted to be a writer and speaker, and now I am. My ichthyosis hasn't stopped me; in fact, it's got me places. Looking different *will* get you noticed.

Try not to compare yourself to others too much. You're who you are – an amazing human being with so much to offer the world – and they are who they are. You may take a little more time to do things – and that's OK. The gold medal will be waiting for you. Sometimes it will be hard not being able to do things the same as others are doing – like going out in the heat, wearing sleeveless dresses and playing a lot of sports (those are the things I couldn't do – you may be able to do them). Try modifying some of these activities – like going to play outside when the sun goes down, wearing layers, and choosing a sport that doesn't hurt your skin too much.

My top two tips for daily care are: eat a good diet with plenty of fresh fruit, vegetables and protein. Ichthyosis means our bodies need lots of nutrients to grow new skin. I've also found that using sulfate-free shampoos and bath products is gentler on the skin and makes my hair grow better.

Have a laugh at yourself. There are lots of funny moments having ichthyosis. And seeing the funny side can help you through the dark days.

You don't have to explain the way you look to everyone who asks. It's none of their business. Just because you're used to being asked, doesn't mean you're going to be OK with being asked. You have the right to educate people on your own terms.

But when you do explain yourself, be polite (unless they aren't, and even so, be polite because it will make them feel worse!). Explain your needs to those who need to know and will help you. Your teachers and your future employers. It makes life a little easier for everyone.

Medical technology is advancing all the time. You may be asked to be involved in treatment trials or new creams. While actively seeking a cure hasn't been something that has interested or fulfilled me, I encourage you to try new things that may improve your life. But don't push yourself too much – sometimes seeking a cure can tire you out and compromise the great life you're already living.

Join a support group – you might be able to find one through hospital or online. If it doesn't work for you, you don't have to stay. Even just having a few people with ichthyosis in your life, in an informal way, can make a difference. Go on camps. No one will get you like others with similar conditions get you. And find a mentor who you can look up to and who can guide you. They'll benefit from this relationship as much as you will.

Wait until you are fully ready before travelling overseas. Travelling will be one of the most amazing things you'll ever do.

But cultural differences will mean that your appearance will make it hard to travel. You will need to be assertive and resilient. But when you do go, enjoy the wonderment of it all.

When you are upset, talk to someone. Tell your parents or your family, a teacher or adult friend you trust. Write your feelings down, or draw them in a picture. If things get really bad for you, talk to a professional counsellor. Don't keep your sad or angry feelings inside. You don't have to be alone.

There's beauty in difference. You're beautiful inside and out. Be proud of who you are. Look the world in the eye and smile.

Love,
Carly

Afterword: Finding pride

Some people have told me that they wish they had my confidence, my ability to tell my story so publicly, and my ability to stay positive. I can say, it's taken practice.

You don't have to do things my way. You don't have to have the same beliefs or acceptance as I do. But I do encourage you to believe in and accept yourself. Don't spend so much time hiding your body by covering up. It's much more freeing being comfortable in your skin than worrying and wishing it away. Wear that summer dress — sleeveless or with layers — and forget those who have told you that you shouldn't.

Start telling by your story in a small way. Write it down for yourself. If you haven't told your best friend or partner about your impairment, tell them. If you want to do media, find someone in the media who you trust.

If you feel confident to, share your experience with someone who might be facing something similar – a new parent, perhaps. When I reached out to a father of a newborn with ichthyosis, he said that he was so thankful and it felt like he was getting a hug from the world.

Take a selfie, post it – unfiltered – on your social media. You never know who else it might empower to show their face and feel they're not alone. Practise your pride – this takes time.

Find role models. Connect with others who are disabled – the internet is great for this. Read books and blogs. Watch the Paralympics. Share their pride. I am always amazed that while we are all different, we can relate because of the social model of disability.

It can help to have a box of tricks for the hard days. A list of standard answers or actions, so you can be on autopilot when the stares and comments get you down.

Have a standard, simple answer like 'I was born like this' or 'It's just a skin condition'.

Ignore them – there's no need to satisfy everyone's curiosity.

Address the comments and stares in one fell swoop – be in control of your story. Write a short piece in a school or work newsletter or on Facebook, or do a talk to the class or workplace, or play the movie *Wonder* with a pre-statement like, 'What Auggie experiences is what it feels like for me.'

Find something in common with the person who points out your difference. Often when a small child asks me about my face I'll say, 'I was born like this, like you were born with blue eyes.'

Write down a list of good things about yourself and reflect on those when you feel down.

Express yourself through drawing, painting, music or writing.

Connect with others. You don't even have to talk about ichthyosis. Just knowing there's someone else that experiences what you do is a good thing.

Remember, you don't owe it to anyone to explain the way you look or make them comfortable in your presence, and you really don't need to apologise.

And it's OK not to want to face the world on a bad day. Place yourself away from people when you eat at a restaurant, if it means you avoid the stares for a moment. Stay home from work if you're too sore. Go do something fun, just for you, and get back out there tomorrow.

Talk to people who understand the intrusiveness of strangers' questions and comments, and who can have a laugh with you at the mean or silly things people say – like when a man on the train asked me if I had been licking lollies, hands down the silliest thing I've been asked about my face.

If you face discrimination, write a complaint letter (and ask if a friend or family member can support you through the complaints process). Or at least write the experience down – to get it out of your system – and post it on social media so that others can see the difficult times you face, and maybe learn from it. Similarly, if you have a great experience, write that down too. Practise your pride – this takes time.

Stop consuming media that erases people like you. Make your own media to ensure people like you are included and visible. Social media is a great way to start – and to get noticed. Making your own media is also a way to connect with and build communities made up of people like you.

Remember, you are not the names people call you, and your body is not repulsive or a magnet for staring. You have every right to take up space in this world, and so you should. You are worthy of love – from others and yourself. You matter and you belong. You are not alone.

I hope that just as I've encouraged non-disabled people to say hello to people whose appearances scare them, that you will be brave enough to say hello to them too.

This pride and confidence I have built in myself took years. Sometimes it wavers – like when the really shit stuff happens – but after a cry, writing it out, a hug and some wine, I come back to pride. It took having the right people around me; respecting my medical choices and identity; seeking mentors in the disability community; and finding myself through my writing. It took looking at my face in the mirror, even when I felt too ugly and ashamed. It took showing up every day, even when I was made to feel I wasn't allowed to be there. It took talking nicely to myself.

I was determined and defiant, and sometimes I swore – because other people had not been nice. But on the whole, I go through my day smiling and greeting people, even when they look worried or fearful when they see me. Because I want to allay their fears and show them that yes, I am happy, and there is beauty where they don't expect it.

I realised that the people who throw their ignorance and hate at me are the ones with the issue, and I must not let them stop me from living my life. I have achieved despite their ableism – not despite my body, my appearance or my disability.

Pride in myself is a lot easier to live with than wanting to change myself. It will be for you too, I promise.

This book has, for the most part, been directed at people who don't have ichthyosis or who are not disabled. I wanted those people to see that the barriers caused by ableism and discrimination are more disabling than my body.

But the truth is, this book for you. I wrote it because I didn't have this book when I was young. I needed a friend on the page. I hope I have been that friend for you.

Pride in myself is a lot easier to live with than wanting to change myself. It will be for you too, I promise.

Acknowledgements

Say Hello is an angry book at times, so thank you to all of you for bringing me happiness and confirmation that there are so many wonderful people out there.

Thank you to everyone who has let me quote you in this book – thank you for telling your story and letting me share it. Erin Kyan, Stella Young, Jeanette and Roger Findlay, Caroline Jones, Ally Grace, Clementine Ford, Brodie Lancaster, Steve Carruthers, Laura Hershey, Tish Peiris, Camille Condon, Christina Ryan, Deborah Farley Adwell, Pip Lincolne, Sarah Blahovec, Lindy West, Larissa MacFarlane, Emily Ladau, Rebecca Shaw, Michelle Roger, Karolyn Gehrig, Savanna Addis, Drisana Levitzke-Gray, Sonia Marcon, Laurie Ann, Siljie Breines, Stacey Leigh Cash, James Partridge, Roni and Corbin Bowden, Rebekah Stewart, Jacki Petty, Alaina Leary, Professor Ingrid Winship, Jeff Gridley and Kaysie Berry. Thanks to Jessica Walton who read my words about beauty privilege before I sent it to the editor, and was honest, kind and thought provoking.

Thank you everyone who has read my blog and media articles, and who follows me on social media. Blogging led to a freelance career in the media, as well as many more exciting things. It has also brought me some wonderful friends. And this book wouldn't have happened without blogging. It still blows my mind when strangers stop me on the street to say they follow me on the internet – I hope that never stops happening.

Thank you to Jacinta di Mase who I met virtually, while I live-tweeted your words at the diverse women in media day at the Wheeler Centre in September 2016. Several months later, when I had publisher interest in this book when it was just a few notes on my iPad, I called you and asked what I should do. You immediately said yes to representing me. Thank you for your wisdom about contracts and royalties and all the things I don't understand.

To Danielle Binks at Jacinta di Mase Management – my agent, fashion advisor, curly girl empathiser and friend. I love that you give me pep talks about my work as well as advice on whether I should buy that dress. May we continue to wear the same outfit at the same event for many more years. Thank you for always cheering me on.

To Catherine Milne at HarperCollins – Jacinta was right when she said you're very cool. Thank you for believing in *Say Hello* from the start. You've been so warm and collaborative.

To Nicola Robinson, my editor at HarperCollins. You've been so patient with my ridiculously busy workload, and kind and gentle with your suggestions. You've asked all the right questions to draw more words out of me, and said FUCK in all the right places in the margins, and you've become my mum's biggest fan. Thank you for getting *Say Hello*, and me. I've loved working with you.

To Hazel Lam, HarperCollins designer extraordinaire – I LOVE the cover and page design of *Say Hello*. It is so very me.

To Lara Wallace, HarperCollins publicist – it has been fun working on marketing and publicity. I can't wait to tour this book with you!

To my teachers – I'm thankful for your education and mentoring. Your wisdom has stuck with me for years. Mrs Crossley at Murray High School – thank you for giving me the love of literature including *The Handmaid's Tale*, John Donne, Douglas Stewart and *Jane Eyre*, and for encouraging me to write. To the lecturers at La Trobe University – that eCommerce degree was never for me, but I'm glad I did it. Hey look, I'm finally using eCommerce by selling my book online. Marianne Dayrit Sison and Matthew Ricketson at RMIT University – your encouragement during my studies and after graduation has been invaluable.

To Writers Victoria (especially the Write-ability program), Melbourne Writers Festival, Emerging Writers Festival, Melbourne Fringe Festival, Arts Access Victoria and the Australian Writers Centre – thanks for giving me a place at the table, and for helping me craft and perform my work in your spaces.

To Viv Daniels and Donna Ross. You were there during the time I needed women leaders most. Thank you for guiding me in my mid-twenties, for the breakfast meetings and Pink concerts, fun work and friendship.

To Layne Beachley and the staff, mentors and alumni at the Layne Beachley Foundation. It was your grant and mentorship that helped me get to England and America, to work out my direction as an appearance activist.

To Dr Vine, Dr Rennick, Dr Douglas in Albury – thank you for treating me when I was a child. To Dr Varigos, Professor Winship and the Dermatology team at the Royal Children's and Royal Melbourne hospitals – thank you for not just seeing me as a patient, but regarding me as a teacher. You understand that skin conditions are not just cosmetic, and know that I need medical and psychological support. You see me at my worst and my best and you make going to hospital a pleasure.

To the friends I made working at Kmart, in the Australian Public Service and at Melbourne Fringe. You make work a joy, and make me feel valued and included. To Mick Fallon who gave me the confidence to work a creative freelance life by telling me to charge more money for my work.

To Joanne Morris who invited me to come and work in Chantilly Studio to work alongside other creatives. I got most of the first draft of *Say Hello* done there, with the help of baguettes, tea and the lovely Chantilly folk asking me about my word count. It was there where I cried when I reached 50,000 words.

To Clare Bowditch, Jenny Noyes, Claudine Ryan, Candice Chung, Yasmin Noone, Nina Mills, Natasha Mitchell and the other editors who asked me to work with you in the media – thank you for valuing my work so much that you want to share it with your audiences.

To Ginger Gorman, Maggie Alderson, Namila Benson, Clementine Ford, Jamila Rizvi, Tara Moss, Beverley Wang, Yasmin Abdul Magied, Maxine Beneba Clarke, Pip Lincolne, Tracey Spicer, Julie Inman Grant, Celeste Liddle, Van Badham – you are the women in the media whose work I admire and I'm proud to call you friends. Thank you for all the advice and support.

To the *You Can't Ask That* team – Kirk Docker, Aaron Smith, Scott Mitchell, Carly Schmidt and Jess Cohen – thanks for asking me on the show; it changed my life. The other wonderful thing to happen since *You Can't Ask That* is the strong bond that has formed between two other participants in the facial difference episode – Ellen Fraser-Barbour, Belinda Downes and me. Ellen and I have met many times – giggling as we shop and having deep conversations over wine; and I met Belinda twice when I went on a work trip to Newcastle. But most days we have a group chat. There are things these women just get, especially the microaggressions. We talk things through, and I always feel better knowing I can turn to you. How lucky we are to have each other to relate to and laugh with so much.

To Stella Young – thank you for helping me see disability and myself differently. Thanks for asking me to write for the ABC on your groundbreaking platform *RampUp*. I read your words often and each time I learn something new. You changed the world. To Lynne and Greg Young – thank you for giving me permission to use Stella's words, and for the chats by email.

To the disability community – thank you for giving me a place that feels like home, and for helping me grow, learn and do better. Academic and musician Anthea Skinner once said that disabled people often don't grow up knowing their culture, so it's up to us all to foster that sense of culture and identity for each other. I think of her words often, and strive to do it in my work.

To the ichthyosis community – thank you for your friendship, advice and for understanding what it's like to live in this skin. I know that sometimes our perspectives differ, but I want you to know how grateful I am that I found you.

To all of my friends for believing in me, cheering me on and keeping me grounded – especially Camille Condon, Jason-Scott Watkins, Andrew Bayley, Cassie Morrow, Sandy Lowres, Sandra Reynolds, Annie Nolan, Jess Billimoria, Trudie Harris, Louis Rowe, Michelle Roger, Elisha Friday Wright, Shane Westmore, Natasha Reid, Debra Cerasa, Carly-Jay Metcalfe, Linda Roxburgh,

Jarrod Marrinon, Sonia Marcon, Fiona Mount, Amber Walsh, Ben and Laura Farnsworth and kids, Pauline and Ben Findlay, Leona Tooley, the Kirley family, the Jones family, Brigette Milne and the Milne family.

To my parents Roger and Jeanette Findlay – you are the best parents I could ever wish for, even when I thought you were really strict and embarrassing. Thank you for continually believing in me and being my biggest supporters. How lucky I am. Thank you for everything.

To Adam, for loving me, for wanting to take my soresies away, enjoying food as much as I do, and talking about handyman projects to take my mind off mean people on social media.

To the challengers and detractors – thank you for giving me something to write about.

Suggested resources

DISABILITY ORGANISATIONS
Council for Intellectual Disability nswcid.org.au
Disabled Persons Assembly New Zealand dpa.org.nz
First People's Disability Network fpdn.org.au
Pain Australia painaustralia.org.au
People with Disability Australia pwd.org.au
Women with Disability Australia wwda.org.au

YOUTH DISABILITY AND CHRONIC ILLNESS
SUPPORT ORGANISATIONS
Children and Young People with Disability Australia cyda.org.au
Chronic Illness Peer Support Program rch.org.au/chips
Livewire livewire.org.au
Youth Disability Advocacy Network ydan.com.au
Youth Disability Advocacy Service ydas.org.au

ICHTHYOSIS AND APPEARANCE DIVERSITY RESOURCES

Australian New Zealand Ichthyosis support group
facebook.com/groups/Australianichthyosis/

Centre for Appearance research www1.uwe.ac.uk/hls/research/
appearanceresearch.aspx

Changing Faces changingfaces.org.uk

Royal Children's Hospital Ichthyosis information hrch.org.au/
kidsinfo/fact_sheets/Ichthyosis/

YP Face It ypfaceit.co.uk

MENTAL HEALTH AND ESAFETY

Esafety commissioner esafety.gov.au

Kids Helpline 1800 55 1800

Lifeline 131114

DISABILITY ARTS AND MEDIA

ABC Ramp Up abc.net.au/rampup (This is now defunct – bring it
back ABC! – but the content is archived.)

Arts Access Victoria artsaccess.com.au

Disability Leadership Institute disabilityleaders.com.au

Disability Visibility Project disabilityvisibilityproject.com

Positive Exposure positiveexposure.org

Quippings – Disability Unleashed facebook.com/quippings/

Ramp Your Voice rampyourvoice.com

Rooted in Rights www.rootedinrights.org

We Need Diverse Books diversebooks.org

Writeability writersvictoria.org.au/support/fellowships/write–ability–
fellowships

ROLE MODELS

Sarah Blahovec twitter.com/sblahov

Keah Brown keahbrown.com

Belinda Downes facebook.com/coffeewithbelindadownes/

Ellen Fraser-Barbour facebook.com/Ellens-
   Agenda-810554249117392/

Laura Hershey – You Get Proud by Practicing laurahershey.com

Karolyn Gehrig karolyngehrig.com

Ally Grace suburbanautistics.blogspot.com

Erin Kyan ErinKyan.com

Emily Ladau wordsiwheelby.com

Alaina Leary alainaleary.com

Andrew Pulrang disabilitythinking.com

Michelle Roger bobisdysautonomia.blogspot.com

Lindy West lindywest.net

Maysoon Zayid www.maysoon.com